Total Hockey Conditioning

From Pee-Wee to Pro

Tudor Bompa, PhD

&

Dave Chambers, PhD

KEY PORTER BOOKS

National Library of Canada Cataloguing in Publication

Bompa, Tudor O., 1932-
    Total hockey conditioning : from pee-wee to pro / Tudor Bompa and Dave Chambers.

Includes bibliographical references and index.
ISBN 1-55263-256-3

1. Hockey—Training. 2. Physical fitness. I. Chambers, Dave, 1940– II. Title.

GV848.3.B65 2003   613.7'11   C2003-903356-2

The publisher gratefully acknowledges the support of the Canada Council for the Arts and the Ontario Arts Council for its publishing program.

We acknowledge the financial support of the Government of Canada through the Book Publishing Industry Development Program (BPIDP) for our publishing activities.

Key Porter Books Limited
70 The Esplanade
Toronto, Ontario
Canada M5E 1R2

www.keyporter.com

Design: Jack Steiner
Electronic formatting: Heidy Lawrance Associates

Printed and bound in Canada

03 04 05 06 07 5 4 3 2 1

Contents

Components of Fitness

The game of hockey requires a skill level as high as any competitive sport. Forwards and defensemen must have the technical skills of skating, puck handling, passing and receiving, and shooting and checking, as well as understanding and carrying out strategy and team play. The goaltender must also possess the skills of skating, quickness, reaction time, and flexibility to stop pucks moving as fast as 100 miles (160 km) an hour.

Fitness is a key component for success in ice hockey and optimal performance is determined by levels of fitness. The short bursts of activity on the ice, ranging from a shift of 30 seconds to 1^1/$_2$ minutes, include stops, starts, and bursts of speed; physical battles along the boards, in the corners, and in front of the net; and some gliding and stopping, and short stoppages in play for face-offs. The players are rested on the bench for two to three minutes and return to play for their next shift on the ice.

Ice hockey is basically a strength, muscular endurance, speed, and power activity, demanding high levels of energy followed by a recovery period to restore this energy. A well-designed fitness program—to promote agility, flexibility, and improve movement time—is also essential for all ice hockey players, and it is important to realize that different age groups require different types of training programs.

Strength

Strength, which is the ability to apply force, should be developed in the upper and lower body and the trunk area. Strength is important in all aspects of ice hockey including skating, shooting, and checking. Abdominal strength, particularly rotational abdominal strength, should be emphasized as well to avoid injury such as tearing the abdominal wall. Generally, 40% of the training time should be spent on the upper body, with the remaining 60% devoted to the lower body and trunk.

Power

Power training occurs after a base of strength has been built. Power encompasses both strength and speed. Power training, then, involves moving weights or the body quickly to simulate or actually execute movements that are used in hockey.

Speed

Speed relates to applying a force to a mass quickly; power and correct technique are key factors. Power and strength training will increase speed. Technique is also important, however, and doing a large number of repetitions of a movement correctly in addition to power and strength training are essential for increasing a player's speed.

Muscular Endurance

Muscular endurance is the ability to make repeated contractions and/or movements. It is developed by performing a large number of movements (20 or more) using weights or the body. Strength is an important factor in muscular endurance, and regular strength training also improves muscular endurance.

Flexibility

Flexibility is important in ice hockey to ensure a full range of motion in all movements and to prevent injuries. Flexibility exercises also reduce muscle soreness and should be performed daily with all fitness programs.

Agility

Agility is the ability to change direction quickly and is an essential factor in ice hockey. Strength, power, and reaction/movement time all contribute to agility. It can best be improved by practicing a movement pattern correctly at increasing speeds.

Movement Time

Movement time may be defined as the period from receipt of a stimulus to the end of the movement. It is essential in most aspects of ice hockey, but especially important in goaltending. Movement time involves both reaction and response time. Reaction time begins when a player receives a stimulus and ends at the initiation of movement, while response time spans the initiation of the movement to the end of the movement. Current research supports the fact that practice has little effect on reaction time, whereas it directly affects response time. Movement time can be improved by repeated practice of the correct movement pattern.

THE ENERGY SYSTEMS

Energy systems have one primary purpose: to supply a chemical compound named adenosine triphosphate (ATP), which when broken down supplies the energy for muscle contraction to take place.

There are three energy systems in the body that supply ATP. Two of these systems are designed for very short periods during which the oxygen we breathe is not used, and they are called *anaerobic* systems. The third system, which uses oxygen and is utilized in longer-duration activity lasting for more than $1^1/2$ minutes, is called the *aerobic* system. This system is also essential for the recovery and replacement of ATP.

Playing hockey utilizes all three systems and they should all be trained. Here is an outline of the energy systems and their time duration.

Anaerobic
1. Alactic (also called ATP/PC or phosphagen) System: First 10 seconds of vigorous work and contributes for up to 30 seconds.

2. Lactic (also called glycolysis or lactic acid) System: Kicks in at or before 10 seconds of vigorous work, is predominant from 30 to 90 seconds, and contributes for up to three minutes. Produces lactic acid, which is a major contributor to fatigue.

Aerobic
3. Oxygen (aerobic) System: Kicks in after 90 seconds of vigorous work and is the major contributor after three minutes. This system is a key factor in recovery.

Although all three energy systems supply ATP, they act alone only in a very short burst activity lasting either a few seconds (alactic) or in longer endurance activities with a steady pace over three minutes. From a few seconds to three minutes, there is an interaction of the energy systems as shown in Table 1.1.

PRINCIPLES OF TRAINING

Overload: The practice of continually increasing stress to produce a change.

Frequency: Training should occur frequently and be spread over a relatively long period of time.

Duration: Total time spent at overload should be sufficient to produce training effects.

Intensity: The intensity of the training refers to the work performed per unit of time. The greater the amount of work, the greater the intensity.

Volume: Training volume is a measure of the total amount of work performed in a training session. Frequency and duration have a direct effect on the training volume.

Rest Periods: Recovery between exercise, and between training sessions, is an important factor for the success of a training program.

Specificity: In certain segments of the program, training movements should closely simulate the movement and speed used in the sport.

Progression: Progression should be gradual and logical.

Adaptability: Training programs should be flexible and adapt to the individual, accommodating individual differences.

Monitoring: Monitoring and/or testing is one method to measure with certainty whether a training program is working.

STEP-TYPE LOADING

Step-type loading is an important concept when applying the principle of load progression. The step-type loading approach allows for the training load to be increased for three weeks in succession followed by a fourth week of lesser load. This allows the body to compensate and regenerate to prepare for further load increases in the following weeks of training, as shown in Figure 1.1.

TABLE 1.1 Relationship of Performance Time to Energy Systems Supplying ATP

Performance Time	Major Energy System(s) Supplying ATP
Less than 10 seconds	Alactic
10 seconds to 90 seconds	Alactic and lactic
90 seconds to 3 minutes	Lactic acid and oxygen
More than 3 minutes	Oxygen

FIGURE 1.1: The Increase of Training Load in Steps (Step Loading)

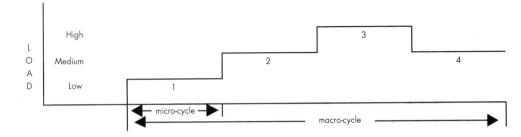

Although the increase in load in training progresses in steps, in a training plan of longer duration the line of the load rating is curvy, as shown in Figure 1.2.

FIGURE 1.2: The Curve of the Rating Load

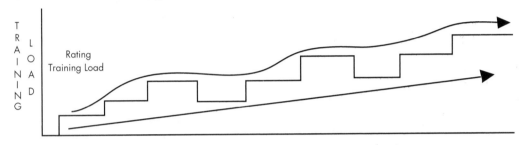

Variations of the Step Method of Loading

Although the Step-Loading Method is the basic concept of increasing the load in training, variations of this method are also used.

A different model can be used for younger players, where the first step is low intensity, the second is either medium or high, and the third is low again, as shown in Figure 1.3. The advantage of using this load pattern, especially for young players in the early stages of development, is that taxing and stressful higher training occurs every second week. At the same time, a regeneration cycle occurs every second week, after high- or medium-intensity training.

FIGURE 1.3: A Suggested Loading Pattern Model for Young Players

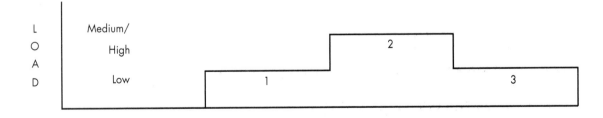

For advanced and experienced elite hockey players, the flat model of loading as shown in Figure 1.4 is recommended. In this model the first three steps are of high demand, volume, and intensity, intended to challenge a high level of adaptation, followed by a week of regeneration and relaxation.

In Chapter 2, these training principles presented here will be applied in a yearly training plan.

FIGURE 1.4: The "Flat" Loading Pattern

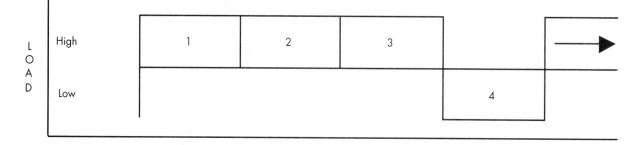

Planning–Periodization of Hockey Training

Those who fail to plan, plan to fail.

PLANNING

Planning involves determining in advance what is to be done, how it is going to be done, and who is going to do it. It involves setting goals and objectives, and making day-to-day decisions on how these objectives can be reached.

Most successful organizations, in both sports and business, include short-term, intermediate, and long-term planning as integral stages of growth of their organization.

Successful hockey coaches are likewise efficient at planning and organizing.

Probably the most important aspect of planning for the coach is developing a training program for the players. Making an annual plan is the first step. Once it has been established, all other planning can take place. Developing weekly and daily training plans is the next essential step. All other aspects of the sport organization, such as game dates, travel and accommodation, training camps, player selection, publicity, and support staff, must be carefully planned as well.

A training program organized and planned over a year is a necessary requirement for anyone who intends to maximize his or her fitness and skill.

The main objective of training is to enable players to reach a high level of performance throughout the regular season and to peak during playoff competition. The entire training program has to be properly periodized and planned so that the development of skills and physical factors (i.e., strength, power, speed, etc.) proceeds in a logical and methodical manner.

PERIODIZATION

Periodization, a term that is becoming more recognized in hockey circles and has its origin in the former Eastern Bloc countries, takes its name from a "period" of time, which in training is called a training phase. Periodization is a systematic division of the training year into phases that allows the coach to develop the players to perform at their optimum

for the league games, and at peak for playoffs and important tournaments.

The annual training plan is conventionally divided into three main phases of training: preparatory or off-season, competitive or league schedule, and transition, which occurs immediately after the season ends and before off-season training begins (Figure 2.1).

The annual plan is further divided into "macro-cycles" (two to six weeks) and "micro-cycles," or weekly training plans (Figure 2.2). The micro-cycles are made up of daily practice plans that include training units, or lessons, directed toward achieving a training objective, which could be technical, tactical, or physical.

CHARACTERISTICS OF THE VARIOUS PHASES

Preparation Phase

During the preparation phase, the foundation is built for development of the hockey player in the off-season. Physical, technical, tactical, and psychological areas are developed during this phase. An emphasis is placed on high volume, which in the physical area should result in a greater resistance to fatigue.

The player during this phase is to:

1. Learn about the importance of and improve general physical preparation.

2. Improve the physical factors required by hockey such as strength, speed, power, aerobic and anaerobic endurance, agility, and flexibility.

3. Develop and/or improve technique.

4. Determine and know the basic tactics to be employed in the following phase. In hockey this phase should last three to four months or longer. As seen in Figure 2.1, the preparatory phase is divided into two sub-phases.

FIGURE 2.1: The Training Phases of the Annual Plan for Ice Hockey

May	June	July	Aug.	Sept.	Oct.	Nov.	Dec.	Jan.	Feb.	Mar.	Apr.
	Preparation				Competition						
Transition	General		Specific	Pre-competition	League Games					Taper	Playoffs

FIGURE 2.2: The Periodization of the Annual Plan into Phases, Sub-phases, Macro- and Micro-cycles

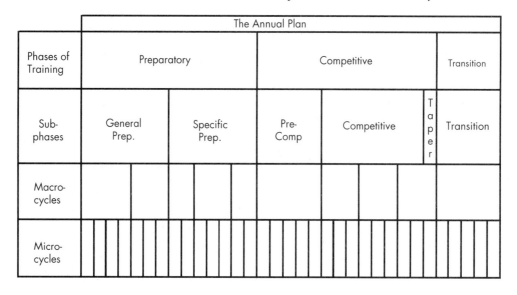

General Preparation Phase

The objective of this phase is to develop a player's general physical preparation, improve basic technical skills, introduce individual basic tactics, and develop and improve basic mental skills.

The prime concern in this phase, however, is the development of a high level of physical conditioning on which the player can build in future phases. This stage is characterized by a gradual and progressive increase of volume at medium intensity. In this phase, the number of training hours from one stage to the next should be raised with each macro-cycle (two to six weeks), which allows the player to improve his or her general work capacity. Coupled with this high volume of work are the psychological aspects of drive and determination to complete the program.

In most cases the time allocated to this phase should be one-third of the total time of the preparatory phase. No games are included in this phase.

Specific Preparation Phase

While the objectives of the specific preparation phase are similar to those of the general phase, the training is game-specific. The volume remains high, and 70% to 80% of the exercises are sport-specific. Toward the end of this phase, volume starts to diminish by 20% to 30% while intensity increases. This phase links the various physical factors such as strength and speed, and applies them to the technical skills of hockey. Mental preparation begins to deal with game-like situations, and team tactical involvement is introduced, with some actual games being played on an informal basis. Physical, technical, and psychological evaluation may take place at the end of this phase.

Competitive Phase

In the competitive phase (league games), the level of physical conditioning must be maintained and improved as technical and game-specific training takes place. In this phase 90% of the training is hockey-specific, and the technical, tactical, and psychological training must be brought to the next level. The ultimate objective is to peak for the playoff games. In this phase, intensity is high while total volume of work is lowered.

The player during this phase is to:

1. Continuously improve physical abilities and psychological techniques in accordance with the specifics of hockey.

2. Perfect and consolidate technique.

3. Feature and develop tactics, and gain competitive experience.

4. Maintain general physical preparation.

This period usually lasts from four to six months, depending on how a league is organized.

Pre-competitive Sub-phase

This phase usually lasts from four to six weeks and consists of a higher-than-normal volume compared with the main competition period. It also includes non-league or exhibition games that test all the elements of physical, technical, tactical, and psychological training developed in the preparation phase. The coach should also try to improve all or most of the technical, tactical, and physical deficiencies noticed during the exhibition games prior to the start of the league games. Physical preparation, although not as high-volume as during the preparation period, remains a major focus.

Main Competitive Phase

Specific hockey-related exercises are included in this period for 90% of the time, with the intensity levels reaching their highest two to three weeks before competition.

The weekly training (micro-cycles made up of daily practice plans with various training units) should reach maximum intensity two to three times during the week, depending upon the total number of practices. The stress levels should be varied (showing an undulating line if graphed), and rigorous and lighter days should be planned for regeneration. Ideally, games should build in order of importance and/or difficulty, or alternate between stiff and easier competition. This can be achieved by adding tournaments and exhibition games, but cannot be done with a set league schedule. Maintaining physical preparation should be highlighted with specific strength and endurance work.

Tapering

After an extensive competitive period a tapering or unloading period of one to two weeks' duration should precede the playoff period. Both volume and intensity are reduced during this period, and not more than two intense training periods per week (micro-cycle) should be included. Any physical-conditioning maintenance programs, such as strength training, should be stopped in the second week to have players well rested for the playoffs.

In addition to the reduction in volume and intensity, more tactical and psychological training, including relaxation techniques (already learned) may be included.

TRANSITION PHASE

This period usually lasts four weeks, and not longer than five weeks. The first week is a detraining and evaluation period, during which exercise should be moderate and non-sport-specific. The second week should be a resting period. The following two to three weeks are made up of active rest, and exercising at a frequency of three times a week at about half the competitive phase volume. The training and exercise environment should be changed, if possible. It should be noted that this phase is not a total rest period, since the gains made throughout the training year should not drop too far below the maintenance level. Players who follow this regimen are found to be more physically and psychologically prepared for the beginning of the new preparatory phase.

Table 2.1 summarizes the objectives of the various phases of the annual plan.

The objectives of the physical performance factors in the phases of the annual plan are summarized in Table 2.2, and all factors, including techniques, tactics, strategy, and nutrition, in Table 2.3.

TABLE 2.1: Objective of a Periodized Annual Plan

Phase	General Objectives
Preparatory	
General	To develop basic technical skills and general fitness.
Specific	Increase the volume of specific training. To perfect technique and basic tactics, and to develop sport-specific fitness. Increase game-specific intensity.
Competitive	
Pre-competitive (exhibition games)	To make training competition-specific. Test all game-related factors.
Competitive (league games)	Maximize performance to qualify for the playoffs.
Tapering	To maximize competitive performance and to regenerate in preparation for playoffs.
Transition	To allow active rest and for the maintenance of training gains.

INTEGRATED PERIODIZATION®

For far too long, sport scientists and practitioners alike have focused on certain aspects of the periodization process without integrating all of the elements into a whole. Coaches and staff can utilize integrated periodization to assimilate knowledge that sports scientists have generated.

Sport psychologists, physiologists, and nutritionists have often developed their areas of knowledge without being too concerned about the need for a planning–periodization process and recognizing that there are specific objectives for each phase of the training plan. The mental/psychological training considers the athlete its main focus, often in connection with the competitive environment. This is also true for nutrition. Sport scientists should, however, be aware that athletes and coaches need their help throughout the annual or long-term training process and not just prior to competition.

Integrated periodization represents the process of combining all of the components of hockey training into a whole and matching them according to the periodization of the various physical factors such as strength, speed, power, endurance, flexibility, etc. It is the periodization of these abilities that actually dictates the diet to be used, and the psychological skills best suited for a given training phase. What is critical for a coach, therefore, is to learn what kind of diet to use and which psychological skills are the optimum when training aerobic endurance, maximum strength, or any other combination of such abilities. Armed with such information, the coach will be able to improve players' abilities and, as a result, their performance.

TABLE 2.2: Objectives of the Physical, Technical, and Tactical Factors in the Annual Plan

Period / Phase ⟍ Performance Factor	Preparatory		Competitive			
	General	Specific	Pre-Competitive	League Games	Taper	Transition
Technical/Tactical Development:						
* Techniques	* initiate the development of techniques (on- and off-ice)	* emphasize the development of techniques (on-ice)	* develop and refine techniques * test skills and efficiency	* refine techniques		
* Tactics	* initiate the development of tactics (on- and off-ice)	* individual tactics (on-ice)	* individual and team tactics	* refine individual and team tactics	* develop tactics for the playoffs	
* Strategies	* initiate the development of strategies (on- and off-ice)	* design team strategy	* work on team strategy	* maximize team strategies * win as many games as possible to qualify for playoffs	* develop strategies for the playoffs	
Physical Preparation						
* Aerobic	* high volume of aerobic base	* continue to train aerobic base	* maintain aerobic base	* maintain aerobic base	* reduction of training volume and intensity	* maintain a level of fitness while avoiding staleness through a variety of recreational activities
* Anaerobic		* train specific energy systems	* train specific energy systems	* maintain specific energy systems		
* Speed		* train specific speed	* continue to train speed	* maintain specific speed		
* Strength	* AA	* train MxS	* maintain MxS	* maintain MxS		
* Power			* conversion of MxS to P	* maintain power		
* Flexibility	* train flexibility	* train flexibility	* train flexibility	* maintain flexibility	* maintain flexibility	* maintain flexibility
* Nutrition	* initiate a nutrition education program * phase specific nutrition plans	* phase specific nutrition plans	* specific nutrition plans	* specific nutrition plans		

NOTES:

AA = anatomical adaptation (basic strength training)

MxS = maximum strength (loads over 80% of one repetition maximum, or 1 RM)

P = power

Table 2.3 illustrates a model of integrated periodization for hockey. The chart is divided into traditional training phases and sub-phases. Under periodization we discuss, from the top down: periodization of speed and endurance; periodization of strength; psychological periodization; and periodization of nutrition. Each of these elements of periodization will be discussed in detail in the following chapters. Read about them, absorb them, and, most importantly, use them in your own programs.

TABLE 2.3: A Model of Integrated Periodization for Hockey

		May	June	July	Aug.	Sep.	Oct.	Nov.	Dec.	Jan.	Feb.	Mar.	Apr.
	Training Phases	Preparatory					Competitive					T	Trans
	Sub-phases	General	Specific			Pre-Comp	Official/League Games					Play-offs	Trans
P E R I O D I Z A T I O N	Periodization of speed and endurance	aerobic endurance	Anaerobic Max. speed short Maintain aerobic endurance		Anaerobic Max. speed short medium long Maintain aerobic endurance		All in age-specific proportions					/	Play/Fun
	Periodization of strength	AA	MxS	P	MxS	Conv to P	Maintenance Power/MxS						Comp
	Mental (M)/ psychological periodization	Eval. M skills Learn new M skills Quiet setting	M skills to attain training objectives Visualization Imagery Relaxation Energy management			M rehearsal Energize Positive self-talk Visioneering Focus plans Simulation Coping	M skills to cope with specific opponents Stress management/relaxation Energizing Focus plans Mental rehearsal Motivation—positive thinking/optimism Positive thinking/optimism						Active rest Regen. De-stress
	Periodization of nutrition	Balanced diet	High carbo-hydrates High protein	High carbo-hydrates High protein	High carbo-hydrates High protein	High carbo-hydrates	Fluctuate according to the schedule of games (high carbohydrates)					High carbo-hydrates	Balanced diet

NOTES:

M = mental skills

* Mental skills to aid regeneration/stress management, positive talk, visualization

THE MACRO-CYCLE

The macro-cycle refers to a training phase of two to six weeks' duration. A sub-phase, such as general preparation, pre-game or exhibition games, and the transition phase could often very well be a separate macro-cycle. The specific preparatory phase could be divided into two such phases, whereas the long phase of league games could represent more than four to five phases.

The structure of a macro-cycle depends on the specifics of training of a given phase.

Macro-cycles for the Preparatory Phase

As the scope of training for the preparatory phase is progressive adaptation, and specific conditioning is improved to the highest level possible through the development of the dominant physical factors such as strength, power, speed, endurance, etc., macro-cycles are of two kinds.

Developmental macro-cycles, where training demand is increased in steps, is shown in Figure 2.3. The first example (Figure 2.3a) refers to a 4:1 structure where the load is increased in four steps, with one week of regeneration at the

FIGURE 2.3: Two Examples of Developmental Macro-cycles (a) 4:1 and (b) 3:1

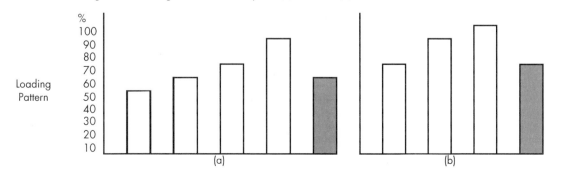

FIGURE 2.4: Examples of Two Variations of the "Shock" Macro-cycle, Where (b) Is of Much Higher Demand

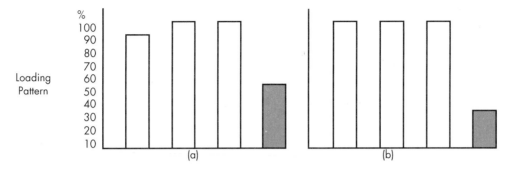

end. Such a structure is recommended mostly for the early preparatory phase when players are still quite fresh and training demand is not very challenging. The 3:1 structure (Figure 2.3b) is suggested for younger players and for most of the preparatory phase for all other players, often in alternation with "shock" macro-cycles (Figure 2.4). If the fatigue level is higher than expected, the regeneration week could be decreased below the suggested levels.

Shock macro-cycles, where training is at the highest level of tolerance, are very demanding and could be planned for players at the provincial/state, university, or professional levels. As suggested by Figure 2.4, maximum demand can be maintained for two weeks (Figure 2.4a) or even three weeks (Figure 2.4b), which allows a coach to plan some two to three shock macro-cycles during the preparatory phase from mid-June to the first half of August.

Shock macro-cycles have to be used with caution, without any exaggeration, since they are very taxing both physically and psychologically. It is strongly suggested that the coach always observe the regeneration cycles. If high levels of fatigue are visible, we recommend that players be given two weeks of regeneration rather than one.

While the three weeks of the shock macro-cycles are 95% to 100% of one's training tolerance, the regeneration

TABLE 2.4: An Example of a Macro-cycle in which the Schedule of Activities Is Listed (Wise, G. 1996)

JANUARY						
Monday	Tuesday	Wednesday	Thursday	Friday	Saturday	Sunday
		1 OFF New Year's Day	2 Practice 4 - 6 pm	3 Practice 4 - 6 pm	4 Moscow Dynamo @ York 2 pm @ Ice Gardens 12:30pm	5 OFF
6 Practice off-ice 4 - 6 pm	7 Practice 4 - 6 pm	8 Practice 4 - 6 pm	9 Waterloo @ York 7:30 pm @ Ice Gardens 6:00 pm	10 Practice 4 - 6 pm	11 York @ Laurier 2 pm Depart 10 am	12 OFF
13 Practice off-ice 4 - 6 pm	14 Practice 4 - 6 pm	15 Practice 4 - 6 pm Depart for Sudbury 6:30 pm	16 York @ Laurentian 7:30 pm	17 Practice 4 - 6 pm	18 Laurentian @ York 5 pm @ Ice Gardens 3:30 pm	19 OFF
20 Practice off-ice 4 - 6 pm	21 Practice 4 - 6 pm	22 Practice 4 - 6 pm QUAA All-Star Game @ York Ice Gardens 7:30 pm	23 York @ Guelph 7:30 pm Depart 3 pm	24 Practice 4 - 6 pm	25 York @ Toronto 7:30 pm @ Varsity Depart 5 pm	26 OFF
27 Practice off-ice 4 - 6 pm	28 Practice 4 - 6 pm	29 Practice 4 - 6 pm	30 Practice 4 - 6 pm	31 Queen's @ York 7:30 pm @ Ice Gardens 6 pm		

cycles have a lower demand than normal, in the range of 30% to 45%. This really allows players to remove the fatigue, replenish energy stores, relax mentally, and rebound before another shock macro-cycle is planned.

Macro-cycles for the Competitive and Transition Phases

The structure of a macro-cycle for exhibition and league games is dictated by the schedule of the games. Since each league has its own schedule of games, and therefore there is not one ideal type of macro-cycle to be followed by everybody, we will discuss this subject in more detail under the topic of micro-cycles. A simple macro-cycle is presented, however, in Table 2.4, in which the coach shows the schedule of games and training activities without referring to their intensity, demand, or type of work.

The objectives of the transition phase have been discussed earlier in this chapter. Figures 2.5 and 2.6 show the intensities and loading patterns for four weeks and five weeks respectively. Please note that the first week has the lowest intensity, where the scope is to remove the fatigue from the body and mind, ideally in a very relaxing, no-pressure environment.

In the next two to three weeks, low-intensity training can be started two to three times per week, with activities completely different from the game of hockey. Swimming, soccer, or any type of physical activity the players want to do is appropriate. They should be allowed to make their own decisions to perform whatever is pleasing to them, and for as long as it is fun and relaxing.

THE MICRO-CYCLE

The micro-cycle, or weekly training plan, along with the chart of the annual plan, are the most important and functional planning tools the coach can use to create a training program.

Not all micro-cycles are the same. Their structure, difficulty, and loading pattern vary according to the training phase, the players' ages, and the classification/league. It is equally important that the intensity of training sessions varies according to energy systems taxed, and to alternate heavy, taxing days, with regeneration days.

For the purpose of presenting more complete information about the micro-cycle, many important elements of this training phase are discussed. Not everything in this section, however, matches the needs of all coaches. This is why it is suggested that you read everything, and then apply these concepts to each individual's needs and training circumstances. In addition, the suggested fitness programs at the end of the book will shed more light on the theoretical discussions presented in the earlier chapters.

FIGURE 2.5: A Suggested Loading Pattern for a Four-Week Macro-cycle for the Transition Phase

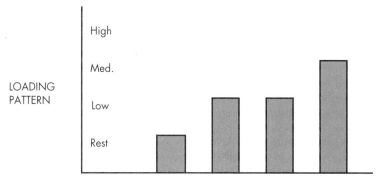

FIGURE 2.6: A Suggested Loading Pattern for a Five-Week Macro-cycle for the Transition Phase

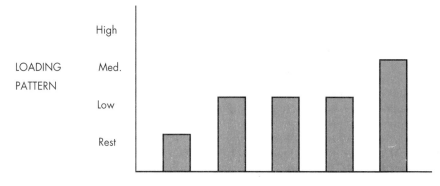

The Classification of Micro-cycles (a week of training)

Like every other plan a coach makes, a micro-cycle plan is a projection of what a coach would like to do in that week. Although a coach spends a lot of time completing the plan, it should be recognized from the beginning that its application has to be done with a great deal of flexibility. The plan must be adjusted to the team's state of body and mind, and especially to the players' fatigue level.

When you create a micro-cycle, you must consider the phase of training, the needs of the team, and the training priorities (technical versus physical; or strength versus endurance, etc.).

The criteria we use to classify micro-cycles are based on:

- The number of on-ice and off-ice training sessions per week.

- Micro-cycles for the preparatory phase, illustrating how training demand per session alternates between high, medium, and low.

- Micro-cycles for exhibition and league games, where training demand has to take into consideration the number of games per week.

- Regeneration micro-cycles.

- Tapering micro-cycles for championship/playoff games.

- Playoff micro-cycles.

As you know, training in hockey is complex, incorporating technical, tactical, and physical training, as well as the volume intensity and psychological stress. When the coach creates a micro-cycle, he or she has to consider all the above elements, which we will call the overall demand in training. Every single element has to be properly regarded to better monitor the overall demand in training and how it is affecting the players' level of fatigue, weariness during training and games, and ability to cope with all these stressors.

Classification based on the number of training sessions per week.

Figure 2.7 considers two on-ice and two fitness sessions, while Figure 2.8 has three on-ice and two fitness sessions, and Figure 2.9 has three on-ice and three fitness sessions. These are typical examples for teams that cannot have more ice time. The fitness sessions can, however, complement the overall preparedness of a team. Obviously the days and time of day for training could be different from our examples.

FIGURE 2.7: A Structure of a Micro-cycle with Two On-ice Sessions and Two Fitness Sessions

	Mon.	Tues.	Wed.	Thurs.	Fri.	Sat.	Sun.
A.M.						Fitness	
P.M.	Ice	Fitness		Ice			

FIGURE 2.8: A Structure with Three On-ice Sessions and Two Fitness Sessions. (If ice time is not available more than twice a week, you can organize three fitness sessions.)

	Mon.	Tues.	Wed.	Thurs	Fri.	Sat.	Sun.
A.M.	Ice			Ice		Ice	
P.M.		Fitness			Fitness		

FIGURE 2.9: A Micro-cycle with Three On-ice Sessions and Three Fitness Sessions

	Mon.	Tues.	Wed.	Thurs	Fri.	Sat.	Sun.
A.M.	Ice		Ice		Ice	Fitness	
P.M.		Fitness		Fitness			

Other structures are also possible, especially for elite teams such as professional, university, and provincial/state leagues, or for camps (Figures 2.10 and 2.11).

FIGURE 2.10: A Suggested Structure with Four On-ice Sessions and Two Fitness Sessions

	Mon.	Tues.	Wed.	Thurs	Fri.	Sat.	Sun.
A.M.		Ice		Ice		Fitness	
P.M.	Ice		Fitness		Ice		

FIGURE 2.11: Elite Players Can Train between Eight and Nine Sessions per Week during Camps

	Mon.	Tues.	Wed.	Thurs	Fri.	Sat.	Sun.
A.M.	Fitness	Ice	Fitness	Ice		Fitness	
P.M.	Ice		Ice		Ice		

Other combinations are possible, including on-ice training with fitness (i.e., strength training) afterwards. If, however, the players are fatigued from a demanding on-ice training, then the fitness program takes the back stage.

The suggestions made in Figures 2.9 to 2.11 might be a shock to many coaches who view training for hockey quite differently. We would like to remind them, however, that players in soccer and other sports train daily, whereas athletes from several individual sports train twice a day, year round.

It is not possible to have a higher rate of improvement without finding more training time, and if ice time is scarce, fitness programs are always easier to organize. If elements of speed, endurance, and strength/power can be trained off-ice in two to four sessions per week, then in two or three on-ice sessions you can dedicate the time to technical and tactical skills and/or drills only.

If athletes from other sports can do it, so can hockey players. Just try to break the tradition of training only two to four times per week and you will see the difference.

Classification based on training demand.

Of all the types of micro-cycles presented below, the coach has to apply them to his or her own conditions, number of training sessions per week, as well as age group. Training demand varies between high (H), medium (M), and low (L).

FIGURE 2.12: An Example of a Micro-cycle with Three Training Sessions per Week

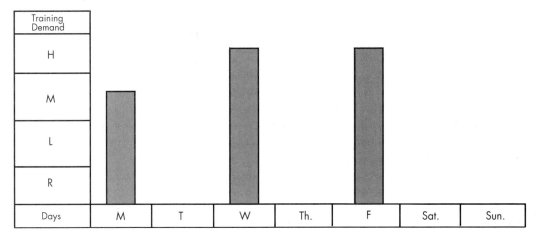

FIGURE 2.13: Exemplifies a Micro-cycle with Four Training Sessions: Two M and Two H. (Under certain circumstances—i.e., a very demanding week—the above can be changed to three, or even four, high-demand training sessions.)

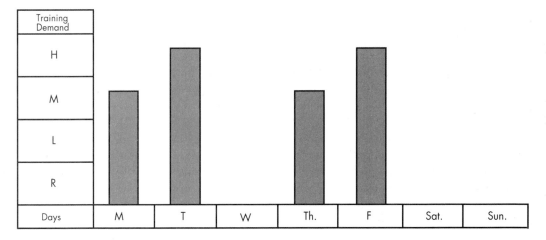

FIGURE 2.14: A Five-session Micro-cycle of High Demand. (For a fatigued team, the Wednesday training session could be of M or even L demand.)

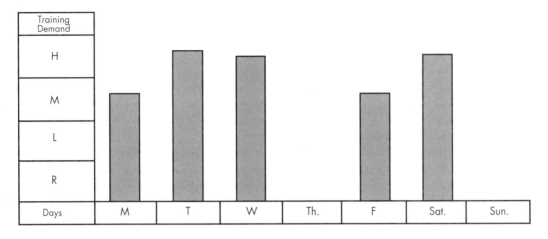

FIGURE 2.15: An Example of an Elite/Provincial/State-Level Team with Daily Training Sessions. (The L demand days are necessary to regenerate and rebound physically and mentally for the H demand days.)

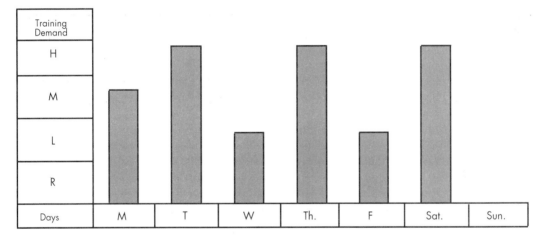

Classification of micro-cycles for exhibition and league games.

FIGURE 2.16: A Suggested Micro-cycle with One Game and Two Training Sessions. (The Thursday session to be M or even L in order to avoid possible fatigue build-up prior to the game.)

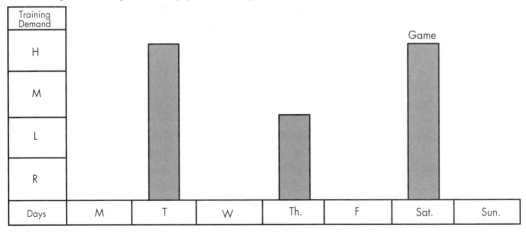

FIGURE 2.17: A Micro-cycle of One Game and Three Training Sessions. (If the team is still fatigued from the previous game, the first session (T) could be of L demand.)

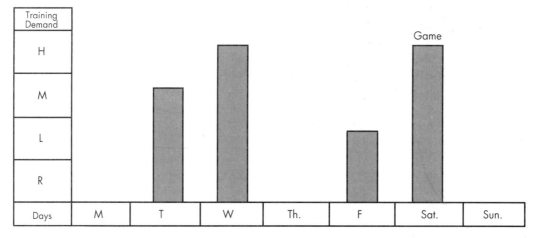

FIGURE 2.18: A Suggested Micro-cycle with One Game and Four Training Sessions. (The L demand session for (M) is intended to give the team extra time to remove fatigue before any training with an M or H demand.)

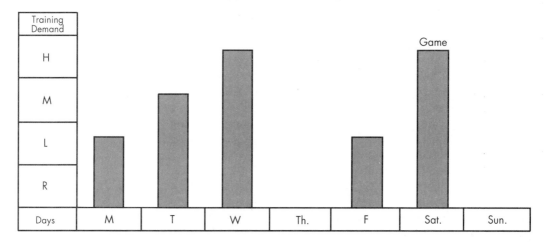

FIGURE 2.19: An Example of a Micro-cycle with Two Games and Two Training Sessions. (The F session can be changed to L demand.)

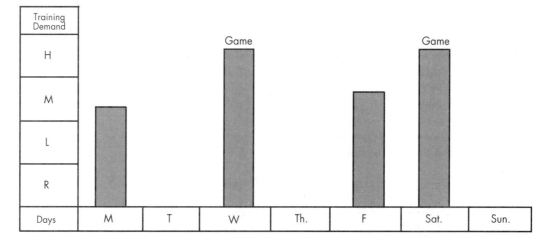

FIGURE 2.20: An Example of a Micro-cycle for an Elite Team (Professional, Junior) with All Games Held on the Road

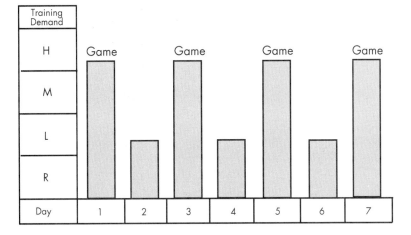

Although Figures 2.12 to 2.20 illustrate various planning possibilities for a micro-cycle, we did not exhaust all variations available for a hockey team. Our intent is to share with you a concept in planning. As you take control of this planning concept, you should adapt it to your own needs and specific training, and other conditions.

The examples in Figures 2.19 and 2.20 are typical for teams playing two or three games per week (professional, university, or junior hockey). When one has to plan the demand in training for such teams, the coach must also consider the time spent on traveling and the fatigue induced by it as well by two demanding games. This is why the suggested demand in training is not very high.

Certainly, it is easy for us to suggest high-demand training sessions once or even twice a week; however, such a program is unrealistic to say the least. The fatigue induced by two games, travel, and high-intensity training will progressively, over time, take the team to exhaustion, over-reaching, and ultimately to overtraining. Under such conditions the team may drastically decrease its chances to make the playoffs.

The only solution for professional, university, and junior teams is a longer and more solid preparatory phase. The fitness level accumulated in this phase will provide a stronger base for the long competitive phase. If, however, you want to plan one or two sessions with higher-intensity drills, you can do so under the following conditions:

- decrease the total training time of training sessions, and/or
- plan only a few drills with high intensity, and/or
- have a longer rest interval between the drills (three to five minutes).

Note: The rest interval can consist of low-intensity drills such as shooting or tactical preparation.

Whether you have a micro-cycle with two or even three games, we strongly advise that you train every day you are able to, with low-demand, light, and aerobic types of training sessions. This type of activity facilitates a better replenishment of glycogen stores than no training at all. Even if you have traveled back home or to another city to play, take time for a 45-minute session. This should consist of 15 to 20 minutes for warm-up and very active stretching, with the balance of the time spent on low-intensity aerobic drills. Some of these drills could be modeled on the tactics you may apply on the next game.

As well as the attention given to low-intensity, short aerobic sessions dedicated to the faster facilitation of energy stores (glycogen) replenishment, maximum attention should be given to the nutrition plan for your players. For further information please refer to our chapter on nutrition.

Regeneration Micro-cycles

You may recall the discussion in chapter one regarding how the load in training (step loading) is increased. Regardless of which loading method you use, we have constantly proposed that after exposing your players to the highest loading step, you should plan a regeneration micro-cycle.

As players are challenged with higher workloads, they experience a high degree of physical and mental fatigue. To avoid critical levels of fatigue, over-reaching, and ultimately overtraining, a regeneration week must be planned. This strategy of a low-demanding week is possible only during the preparatory phase. As soon as your team starts playing games, the structure of micro-cycles is dictated by the games' schedule. Under such conditions, the structure of micro-cycles has to follow one of the options discussed above (classification of micro-cycles based on training demand).

The objectives of regeneration micro-cycles are to:

- remove the physical and psychological fatigue,
- replenish the energy stores in order to resume a new and energized step-loading, and
- allow players to relax mentally.

These objectives can be accomplished through decreasing, by one or two sessions, the number of weekly training sessions—for instance, from six to four, or four to two—or, if you train three times a week, from three to two. It is equally important to decrease the duration of training sessions by 20% to 30%, as well as the total demand of each training session. The benefit of this approach is usually not realized in the first, but rather in the second, part of the week. If you want any higher intensity to spark your training it must, therefore, be done in the second part of the week, with much longer rest intervals between the drills you plan.

During this week, even the coach has to be informal and project a relaxed attitude and optimism.

As a result of implementing all the above methods, the team will be able to rebound energetically and mentally, and be ready for another two to three weeks of being challenged to their highest levels of tolerance.

Tapering Micro-cycles

The only time tapering micro-cycles are used in hockey is before league playoffs or an international competition such as the World Championships and the Olympic Games.

As playoffs for league championships immediately follow league games, tapering may start either seven to 10 days prior to the playoffs or as soon as a team has qualified. If a team qualifies for the playoffs in the very last game of the regular season, then the coach does not have any time at all to taper.

The objectives of regeneration micro-cycles are to:

- remove the physical and psychological fatigue,
- replenish the energy stores in order to resume a new and energized step loading, and
- relax players mentally.

Before examining the above two options, we would like to share with you the main objectives of a tapering strategy:

- To facilitate the removal of physical and mental fatigue accumulated during the league games through training sessions of lower intensity.

- To replenish the energy stores, which is easier to achieve with low-intensity sessions.

- To create for the players an environment of positive thinking and optimism and a desire to play the best games possible.

- To design and practice the tactics to be used in the first playoff games.

- To design the diet, mental training, and recovery strategy as per Chapters 10, 11, and 7 respectively.

Let us now examine the two tapering options available to you.

1. A 7- to 10-day tapering strategy for the playoffs, as shown in Figure 2.21.

FIGURE 2.21: A Suggested Tapering Strategy for League Playoffs

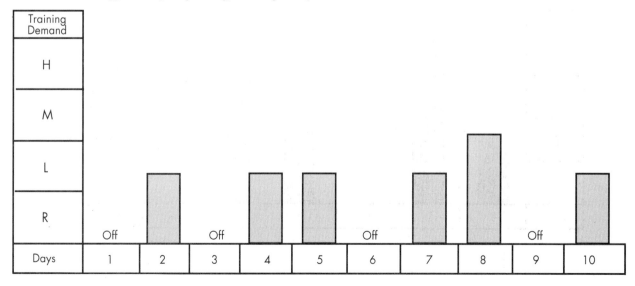

You can see from examining Figure 2.23 that in the first seven days there are consistent alternations of days off and low-intensity training sessions. There is only one medium-intensity session toward the end of the program, assuming that fatigue has been removed from body and mind, and energy stores replenished.

If you realize that the players have recovered better and faster, you can use some high-intensity drills, but not a high intensity and longer training session. The few high-intensity drills must, however, be short—less than 30 seconds—and incorporate a longer rest interval than usually observed for such drills (i.e., three to five minutes between drills for a full recovery). You should always remember that tapering does not have the objective to actually train the team—it is too late for that. Rather its scope is to get the team physically and mentally ready for the most important games of the year. At this time of year it is *better to undertrain than overtrain*! The more highly demanding training sessions are, with longer high-intensity sessions, the higher the level of fatigue accumulation. As a result of this, the probability of an unsuccessful outcome in the playoffs is higher.

2. The earlier qualification for playoffs is often the case for the leading teams of the league. While your team still has to play the remaining league games, you can take some measures to prepare for the playoffs. In your strategy to prepare the team for the playoffs you should consider the following:

- Winning all the remaining games should not be an objective. You have already qualified.

- It is more important to have a fresh, rested, and ready team than to constantly be obsessed by winning. Often, the league-leading team can be eliminated in the first playoff round.
- For the remaining league games give more playing time to your second, third, and fourth lines. Save the energy of your best players and goalie.
- In your training sessions prior to the playoffs you should have shorter and lower-intensity practices. Pushing for high intensity all the way results in a high level of fatigue.
- Your best players may be more fatigued than the third- or fourth-line players. Consequently, you should have an individualized program for each category, in which the best players have shorter, less intensive training sessions.
- Remember that winning the playoffs is your goal. Everything else is secondary; therefore, intelligently prepare the team to achieve your main goal of the year.

Playoffs Micro-cycle

Whether for league, national, or international championships, playoffs determine the winning team. As such, the schedule is extremely taxing, with players having to play every second day, and in many instances having to travel. Often, the successful team may be the one whose coach knows how to organize training between playoff games. Figure 2.22 illustrates a possible micro-cycle for the playoffs where the days are given numbers rather than the typical weekdays.

FIGURE 2.22: A Typical Micro-cycle for the Playoffs, with a Duration of One to Several Weeks (G = game)

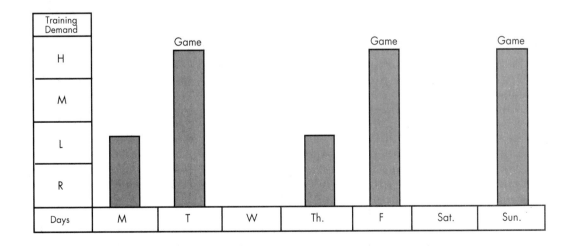

As seen in Figure 2.22, no high-intensity sessions are suggested between the games. It is not necessary to plan any high-intensity training sessions during the playoffs because the players play with high intensity in every single game. To do the same in training would be a gross mistake, which the team might pay for toward the end of the playoffs.

A low, aerobic type of intensity has the benefit of facilitating faster replenishment of energy stores, which is superior even to a complete rest day. It is equally important for the coach to plan relaxing, simple, low-intensity workouts, where the plan for the training sessions should be:

- Do 20 to 30 minutes of low-intensity, relaxing, and easy stretching, warm-up.
- Practice, at low intensity, tactical elements to be used in the next game.
- Create a low-stress environment.
- At the end of the session use massage and heat therapy to relax the muscles and the mind (please refer to Chapter 7).

THE TRAINING SESSION PLAN

How you practice is how you play.

The training session can be described as the main tool used to organize the daily program. Planning the daily practices, and the effective use and progression of drills, are intricate parts of a coach's responsibility. Game day, as many coaches comment, is only the result of all the hard work, preparation, and dedication of players and coaches.

The individual practice is one part of the total plan. Part of each practice should be the development of individual skills (technical), as well as team play and systems (tactical), and conditioning. The coach can also address the strategy part of the game in practice. Besides having a set plan for each practice, consider the weaknesses you have observed in the play of your players in previous practices and games.

Plan the practice according to your philosophy of teaching as it relates to the amount of activity and flow. Also consider the skill and physical development level of the players, and confirm that the equipment and facilities are in proper order to ensure the safety of the players.

Make skill or technical development a part of most practices. Skill progression and other suitable drills should be part of the plan; vary the drills that teach the same skill to prevent boredom. Systems and team play should be part of the tactical development of the practice for hockey. Make sure that systems fit the players' age and skill levels, and progress from the simple to the more complex.

Include some physical preparation (conditioning) in each practice. Take into account the conditioning effect of each skill drill and team drill when you design the practice. Consider such factors as energy systems, strength, and flexibility.

Remember the mental aspect of practice. Include, as part of the general plan, tactics and strategy discussed and practiced during the training period.

Evaluate each practice after it has been completed, and use this information to plan the next. Although you should plan for the whole year, your weekly micro-cycle planning must be flexible enough to accommodate day-to-day changes, and to adjust to the strengths and weaknesses of the players and the team.

Designing an effective training session:

- Set the goals and objectives of the training session. Inform the assistant coaches and players of what you are trying to accomplish.
- Plan a general progression through the session, from individual skills to team play.
- Arrive early and be available.
- Project a good mood. Use idle chatter to create a feeling of ease at the beginning of the practice.
- Teach new skills and drills early in the practice, when the players are rested.
- Keep all the players active in the practice.
- Give clear, concise instructions throughout the practice, and be in command.
- Use effective teaching formations, and make sure you have the attention of all players when you are speaking to them.
- Explain and demonstrate skills and drills clearly. Have the players perform the drills immediately after your explanation.
- Be concise, keeping explanations from 30 to 90 seconds.
- Keep your assistant coaches informed and use them effectively. Keep them active in all drills and make them part of everything you do.
- Keep the players active and use the entire training surface. You may wish to use the full training area for team drills and different parts for individual skill drills.
- Observe, evaluate, and give feedback throughout the practice. Assistant coaches should be involved in this process as well.

- Keep drills effective, competitive, active, and challenging.

- Be positive and upbeat. Greet the players, using their first names, before or at the start of practice. Use voice communication throughout the practice at the proper times. Use voice communication more frequently early in the practice to get the players going and establish a good rapport.

- Include a warm-up and cool-down in each practice.

- The warm-up should include stretching, and the cool-down should follow the reverse order of the warm-up.

- Use mass stretching and/or a fun warm-up drill to get the team together and ready for the main part of the practice.

- Include a fun drill in most practices.

- Stop the drills when a common error or lack of effort is apparent.

- Choose drills for their conditioning features, or use a conditioning drill or drills at the end of practice.

- Speak to players as a group at the end of the session.

- Discuss the practice, upcoming games, general information and so on.

- If time permits, have certain players work on specific skills with the assistant coaches after practice.

- If possible, after practice provide an area for additional strength, anaerobic, and aerobic conditioning.

- Conduct individual meetings with players before or after practice, if time permits.

- Meet with assistant coaches, and possibly the captains, to discuss and evaluate the practice and plan for the next practice or game.

- Demand excellence. Repeat a drill until the players get it right.

- Use the chart of the training session (Table 2.5) for planning your daily program.

TABLE 2.5: Chart of the Training Session

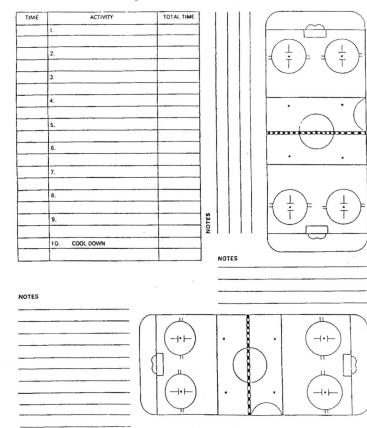

CHAPTER 3

Training for Strength and Power

Strength and power are two of the most important elements required by hockey players. No player can skate fast, shoot the puck forcefully, or change direction quickly without reaching a high level of power.

In simple terms, strength is the ability to apply force against resistance. Power, on the other hand, is a combination of strength and speed, or the ability to apply force as quickly as possible (often called explosive force). In hockey, the more forcefully a player wants to shoot the puck, or the faster he or she wants to skate, the more he or she will require by degree a higher level of power.

In strength training, specific terms are used to define different types of strength:

Absolute strength is used to define the maximum force a player can display, irrespective of body weight. This type of strength will always favor a player who is tall and heavy.

Relative strength, on the other hand, is defined as the maximum force a player can generate per unit of body weight. A big body size is not as important since lighter players can generate more relative strength. For instance, if you test two players of different body weight in power skating, the chances are that the lighter player, with higher relative strength, will be the faster of the two. In hockey, therefore, there are game situations in which relative strength is more important, and in this respect this book will help you to improve your players' relative strength.

Maximum strength refers to peak force, the highest load a player can lift in a given exercise. This is his or her 100%, or one repetition maximum (1RM). This is extremely important to know throughout phases of training. Maximum strength does improve from phase to phase, and it must be tested periodically in order to calculate the load used in a given training session. The development of maximum strength is essential if a player wants to constantly increase power from year to year.

Power-endurance refers to the ability of a player to apply power repetitively as in longer-duration power skating, with many stop-and-go situations as in a very dynamic shift.

Strength should be viewed as a step to power. Strength has to be converted and transformed into power and power-endurance to provide the real essentials needed in the game of hockey. This is accomplished through specific methods, and especially as a result of implementing the concept of periodization of strength.

TYPES OF MUSCLE CONTRACTIONS

As a player is exposed to strength training, he or she may perform isotonic, isometric, and isokinetic contractions.

Isotonic contractions are usually defined as those in which the muscle exerts a constant tension. Common free weights and various weight-training machines are usually referred to as isotonic. Isotonic contractions are performed in three ways: concentric, eccentric, and plyometric.

Concentric contraction refers to contractions in which the muscle length shortens. This occurs when the muscle tension overcomes the resistance (the weight).

Eccentric, or negative, contractions are those in which the muscle lengthens. Muscle tension is greater during an eccentric contraction than during a concentric or isometric contraction.

Isometric, or static, contractions occur when the muscle develops tension without changing its length. Thus, the muscle is unable to generate enough force against an object to cause movement. This type of resistance training is usually performed against an immovable object such as a wall, a barbell in a locked position, or an overloaded weight machine, where movement is impossible.

Isokinetic contractions are performed at a constant speed in a full range of motion. There is no set resistance as the resistance varies to keep the speed constant. A reaction force equals the force applied to the equipment, making it possible for the muscles to exert a continual force throughout the range of motion. The Cybex machine is one common example of an isokinetic device.

Plyometrics refers to a concentric contraction immediately preceded by an eccentric contraction. One-leg and two-leg hopping, and jumping from benches, are examples of plyometric-type exercises.

DESIGNING A STRENGTH PROGRAM

To design an effective training program, the coach should consider the following steps.

Step 1:   Since strength training should be phase-specific, you should decide upon the type of strength you would like to develop in your athletes. The periodization of strength discussed later in this chapter will help you to select the type of strength for a given training phase.

Step 2: Select the exercises. Identify the muscle groups you will target in a particular training session as well as individual needs, which might depend on individual strengths and weaknesses. The selection of exercises is also phase-specific, with exercises often varying from phase to phase.

Step 3: Test maximum strength, or one repetition maximum (1RM), for each exercise. This is done by progressively finding out the highest load a player can lift in one attempt. Knowing 1RM is essential, as training sessions may use different percentages of 1RM. Loads are often chosen randomly, or by following the programs of other players. By finding out each player's 1RM, the coach is able to easily specify the load to be used by each player. This method is the most objective.

There is an unfounded belief among coaches and players that testing for 1RM is dangerous because an athlete might be injured if a maximal lift is used. Keep in mind, however, that a test for 1RM should normally be performed after a thorough warm-up, and after increasing the load progressively. If the coach is still reluctant to test 1RM, however, another option is to test for 3RM or 5RM, then look at the equivalent 1RM (please refer to the Appendix).

Step 4: Develop the actual program by using Table 3.4 and by suggesting the number of sets and reps for each exercise.

Step 5: Test to recalculate 1RM. Since players' strength capacities constantly change (improve), a test to recalculate 1RM should be done in each macrocycle (two to six weeks), and normally at the end of the regeneration cycle, when the players are more rested.

The above steps are usually taken during the preparatory phase. As soon as players begin league play, a maintenance program has to be put in place, but without testing again for 1RM. For load calculations the coach can use the information from the last test.

PROGRAM DESIGN

In order to design a strength training program, there are several elements you must consider, as listed below.

The Load

The load, or intensity, in strength training is really expressed in percentage of 1RM. The load used in training refers to the actual weight lifted in a given exercise. As suggested by Figure 3.1, the following loads are used in strength training.

Supermaximum is a load that exceeds one's maximum strength. Loads between 100% and 125% should be used in most cases, by applying the eccentric method. When using supermaximum loads it is advisable to have two spotters, one at each end of the barbell, to assist or guard the performer and prevent accidents. For example, by employing the eccentric method in bench press, a barbell may fall on the performer's chest if not spotted.

Only those players with a strong background in strength training should use supermaximum loads during maximum strength development. Most other players should be restricted to a load of up to 100%.

Maximum load refers to a load of 90% to 100% of one's maximum, and is used to develop maximum strength.

Heavy load is between 80% and 90% of one's maximum, also with the purpose of developing maximum strength.

Medium load refers to a percentage between 50% and 80% of 1RM, and is used in developing power.

Low load is considered to be any load between 30% and 50% of 1RM, which is useful in the development of both power and power-endurance.

TABLE 3.1: The Load Used in Strength Training

Intensity Value	Load	% of IRM	Type of Contraction	Training Benefits
1	Supermaximum	> 105	Eccentric/Isometric	Maximum strength
2	Maximum	90–100	Concentric	Maximum strength
3	Heavy	80–90	Concentric	Maximum strength
4	Medium	50–80	Concentric	Power
5	Low	30–50	Concentric	Power-endurance

The load should also be related to the type of strength being developed, and more importantly to the sport-specific combination resulting from the mixture of strength with speed, and strength with endurance. The load will not, however, be the same throughout all phases of training. On the contrary, the application of the concept of periodization will alter the load according to the goals of each training phase.

It is also extremely important to mention that the type of strength training used and the load are age-related. No matter how obvious, we have to state very clearly that young players should be exposed to a *progressive* strength training program—one that is developed with care, and requires patience from all individuals involved including players, parents, and coaches. To eliminate confusion, and to specifically address the needs of strength training for hockey, we invite you to examine our suggested, although not comprehensive, training programs for different age groups (see Fitness Program in Chapters 13 to 17).

The Number of Exercises

The key to an effective program is an adequate selection of exercises. Some coaches often overlook setting an optimum number of exercises. In their desire to develop most muscle groups, or through a bodybuilding approach, they select too many exercises. Obviously, the outcome is an overloaded and fatiguing training program with a questionable effect.

The selection of exercises must take into consideration the player's age and level of performance. The development of a solid foundation is one of the main objectives of a training program designed for young players. Without such an approach, consistent improvement will certainly be less likely. As far as strength training is concerned, therefore, the coach should select many exercises (9 to 12) that address the main muscle groups of the body.

Training programs designed for Junior A, university, or professional player should follow a completely different approach. The main objective of training for these players is to increase performance to the highest possible level. Strength training has its role in accomplishing such an objective. A strength program for elite-class players, especially during the competitive phase, has to be very specific with only a few exercises (three to six) directed precisely to the main muscle groups. Proportions of 60% for legs and 40% for upper body are advisable, starting from the mid-preparatory phase.

The Order of Exercises

Exercises should be planned so that the performer is constantly alternating between limbs and muscle groups, to ensure a better recovery. If all parts of the body are utilized, the following order is suggested: legs, arms, abdomen; legs, arms, back, etc. This order refers to one session. Coaches should resist the influence of bodybuilding, which applies the so-called split-routine. This involves certain muscle groups in one day, say chest and shoulders, then arms and back the next day, and legs on a third day.

Such a method is not recommended for hockey, where strength training is performed two to three times a week at best. For example, by applying the split-routine, the legs would be trained just once a week. This is quite inappropriate and the training benefits are questionable. The coach should, therefore, train all of the major muscle groups used in hockey in every strength training session. To ensure efficiency, exercises have to be multi-jointed and therefore involve many muscle groups (i.e., squats).

Another important training concept is the alternation of exercises. As seen in our suggested programs, each chart has the exercises listed from top to bottom. When working out, players should perform the first exercise and take the suggested rest interval, then move down to the next exercise. The advantage of this method, as opposed to doing all sets for the first exercise, is alternation of muscle groups, which results in better muscle recovery. By the time exercise number one is performed again more time has passed, allowing the muscles to better rest and recover before performance of another set.

The Number of Repetitions and the Speed of Lifting

The number of repetitions and the speed of lifting depend on the load. The higher the load, the lower the number of repetitions and speed of lifting. Table 3.2 illustrates the number of repetitions for a given load, speed of lifting, and training benefits.

TABLE 3.2: The Load, Number of Repetitions, and Speed of Lifting for Strength Training

Load % of 1 RM	Number of Repetitions	Speed of Lifting	Training Benefits
100	1		
95	2–3	Slow	
90	4		Maximum strength
85	5–6	Medium	
80	8 (10)		
75	10–12		
70	15	Fast	Power
65	20–25		
60	25		
55	25–30	Explosive	Power-endurance
50	40		
40	50		

It is impossible for the speed of contraction for heavy maximal loads of over 90% to be anything but slow; however, the player should focus on applying force against the resistance as aggressively and with the maximum concentration possible. In this way, more muscle fibers are recruited into action, which results in higher gains in maximum strength.

Number of Sets

"A set" consists of a number of repetitions of an exercise followed by a rest interval. The number of sets is related to the type of strength being trained, the total number of exercises, and the number of repetitions per set. As the number of repetitions of an exercise increases, the number of sets decreases. If an athlete is training with a lower number of repetitions per exercise, the number of sets can be increased to five or six. A general strength program usually has between three and four sets.

The training phase is also a factor in the number of sets performed in each training session. In the general preparation phase, the number of exercises is lower, and consequently the number of sets is higher. During the competitive phase, where strength maintenance is the prime objective, the number of exercises and sets is reduced for the one or two workouts per week, and more time is spent on technical and tactical work.

In general, the highly trained player should be able to perform between three and eight sets, depending on the level of training. Beginners should use only one or two sets per exercise each workout.

Rest Intervals between Sets

The rest interval determines the amount of restoration of the anaerobic energy system (alactic and lactic acid) that is achieved, and is of utmost importance in a well-designed strength program. For complete restoration, the alactic system needs up to three minutes, and if this is not allowed, energy depletion will begin in the lactic system. When rest periods are reduced to 30 seconds, and relatively heavy loads are used, lactate levels are high and early fatigue ensues.

Shortening rest intervals can, however, create greater tolerance for the lactic acid system, which is so important for the game of hockey.

Improving Muscular Endurance

Table 3.3, which summarizes rest interval information, is useful in determining the rest intervals for the various strength programs. The central nervous system, including the motor nerve, the neuromuscular junction, and the contractible mechanism, will recover with a rest interval of between four and five minutes.

TABLE 3.3: Suggested Rest Intervals between Sets for Different Loads

Load %	Rhythm of Performance	RI (minutes)	Applicability
> 105 (Eccentric)	Slow	4–5/7	Improve maximum strength and muscle tone
80–100	Slow to Medium	3–5/7	Improve maximum strength and muscle tone
60-80	Slow to Medium	2	Improve muscle hypertrophy
50–80	Fast	4–5	Improve power
30–50	Slow to Medium	1–2	Improve muscular endurance

Activity during Rest

Relaxation exercises, such as shaking the arms and legs, and light massage allow for faster recovery between sets. Walking, stretching, and light muscle contractions also aid in recovery from fatigue between sets as they facilitate lactic acid removal.

Rest Interval between Strength Workouts

It is generally believed that training three times a week, every other day, is the optimum method for efficient strength development. The level of condition, age, the training phase, and the energy source used are important factors in determining the rest days between strength training.

The rest interval between strength training sessions also has to take into account the energy systems being used in the technical and tactical training. Strength training sessions should follow the technical and tactical training, and be on the same day. The next training of this type should then follow 48 hours later to allow for full restoration of the glycogen stores.

Frequency of Strength Training

The frequency, or number of training sessions per week, depends on age, level of performance, and training phase, as in many aspects of training.

Although it is not suggested that tykes (ages 6 to 7) and novice (8 to 9) do classical strength training, they can, however, do general overall developmental exercises. From atom on (10 to 11), simple low-intensity strength training using body exercises (e.g., pushups, situps, etc.) can begin (see Chapter 18).

Hockey players from atom, pee wee (12 to 13), and bantam (14 to 15) can perform two light resistance strength training sessions during the preparatory phase and one or two during league games. From midget (16 to 17) on, to juvenile (18 to 21) and juniors (16 to 20), a more formal and comprehensive program has to be organized, with three strength training sessions per week during the preparation phase and two during league games (see Chapters 16 and 17).

Highly skilled and trained junior players (19 and 20), university teams, and professional players can train three to four times during the preparatory phase, and two times during league games (see Chapters 14 and 15).

Certainly, the planning of strength training during league games has to be flexible and take into consideration the players' level of fatigue, playing schedule, and traveling

schedule. During the preparatory phase, the program has to be more formal and of 1 to 1.5 hours' duration. For league games, the duration has to be substantially reduced to 20 to 30 minutes.

Warm-up and Cool-down for Strength Training

Every strength program should include a warm-up before beginning the strength exercises and a cool-down after the exercises have been completed. The warm-up should consist of a general phase of between 10 and 12 minutes. This should include a light jog, running on a treadmill, or riding a stationary bike for five or six minutes, followed by five or six minutes of stretching. A specific phase lasting up to three to five minutes should follow, using some of the exercises to be performed in training, with loads lighter than those used in regular training.

The cool-down follows the workout and consists of similar exercises included in the general warm-up, such as stretching and light jogging or riding a stationary bike. The cool-down usually lasts five to10 minutes.

Proper Breathing

It is recommended that lifters inhale just before and during the lowering of a weight or resistance, and exhale when lifting. Some breath-holding may occur during the last repetition in a set or during a heavy lift. Breath-holding is not recommended, as it causes an increase in blood pressure and reduces the blood flow to the heart. When the breath is released, blood flow is reduced to the brain, and dizziness and fainting can occur.

Weight-Training Belt

The weight-training belt is designed to help support the lower back. The belt is merely an aid to counteract the lack of strong abdominal and lower-back musculature, and it should be used only in exercises involving the lower back. Strengthening the lower back and abdominal muscles is a better method, however, than relying on the training belt.

Training Log

The training log should be used to record the number of sets, repetitions, and resistances for each exercise for each training session. Keeping this record enables the player to measure the progress in the strength training program and determine the increases in repetitions and load. Short forms such as Table 3.4 are commonly used in a training log. The training log is a good motivational tool to measure progress and evaluate the success of the program.

TABLE 3.4: A Suggested Training Log for Strength Training

Date: _____

Team: _____   Coach: _____

No.	Exercise	Set 1		Set 2		Set 3		Set 4		Set 5		Set 6	
		Load	Reps	Load	Reps	Load	Reps	Load	Reps	Load	Reps	Load	Reps
1													
2													
3													
4													
5													
6													
7													
8													
9													
10													
11													
12													

PERIODIZATION OF STRENGTH/POWER TRAINING

The annual plan, as discussed previously, divides the training year into three main phases: preparatory, or pre-season; competitive, or in-season; and transition, or off-season.

The periodization of strength training can be divided into five phases:

1. Anatomical adaptation
2. Maximum strength
3. Conversion to power
4. Maintenance
5. Transition

Anatomical Adaptation Phase

The purpose of this first phase of strength/power development is to enable tendons, ligaments, and muscle tissue to handle progressively increasing loads. The exercise program should be designed to strengthen the arms and legs, and the core muscles of the body that include the abdominals and lower back, as well as the spinal column musculature. These core exercises strengthen the trunk to support arm and leg movements, as well as prepare the body for the jumping, land-

ing, and falling movements that are part of off-ice training for hockey. All muscle groups should be exercised, and special attention should be paid to the balance between the agonist and antagonist muscles, the balance between the two sides of the body, and strengthening the stabilizer muscles.

The duration of this phase should be eight to 10 weeks for younger inexperienced players and three to five weeks for players who have been strength training for at least four years.

Maximum Strength Phase

The objective of this phase is to develop the highest level of force possible. The body adapts the neuromuscular system to heavy loads and the recruitment of as many muscle fibers as possible in a given movement. The duration of this phase depends on the sport, but usually lasts from one to three months. This phase prepares the body for the development of power, as power is a product of maximum strength and speed. Heavier loads with a lower number of repetitions are used in this phase.

Power Conversion Phase

The main purpose of this phase is to convert or transform gains in maximum strength into power and specific movements. Lighter loads are employed with fast contractions, where the player is exposed to activities in which the nervous system is activated and the speed of the contraction is sport-specific. Weights and plyometrics are used in this phase, along with sport-specific movements using resistance with light weights, elastic tubing, medicine balls, etc. The duration of this phase is usually four to five weeks.

Maintenance Phase

This phase continues throughout the competitive season, usually stopping one to two weeks before the playoffs. Without this phase, strength and power gains can be lessened by a detraining effect.

Usually, four to six exercises performed one to two times per week are sufficient to maintain the strength and power gained in the first three phases. The intensity of the training sessions should remain high, but the duration should be shorter, lasting between 30 and 40 minutes.

Transition Phase

The main purpose of this phase is to remove fatigue, replenish the energy stores, relax, and maintain the fitness and strength levels acquired in the previous four phases. Some strength work should be continued, as without it the detraining effect will cause a loss of muscle size and power. This phase lasts four to six weeks, and the workload is reduced by 50% to 60%.

DETRAINING AND STRENGTH MAINTENANCE

Most players are involved in a strength program during the preparation period of their training program. The questions often arise as to how much strength is lost when a strength program is completed, and what type of maintenance program is necessary during an player's competitive season.

After training ceases, strength declines at a much slower rate than it increases. Strength gained rapidly appears to be lost rapidly, whereas strength gained over a longer period of time declines at a slower rate. Strength gained is lost at approximately one-third the rate at which it is gained.

It is therefore recommended that players strength train at least one to two times per week to maintain the strength gained during the preparation period. Although the intensity, repetitions, and sets remain the same, the volume is decreased.

CHAPTER 4

Training the Energy System

THE ENERGY SYSTEMS

For a coach to design the daily, weekly, monthly, and yearly training programs, it is essential to understand how the hockey player derives the energy to perform. How much work to assign to players, how much rest to allow them, and how to have them at peak energy for games is information the coach must have.

The energy used by the hockey player to move his or her body is derived from the breakdown of the chemical compound named ATP (adenosine triphosphate). ATP is produced in the body by chemical reactions classified as aerobic and anaerobic. Recall from Chapter 1 that aerobic refers to the presence of oxygen and anaerobic refers to the lack of oxygen. The anaerobic system is further divided into alactic and lactic systems. With the alactic system, exercise for a short duration will not produce lactic acid, while the lactic system produces lactic acid, which causes fatigue. These systems are summarized below.

Production of ATP
- Anaerobic (without oxygen)
  - a) Alactic System (without lactic acid)
  - b) Lactic System (produces lactic acid)

- Aerobic (Oxygen) System

Characteristics of the Anaerobic–Alactic System
(also called the ATP/CP or phosphagen systems)

- This system supplies the ATP for all-out effort of up to 10 seconds, and contributes for up to 30 seconds.
- ATP is stored in the muscle cell.
- The breakdown of ATP does not require oxygen.
- Creatine phosphate (CP) is a chemical compound also present in the muscle cell that, with its breakdown, remakes (resynthesizes) ATP.
- The total stores of ATP and CP in the muscle are small so the system is limited. The energy, however, is rapidly available.
- One-half of the ATP used can be restored in 30 seconds of recovery. Almost all is restored in approximately three minutes.

The Characteristics of the Anaerobic–Lactic Acid System (also called anaerobic glycolysis)

- This system supplies the majority of ATP for activities requiring energy for longer than 10 seconds, and contributes for up to three minutes. The system is predominant in intense exercise of 30 to 60 seconds in duration.
- Glycogen, which is stored in the muscle cell, is the immediate source used to generate ATP. Glycogen is the storage form of glucose (sugar). Some glycogen is also stored in the liver and can be converted to blood glucose to assist in the production of ATP.
- More ATP is supplied than with the alactic system, but the supply is also limited.
- A by-product called lactic acid is produced which, when it reaches a certain level, causes muscle fatigue and soreness.
- During recovery, one-half of the ATP is restored in approximately 15 minutes, and 95% is restored in one hour.
- Light exercise aids in the removal of the lactic acid.

Characteristics of the Aerobic, or Oxygen, System

- This system is used to supply energy in prolonged activities, especially over three minutes, and is important in the recovery process.
- It is capable of manufacturing large amounts of ATP by utilizing both carbohydrates (glycogen) and fats.
- It produces no fatiguing by-products such as lactic acid.
- It takes several minutes for this system to become the major producer of ATP, because it takes this long for the oxygen we breathe to be assimilated into the blood and transported to the muscle cell.
- Carbohydrates contribute to the manufacture of ATP early in prolonged activity, whereas fats contribute later. Carbohydrates can produce ATP more efficiently than fats.
- The supply of ATP in this system is unlimited, and it is usually other factors such as lack of fluids or muscle soreness that cause fatigue, rather than a lack of ATP.

Interaction of the Energy Systems

The three energy systems all supply ATP, although the alactic system acts only during a very short burst of exercise lasting a few seconds, while the oxygen system acts in longer-endurance activities with a steady pace. From a few seconds to three minutes there is an interaction of the energy systems to supply ATP, as shown in Tables 4.1 and 4.2.

TABLE 4.1: Relationship of Performance Time to Energy Systems Supplying ATP

Performance Time	Major Energy System(s) Supplying ATP
Less than 10 seconds	Alactic
10 seconds to 90 seconds	Alactic and lactic
90 seconds to 3 minutes	Lactic acid and oxygen
More than 3 minutes	Oxygen

TABLE 4.2: Approximate % Contribution of Energy Systems (The Canadian Hockey Association. Source: *Intermediate Level Course Conductor Manual,* 1989, Overhead #9. Reprinted by permission.)

Work Time Maximal Effort	Alactic Anaerobic	Lactic Anaerobic	Aerobic
5 seconds	85	10	5
10 seconds	50	35	15
30 seconds	15	65	20
1 minute	8	62	30
2 minutes	5	46	50
4 minutes	2	28	70
10 minutes	1	9	90
30 minutes	negligible	5	95
1 hours	negligible	2	98
2 hours	negligible	1	99

The Energy Systems in Hockey

The training of the energy systems is an essential component of the physical training of a hockey player. Hockey is a non-steady state type of activity, where the intermittent actions of the players involve both the alactic and lactic systems (anaerobic) supplemented with the aerobic component in supplying ATP.

Hockey is an intermittent activity where shifts on the ice can last from several seconds to approximately 90 seconds. The shift on the ice can amount to up to 40 seconds of active ice time and 30 to 40 seconds of moderate to low-intensity work, and possible stoppages in play (up to three). The shift has periods of very high-intensity activity of sprint skating, battling for the puck along the boards, and giving and taking body checks. There are also periods of time when moderate activity such as gliding or playing at a moderate pace occur. The average player plays between 12 and 20 shifts a game and has an average rest period of 225 seconds between shifts (Wise, 1993). The rest interval between periods is 15 minutes. It has been estimated that 70% to 80% of the energy for a hockey athlete is derived from the alactic and lactic systems (anaerobic). Although the aerobic energy system supplies only a small portion of the energy for intense effort, it does, however, supply most of the energy needed for moderate activity (gliding and playing at a low intensity). It is also very important for recovery between stoppages of play and the rest time on the bench. The more ice time a player has, the longer the shifts and the shorter the time on the bench, then the more important is the contribution of the aerobic system. The approximate contribution of each energy system for the various types of activity possible in a shift on the ice is shown in Table 4.3.

TABLE 4.3: Approximate % Contribution from Each Energy System for Specific Activities in Hockey (The Canadian Hockey Association. Source: *Intermediate Level Manual,* 1989, 11.10.)

Type of Activity	Energy System		
	Alactic Anaerobic	Lactic Anaerobic	Aerobic
5-second burst	85	10	5
10 seconds of hard skating	60	30	10
30 seconds of continuous activity	15	70	15
1-minute shift of intermittent sprints, coasting and stops	10	60	30
Recovery between shifts/periods	5	5	90

Training the Energy Systems

As mentioned previously, all three energy systems should be trained for ice hockey. The aerobic system should be trained early in the general and specific preparation periods and then maintained as the start of the competition period approaches. The alactic and lactic anaerobic systems should be trained after the aerobic base is built, and the intensity and duration of this training should increase as the competition period approaches.

The Alactic (ATP/CP) System

The alactic system is usually trained with all-out bursts of speed, resistance (strength/power), and plyometric movements lasting between five and 10 seconds, with a work-to-rest ratio of 1:5 or 1:6. The five- to 10-second bursts use the alactic system to supply ATP without entering the lactate system. The rest periods of 30 to 60 seconds allow the ATP to be 50% to 75% restored for the next exercise burst. The total work volume should be 60 seconds for one set (a set being a number of repetitions), allowing three to 10 minutes between sets, which facilitates the total restoration of the alactic system. The training should be related to the movements in hockey, and the intensity should be maximal. The frequency of training should be every other day, or three times per week. Noticeable improvement occurs in eight to 12 weeks. Progression occurs by adding sets, shortening the pause time, and/or increasing the intensity.

Maintenance of this system in the competitive period of training should be done two or three times per week. In detraining, the alactic system maintains 80% to 90% of the gains for the next six weeks, although some losses are evident in the first two weeks.

An example of an alactic workout using quick burst acceleration sprinting would include:

- Duration: 5 to 10 seconds
- Intensity: maximal or near maximal (95%)
- Repetitions: 10 to 20 per set
- Rest between reps: 30 seconds to 2 minutes (shorter for technical/tactical drills)
- Total work time: 75 to 200 seconds
- Total workout time: 10 to 20 minutes

The Lactic System

The lactic system is a major supplier of ATP in intense exercise lasting from 10 seconds to about two minutes, with peak output at approximately 30 seconds. This system is usually preceded in the preparation period with the development of an aerobic training program that acts as a base to build the anaerobic system. The aerobic base allows for a faster and more efficient recovery time between repetitions, sets, and training days.

The intensity of the training should be near maximal and, if possible, the exercises should be specific to the movements of hockey. The training intervals should range from 15 to 90 seconds, with the optimal time being between 30 and 60 seconds. The rest intervals should range from a 1:6 or 1:5 to a 1:3 work-to-rest ratio. Recovery time between sets should range from 10 to 15 minutes, with light skating or jogging, and flexing and stretching being done in the rest

intervals to help in the removal of lactic acid. The total work time should last between 10 and 12 minutes. Training should be done three times per week on alternate days. Recovery of the glycogen stores from intermittent exercise of this intensity takes at least 24 hours.

A word of caution about the training of the lactic system: younger and inexperienced players should reduce the intensity and duration of this type of training. Prepubescent players do not possess the capacity for any noticeable improvements in this system. Their total volume of training should be reduced to less than three minutes, with training intervals reduced to 25 seconds or less, and longer rest times should be provided between sets.

Detraining effects occur more rapidly with the lactic system compared to the alactic system, with 50% of the training gain lost within six weeks of stopping training. Maintenance of the system can be achieved with two or three workouts per week (usually on ice) during the competition period.

An example of a lactic system workout using the mode of skating, hockey drills, or running would include:

- Duration: 15 to 90 seconds
- Intensity: near maximal (95%)
- Repetitions: 5 to 12
- Rest between rep: 1.5 minutes to 3 minutes
- Total work time: 5 minutes
- Total workout time: 45 minutes (approx.)

Modes of training other than skating or running could include swimming, cycling, stationary bike, skipping, and hill running.

The Aerobic System

Aerobic training is important as a means of recovery for intermittent anaerobic sports such as ice hockey. The ability of this system to efficiently take in oxygen and deliver it to the working muscles is important in hockey. An aerobic training base is, therefore, an important part of the training program in the general preparation period. The higher the aerobic endurance, the lesser role the anaerobic system plays, and as a result players will experience lower levels of fatigue.

The aerobic system can be trained using two methods: continuous long-distance exercise, and intermittent interval training. Submaximal continuous exercise (75% MVO_2, approximately 165 beats per minute heart rate) improves the delivery rate of oxygenated blood from the heart to the muscles (central adaptations, i.e., cardiac output). This can be trained using a variety of modes such as running, swimming, cycling, on-ice skating, in-line skating (Rollerblades), and long-duration hockey drills. Intermittent aerobic training trains both the central adaptations (cardiac output and oxygen delivery) and the peripheral adaptations (increasing the oxygen-extraction capabilities of the working muscles). As much as possible, especially from the second part of the preparatory phase on, aerobic training should be hockey-specific (i.e., long-duration drills).

The aerobic (O_2) training we propose in our training programs is slightly different from the traditional North American school of thought. Often, the endurance training program of hockey teams for the preparatory phase is based on two elements: one, a steady-state, continuous run of 30 to 60 minutes, and the other, interval training of 2.5 minutes run and 2.5 minutes rest, repeated several times in a training session.

The importance of endurance training is that it makes a team more consistent throughout the three periods of the game and enables players to cope more easily with the fatigue of training, playing, and traveling. In recognition of this, we propose a slightly different approach in our programs.

We do start the early part of aerobic training with long-duration, continuous activity (running, Rollerblades, cycling, stationary bike, or slide board for the younger players. After four to five weeks of long-distance aerobic training, however, we introduce "long repetitions," or repetitions of 20, 15, 10, and 5 minutes.

There is a great training advantage to continuing long-distance aerobic training with "long reps" and then anaerobic lactic acid system training. One reason is that this provides a far better progression for training the aerobic and anaerobic systems. Another reason is that when training long distance, the heart rate is around 156 to 164 beats per minute (b/m), while during "long reps" training the heart rate is 168 to174 b/m and sometimes even higher. In addition, the mean velocity for "long reps" is much higher than during long-distance training, which means that this type of training is closer to the physiological demand of the game of hockey than long-distance aerobic training. This is also evident in the way the heart responds to the two types of training.

On this more game-specific aerobic base, we then introduce the anaerobic lactic acid system, and later in the preparatory phase, the alactic energy system.

Continuous aerobic training with skating, running, cycling, roller skating, etc., should last a minimum of 20 to 40 minutes and be done at least three times a week on alternate days. Recovery of the glycogen stores takes longer with this type of exercise (usually 48 hours) as compared with intermittent exercise (approximately 24 hours). Improvement comes with increasing the intensity, duration, and/or frequency of the training. The intensity increase is usually 75% to 80% MVO_2 maximal, or heart rate of approximately

168 to 175 b/m. To repeat, several different modes of training can be used effectively to provide variety in training while still achieving improvements in the central adaptation.

Intermittent aerobic training, as mentioned, improves both the central adaptations and peripheral adaptations (oxygen extraction at the cellular level). This type of training allows for higher training intensities and improves the anaerobic threshold (usually approximately 85% of maximum heart rate). Anaerobic threshold is the point where lactic acid begins to build up and interfere with muscle contraction. Improved recovery times also result from intermittent exercise.

Intermittent aerobic training is of two types: training time of two to five minutes, with two minutes being the most common, with a 1:1 work-to-rest ratio; and shorter intervals of approximately 15 to 20 seconds, repeated 20 to 30 times, working at a pace slightly above the anaerobic threshold.

Intermittent aerobic training should always be used after a continuous aerobic training base has been established.

TABLE 4.4: General Guidelines for Training the Energy Systems

System	Duration of Exercise	Work-to-Rest Ratio	Percentage of Maximum Heart Rate
Alactic (ATP-CP)	5–10 seconds	1:5 – 1:6	95–100
Lactic	20–90 seconds	1:5 – 1:3	85–95
Aerobic	20–60 minutes continuous 90 seconds to 5 minutes for drills	1:5 – 1:1	85–90

Interval training is the best method for the systematic training of the energy systems. Although the traditional stops and starts in ice hockey is a form of interval training, a specific system and progression should be devised for their use.

Interval training uses work, interspersed with periods of rest, to achieve the desired improvement. If the intensity is not too high during intermittent work, the level of accumulation of lactic acid is lower than levels that would occur during continuous work. The ATP/CP system is used more extensively and, consequently, the lactic acid system is not fully depleted. Interval training does the following:

- allows the ATP/CP system to be used over and over
- delays the onset of fatigue by not delving so deeply into the lactic acid system

- allows the system to become more tolerant to lactic acid
- works long enough at sufficient intensity to allow an improvement in the aerobic system

The manipulated variables used in interval training are:
- rate and distance
- repetitions and sets
- duration of the relief interval
- type of activity during relief interval
- frequency of training

TABLE 4.5: Interval Training Explained

Terms	Definitions
Work interval	Portion of interval training program involving high-intensity work bursts
Repetition	1 work interval
Relief interval	Time between work interval (can be working, flexing, or light skating/jogging)
Set	Series of work and relief intervals
Training time	Rate at which work is performed

Aerobic training can include skating, running, rollerblading, or cycling. Aerobic training starts with continuous long-distance work and progresses to interval training.

Anaerobic alactic (ATP/CP) and lactic training can include running, skating, rollerblading, or use of the stationary bike. Some guidelines to follow:

- Perform a proper warm-up, including stretching exercises and jogging.
- Wear proper clothing and footwear.
- Work out three times per week.
- Work out on alternate days. Do strength/power training on the other days. Have one rest day after six days of training.
- Finish the workout with a cool-down. Walk, jog, or rollerblade for 1 mile (1 km), and finish with a stretching program.

ALTERNATING ENERGY SYSTEMS AND FITNESS COMPONENTS

Coaches, trainers, and players know that hockey is a very complex sport from the point of view of both the energy systems and technical and tactical skills. Hockey requires both the body and mind to refine a skill, train a given energy system during complex tactical drills, and constantly improve speed and power.

The question, therefore, is how to plan a micro-cycle so that all of the skills and fitness components are trained without overtraining the players. Furthermore, how can this be done to make sure that each energy system has time to restore its energy pools before the next training session or prior to a game?

To answer these questions, the first step is to classify the skills and types of training according to the energy system they require. The classification suggested below (see Table 4.6) represents a general guideline. It can be adapted and applied to specific conditions for more effective planning.

TABLE 4.6: A Suggested Classification of Skills and Physical Training to Be Used for the Alternation of Energy Systems

Anaerobic Alactic	Anaerobic Lactic	Aerobic
Tactical skills; 5–10 seconds	Tactical skills; 10–60 seconds	Tactical skills, long duration
Skills; 5–10 seconds	Technical skills; 10–60 seconds	Technical skills, medium and long duration
Maximum speed/ power skating up to 10 seconds	Speed training 10– 60 seconds	Aerobic endurance/long-duration drills
Maximum strength; 1–2 sets, long rest intervals	Power-endurance	Muscle endurance

As Table 4.6 shows, all the skills and fitness training classified under a given system can be planned in the same day, as they all require the same energy source. Although this is possible, for practical reasons the coach should select only some of these training options for one day and leave the balance to be trained on other days.

The second step is to create a weekly plan (micro-cycle) where the training options from Table 4.6 are alternated to favor the restoration of the energy system required in a given day. When energy is fully restored, the players will feel fully recovered, with all the physical and psychological benefits.

Before we suggest an example of a micro-cycle where the energy systems are alternated, it is important to mention that such training cycles are not planned to occur throughout the annual plan. In deciding when you must plan such a micro-cycle, you must remember that there will be training weeks when you will want the players to fully recover, and others when they must be pushed to exhaustion to challenge the level of adaptation of a given training phase.

Figure 4.7 shows how different types of training can be planned in a micro-cycle during the preparatory phase for a team that trains six times per week. The practice of alternating energy systems can be applied to teams that train three to four times per week (Figure 4.8).

FIGURE 4.7: The Alternation of Energy Systems for Hockey during the Preparatory Phase

Mon.	Tues	Wed.	Thurs.	Fri.	Sat.	Sun.
– T	– TA	– T	– TA	– T	– TA	
– S	– O$_2$ END.	– P/MxS	– O$_2$ END.	– S	– O$_2$ END.	
– P/Mxs				– P/Mxs		

As shown in Figure 4.7, all types of training belonging to a given energy system are planned in a given day. For instance, alactic types of training are planned for Monday/Wednesday/Friday, namely: technique (T), speed (S), and power (P) or maximum strength (MxS). Theoretically, it is possible to train all in the same day, but this is not advisable because such a training session would be far too taxing. To work on certain technical refinements, such as maximum speed, use power skating or fast but short drills. A few sets of power training or maximum strength exercises in the same day is, however, a realistic possibility for more advanced hockey players. Why? Because all the above training options rely on the ATP/CP as fuel, which does replenish relatively quickly.

On Tuesday, the coach can plan tactical (TA) drills, taxing the lactic acid system, followed by either aerobic drills or aerobic training (O$_2$ END). Aerobic training, as planned at the end of the session, helps to remove the lactic acid accumulated in the first part of the session more quickly. Consequently, the energy stores are replenished and recover much faster before the next day's training session.

The same approach is possible for either Thursday or Saturday. Our advice, however, is to plan it for Thursday, since specific aerobic system training, via specific but long-duration drills, also has to be trained at least one a week.

From analyzing Figures 4.7 and 4.8, the coach can see that all energy systems contributing to hockey performance are carefully planned. Furthermore, by following the above approach, all of the energy systems and fitness components prevailing in hockey will be trained. Finally, by alternating the energy systems from day to day, you do guarantee that a given energy fuel will be restored by the next day and players will recover faster. As a result, they avoid lactate fatigue, as well as overall mental and physical fatigue.

FIGURE 4.8: A Suggested Micro-cycle for the Alternation of Energy Systems with Only Four Training Sessions per Week

Mon.	Tues	Wed.	Thurs.	Fri.	Sat.	Sun.
– T	– TA lactic		– T/TA lactic	– T/TA lactic		
– S	– TA lactic		– S	– TA aerobic or		
– P/Mxs			– P/MxS	– O$_2$ END.		

Alternating energy systems and the prevailing fitness components in hockey will actually assist you to better address the needs of training a very complex sport.

TRAINING THE ENERGY SYSTEMS: ON-ICE DRILLS

Anaerobic–Alactic System (short intense work)

Drills 1 to 5

Work-to-rest ratio: 1:6 to 1:5
5 repetitions equal 1 set
Build to 4 sets; i.e., 20 repetitions
Use 4 to 5 groups: one group works while the others rest
Allow for a longer rest/relief period after each set

Anaerobic–Lactic System (medium intense work)

Drills 6 to 30

30 to 60 seconds
Work-to-rest ratio: 1:5 to 1:3
4 repetitions equal 1 set
Build to 3 sets; i.e., 12 repetitions
Use 3 or 4 groups: one group works while the others rest
Allow for a longer rest/relief period after each set.

Aerobic System (long moderate work)

Drills 31 to 33

3 minutes or more of work
Work-to-rest ratio: 2:1 to 1:2
Build to 20 minutes of continuous skating

Note: It is now recommended that players skate lightly every 3 minutes and stretch the back for 10 seconds to prevent or alleviate back pain.

TRAINING THE ANAEROBIC–ALACTIC SYSTEM: DRILLS 1 TO 5

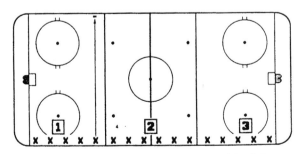

1 Using 3 groups, each group skates 1 width of the ice or from the goal line to the center red line, in turn.
Variation: Each group skates 2 widths of the ice or from the goal line to the center red line and back, in turn.

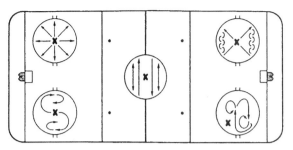

2 Using 5 groups, the players perform a different drill in each circle—stops and starts, figure 8s, speed around the circle, etc.

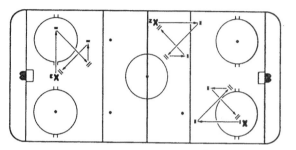

3 Players skate the preset pattern shown, as fast as they can. Run 2 players at a time and then switch to a new set of 2.

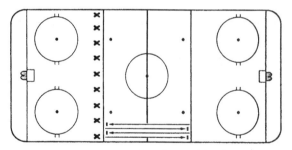

4 Have each group skate blue line to blue line, 2, 3, or 4 in turn.

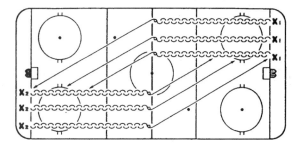

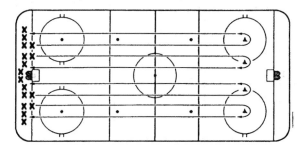

5   From the goal line, X1 and X2 players skate backward to the center red line, pivot, and skate diagonally across the ice to the far corner of the rink.

8   The player skates down the ice, around the pylon and back. The next player in line starts when his teammate crosses the goal line.

TRAINING THE ANAEROBIC–LACTIC SYSTEM: DRILLS 6 TO 30

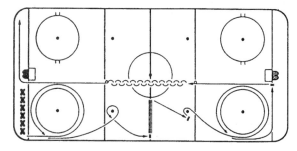

6   Players line up in the corner of the ice. They skate clockwise around the face-off circle, skate to the near neutral zone dot and do a tight turn, skate forward to the center red line, stop, and do stepovers to the edge of the center ice face-off circle. The players skate to the neutral zone dot as shown, pivot, and skate counter-clockwise around the face-off circle. Then the players skate to the blue line, pivot, skate backward to the other blue line, pivot, and skate hard to the goal line and into the far corner.

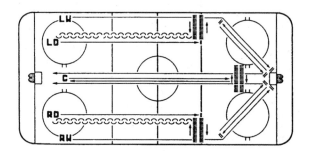

9   Five players go at the same time in this drill. LW and RW skate forward to the far blue line, drive to the net and back twice, and then back to where they started. C skates to the inside hash marks at the far end, does stepovers to the edge of each circle and back to the middle, then returns to the start position. LD and RD skate to the far blue line, do stepovers to the boards and back, and then skate backward to the goal line to the start position.

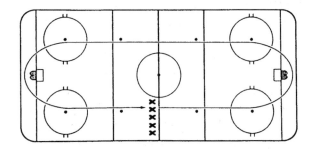

10   Each group skates from 2 to 4 laps around the rink.

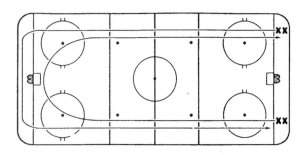

7   Players from one side skate in front of the net, and players from the other side skate behind the net. Players from both sides go at the same time. This can be done with 1, 2, or 3 players at a time.

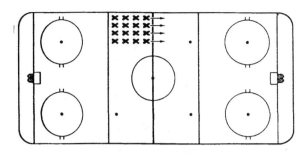

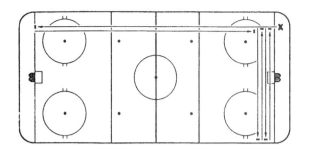

11   The same as previous drill except the team is divided into groups that run relay races. Each group skates 2 or 3 laps.

14   The players skate the length of the ice, stop, and skate back, moving back and forth across the ice twice, and then skate the length of the ice back to the start position.

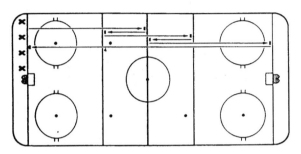

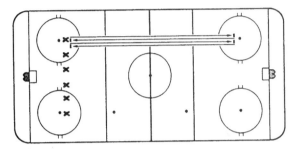

12   Each group skates forward from the goal line to the center red line, back to the near blue line, then to the far blue line, back to the center red line, then to the far goal line, and, finally, the length of the ice.

15   Each player skates from the defensive face-off dot to the one at the far end, 4 times.

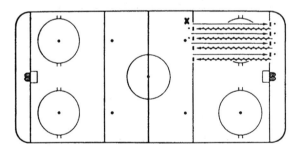

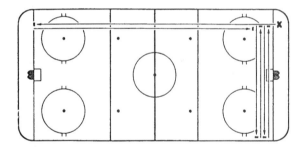

13   Place 5 pucks on the blue line. Players start on the goal line, skate to the blue line, stop, pick up a puck, skate back to the goal line, stop, drop the puck, and repeat until all 5 pucks have been moved. The second group starts on the blue line and brings the 5 pucks back.

16   Players skate the length of the ice and return, and then do stepovers across the ice twice.

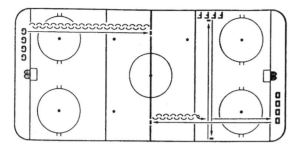

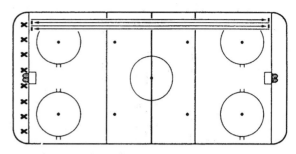

17 *Defense:* Skate forward to the center red line, backward to the blue line, and then turn and skate forward to the goal line. Do the drill 3 times, alternating the pivot to backward position.

Forwards: Skate forward across the rink and back 3 times, touching the boards with their sticks.

Goaltenders: Skate forward to the center red line, drop to both knees holding goal stick and catcher in proper position. Rise and skate backward to the goal line and do a double leg-pad slide to one side. Do this drill twice, but on the second time, switch sides for the slide.

20 Each group skates from goal line to goal line 4 times.

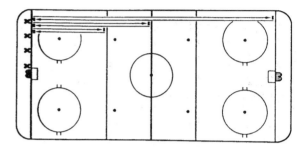

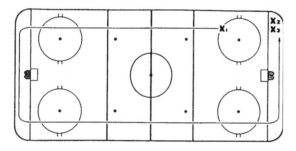

18 Player X1 starts on the top of the circle and 3 or 4 players chase X1 around the ice. The chase players start at the bottom of the circle.

21 Each group skates from the near goal line to the far goal line and back, to the center red line and back, and to the near blue line and back.

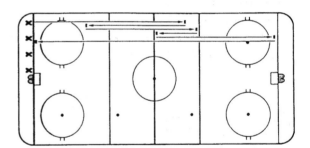

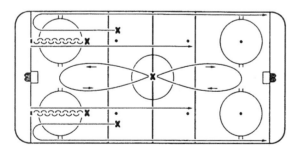

19 Divide the team into 5-player units. Players practice their breakout system without a puck and at full speed.

22 Each group does stops and starts using the entire length of the ice, changing direction on the whistle. Have groups work from 20 to 40 seconds.

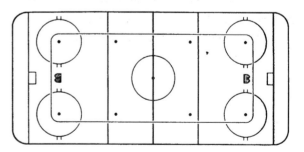

23 Each group skates 3 laps around the defensive zone face-off dots.

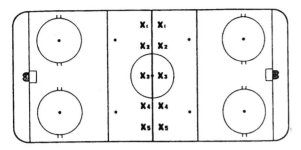

24 Games of 1-on-1 are played all over the ice. Start at 30 seconds and move up to 90 seconds at a time.

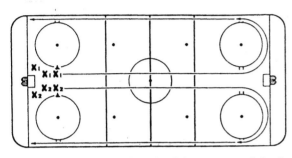

25 X1 and X2 skate the length of the ice, around the face-off circle on their side of ice, and return to the goal line where they started. The next player goes when their teammate crosses the goal line.

Variation: Have players skate hard for 1 length of the ice and return slowly on the outside. Start again when recovered. Repeat for 5 minutes.

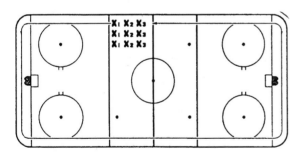

26 The players line up in 3 groups at the blue line. Each group skates 1 lap of the ice as hard as they can, 1 player at a time.

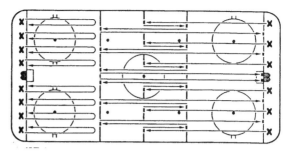

27 (**VARIATION 22**) The players race to the blue line, do tight turns, and then skate back to the goal line. The players then skate to the red line, stop, skate back to the blue line, stop, skate forward to the opposite blue line, stop, and skate to the goal line.

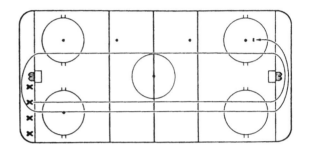

28 Each group skates around the rink behind the nets for 1½ laps, then goes in the other direction for 1½ laps, in turn.

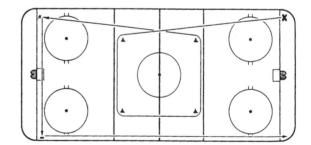

29 Starting in the corner, the players make a full loop in the neutral zone, skate to the opposite corner and stop, skate the width of the ice and stop, and skate to the far end of the ice.

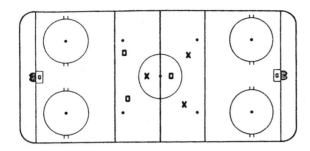

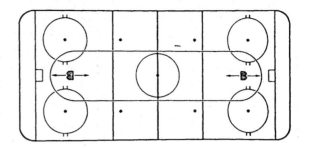

30 Play a 3-on-3 or 4-on-4 scrimmage using the full ice. Players change while the puck is in play. On the change, the puck is passed to the goaltender. On offsides, the puck is passed back to the goaltender and the offending team must move outside the opposing team's blue line. Players scrimmage for 30 seconds to 1 minute, and then rest. Have players come in one end of the bench and out the other. The next 3 or 4 players in order go on the whistle.

TRAINING THE AEROBIC SYSTEM: DRILLS 31 TO 33

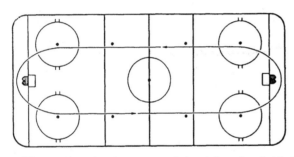

31 The entire team skates around the rink, going behind each net. The players skate for 3 minutes and then change direction and skate the other way for 3 minutes. Continue the drill for 6 to 15 minutes. Move the nets to keep the ice in good condition.

32 The players skate around the rink behind the nets while the coaches move the nets toward center ice as laps are completed. When the nets reach center ice, have the players skate in the opposite direction, and the coaches start moving the nets back down the ice. The drill ends when the nets are back in the start position.

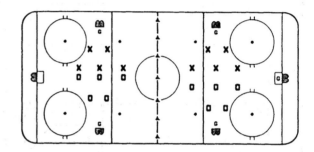

33 The players play two 5-on-5 scrimmages using half-ice. Each game is 10 minutes in length and change lines at the 5-minute mark. The players work for 5 minutes and rest for 5 minutes.

ON-ICE CIRCUIT TRAINING

The following circuit involves all three energy systems. It could be used in training camp or during the season for conditioning and speed/power training.

In this circuit, players work 2 to each station with 30 seconds of work followed by 30 seconds of rest, and then the exercise is repeated. Then the players change stations. Allow 1 minute for rest and changing stations.

1. Players start at the center line and skate to the blue line and back to the center line 4 times. Each tries to pick up a hockey stick and push back the other player.
2. Players play keep-away inside the face-off circle.
3. Players practice continuous breakaways from the center red line; one player chases the other player who shoots on goal, and then they alternate.
4. Without sticks, players try to body check the other man out of the face-off circle.

5. One man skates forward with the puck between the blue lines and passes it to a teammate, who is skating backward. The player skating backward stops and then skates forward with the puck and passes to his partner, who is skating forward.

6. Without using sticks, players fight for the puck along the boards, using their skates.

7. Players practice continuous breakaways from the blue line as pucks are picked up at the side of the net.

8. Players do stops and starts between the end boards and the top of the face-off circle.

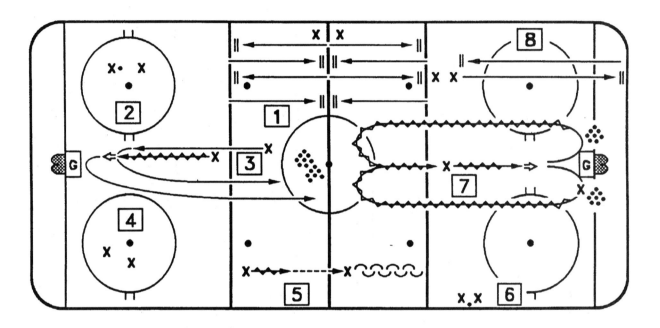

CHAPTER 5

Training for Quickness and Agility

Quickness, high-velocity power skating, reaction/movement time, agility, and quick changes of direction are skills sought after by any hockey player. Off- and on-ice training programs should be geared toward helping players achieve a high degree of skill in these areas.

Quickness in hockey comprises the following five elements:

- reaction/movement time, or how quickly a player reacts to different playing situations, with changes in direction, stopping and starting, etc.
- frequency of skating strides and fast footwork
- skating speed over a given distance
- movement time, especially for a goalie who must move arms and legs quickly to stop the puck
- leg power enhanced by plyometric exercises

Quickness, power, reaction time, and maximum velocity depend on several factors during play. On- or off-ice maximum velocity is often determined by heredity. Players who are top skaters are thought to have natural talent, which in fact means having a higher proportion of fast-twitch muscle fibers than slow-twitch muscle fibers. Maximum velocity is not achieved instantly, however, but rather after an acceleration distance of at least seven to 10 meters. Quickness and high-velocity skating are improved only as a result of increasing power and power-endurance.

Reaction time and movement time are also inherited features. In hockey we can distinguish two types of reaction:

1. *Simple reaction* refers to a predetermined conscious response to a known signal, such as the coach's whistle or the drop of the puck during face-offs.
2. *Choice reaction* refers to game situations that present a player with several options. For example, a defenseman must decide which attacker to take, or a forward must decide what position to take when attacking. Reaction time to a visual stimulus, such as the puck's motion, or when to pass or shoot the puck, is quite short for well-trained players (0.15 to 0.20 seconds) as opposed to beginners (0.17 to 0.27 seconds). This time is even shorter for international class athletes (0.5 to 0.07 seconds).

Movement time refers to the time that elapses between the start and finish of a limb's motion. Quick movement time is essential for many players, and is most important for goalies attempting to catch or block the puck.

A player's ability to concentrate maximally on the task is a determining factor of success for both reaction time and movement time. Fatigue negatively affects one's reaction time, as well the ability to concentrate maximally.

The technique of skating and gliding is a determinant in a player's ability to move fast and react quickly to a game situation, as well as for power skating. The development of the most effective skating technique should be one of a player's major goals in the early years of hockey training. To improve players' game effectiveness, a coach should spend more time training players than having them play a high number of games. Always remember that during the early stages of involvement in hockey, it is training that makes the best players, not playing a lot of games.

TRAINING METHODS TO DEVELOP QUICKNESS AND REACTION

All the methods used to develop quickness, high velocity, and power in skating have these common elements:

Intensity: For development of the above skills, intensity has to be close to or at maximum. When reaction is also trained, whether for skating, specific alactic drills, or combinations, the repetitions must be performed quickly, with good technique and maximum mental concentration on the task at hand. We strongly recommend that any activities performed for the development of quickness and speed be done on the days when players are rested, such as following an off-day or a low-intensity training session, and immediately after a good warm-up. It is specifically necessary for the nervous system to be fresh and therefore capable of concentrating and focusing on the exercise and/or drill you have planned.

Duration: The duration must not be longer than 10 seconds, and normally between five and 10 seconds, since exercises and drills used for quickness use the alactic energy system. In the case of skating for maximum speed, the duration has to allow for the time required for quick acceleration and, of equal importance, the time necessary to reach and maintain maximum velocity. If the duration exceeds 10 seconds, players start to build lactic acid that impairs the development of maximum quickness and speed.

Rest interval: When training for maximum speed, the rest interval between repetitions has to be long enough for an almost full recovery, about four to six minutes. If this is not observed, high-velocity repetitions may be impossible to repeat. Players need not be sitting still or inactive during rest intervals; they can work on their passing and shooting accuracy, but at low intensity and with more time between repetitions of passing and/or shooting.

TRAINING METHODS FOR QUICKNESS AND SKATING SPEED

The *repetition* method is the most important training method for speed training. Players have to perform a certain number of repetitions of fast skating or quickness drills with a set rest interval. These drills are repeated as many times as the coach has planned for that training session. For any training benefit, a given drill and/or skating for speed have to be repeated several times, especially those drills that may have an important technical component. For maximum benefit, similar types of activities have to be repeated several times per week, especially during the preparatory phase.

The *handicap* method allows players of different abilities to work together, provided they all have similar motivation. When a repetition is performed, the coach staggers the players according to their speed and power potentials, and starts them together. The scope of the exercise is to reach the set distance at approximately the same time. This method is often a very successful motivational tool for most players, especially the younger ones.

Relays are extremely effective for the development of quickness and maximum speed, especially for younger players. Organizing the team into equally talented players allows for an emotional involvement, which facilitates competitiveness between relay groups. Relays are organized to be performed with or without a puck. When a puck is used, the relay has to be technically simple, such as using pylons to skate around or change directions, etc.

TRAINING METHODS FOR THE DEVELOPMENT OF REACTION TIME

Reaction time can be developed off- or on-ice for all players, although the players who definitely need a great deal of training are the goalies.

The repetition method is also very useful for the development of this skill. The coach can normally use either sonic or visual stimuli, or rousing methods. For the *sonic* method you can use a whistle, clap your palms, or employ any other instrument that can create a stimulating sound.

Examples:

- The player skates backward toward the coach. At the coach's signal the player turns to face the coach, who indicates with his arm the direction in which the player must quickly move.
- The player skates backward toward the coach. At the coach's signal, the player turns to face the coach, who

passes the puck, which has to be quickly controlled by the player.

- The coach stays behind to the side of the goal. Player skates backward or sideways. At the sound of the whistle the coach passes the puck in a given direction around the goal. The player quickly changes direction toward the goal and shoots.
- Same as above with the intermediary task of controlling the puck while going around a cone, and then shooting to score.
- The player performs reaction drills lying prone on the ice in various positions. At the whistle, the player stands on his or her skates as quickly as possible, and then performs a reaction or technical task as indicated by the coach.
- Have two players push against each other. At the coach's signal, they have to perform a technical or reaction task.
- The player skates in an indicated direction. At the coach's signal, he or she performs a reaction or technical task.

The improvement of reaction time depends very much on how well you prepare and explain the drills and exercises to the players, as well as how focused the players are on the specified task. If a player's concentration is directed toward the exercise and/or drill to be performed rather than on how fast he or she hears and responds to the signal, then reaction time is much shorter. Reaction time is also reduced if prior to performing the drill the player slightly contracts the muscles needed to perform the action. This "set" condition allows the player to contract the muscles needed to perform the task at hand faster.

Choice reaction, which is so specific for hockey, has four segments. The player has to visualize or see the puck or player to take, perceive the direction and speed of the player or puck, select the plan of action, and actually perform it. The first phase, visualization or seeing the puck, takes the longest time. As soon as this is detected, the other three phases are much shorter. For this reason, the visualization phase must be emphasized most during training; for a defensive player, this is to see the moving puck or player. Among the drills you can use are:

- The coach passes the puck toward a player from unexpected positions, sudden directions, or at variable speeds. The player has to quickly get to the puck and take control of it. The drill can then be followed by other technical tasks.
- Use various drills in a reduced playing area where the traffic is quite high. Under this condition the player

has to concentrate maximally to visualize the puck, take control of it, pass, or shoot at the goal.

TRAINING METHODS FOR MOVEMENT TIME

In addition to the traditional drills used to train movement time for a goalie or any other player, you can use the reaction ball (see picture).

Off-ice:

- Throw the ball against the wall and try to catch it as quickly as possible.
- Same as above but hit the ball in a predetermined direction.
- Throw the ball against the floor. From the floor the ball should hit a wall, and then try to catch it.
- Perform all of the above with either hand, or leg.

On-ice:

- Throw the ball on the ice and have one, two, three, or four players battle to take control of it with their stick.
- Throw the ball against the boards, let it bounce, and then have one to four players battle to take control of it with their stick.
- Shoot the puck in the air; players are to block it with a leg, knock it down with a hand, or hit it with a stick.

- Distract the player's concentration (i.e., look at the ceiling), then quickly throw the puck in a given direction. Have the player take control of the puck and shoot at a predetermined part of the goal as quickly as possible.

Drills for reaction and movement time can be performed at the beginning of a training session when the players are fresh or at the end when they are fatigued. Often such drills have to be performed under the conditions of fatigue to train the players for the effort required in the second and third periods. Since variety is important, try to use your imagination to continually come up with new drills.

OFF-ICE DRILLS FOR QUICKNESS AND AGILITY

1. **Stepovers (Carioca)**
   Move laterally, alternately crossing one leg in front and one leg behind.

2. **Shake and Bake (Fast Feet)**
   Short, knees low, running on the spot. Fast movements moving forward.

3. **Stride Crossovers**
   Tape a line on the floor. Stand with feet on either side. Touch right toe to left calf. Alternate.

4. **Forward Crossovers**
   Stand with one foot forward and one foot behind. Switch feet back and forth.

5. Lateral Crossovers
Stand with feet apart. Jump and cross over feet. Land with ankles crossed. Repeat.

6. Backward Crossovers
Moving left, right leg crosses behind left leg.

7. Box Jumps (Single Four)
Using one or both feet, jump from square to square inside a box that is 2 feet (.185) square, taped to the floor as shown.

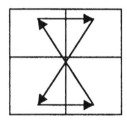

8. Box Jumps (Double Four)
Same as single four, but perform the jumps on both feet, in all possible directions.

9. Slalom
Use a line on a gymnasium floor or tape a 10-foot (3-m) line. With feet together, jump in slalom zigzag fashion across the line while moving forward. Move forward and then backward.

10. Slalom Jump and Sprint
Use a tape or line on a gym floor, or on a field (approx. 10 feet/3 m). Jump in slalom skiing fashion (zigzag), and at the end of the line, sprint forward for 10 to 15 yards (9 to 14 m).

11. Skipping
Skip fast for 30 seconds, then rest for 30 seconds.

12. Squat Thrusts (Burpees)
Stand, squat, thrust legs backwards. Pull knees into a squat position again. Stand up. Repeat.

13. Side Hops (18-inch bench/46-cm)
Side to side with both feet together.

14. Single Hops (18-inch bench/46-cm)
Take off and land on a different foot diagonally and across.

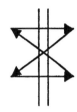

15. Step Hopping
Hop up stairs on one foot and then use both feet. Hop up one step at a time and then two steps at a time.

16. Split-Leg Shuffle
Stand with feet together. Jump and land in a wider stance. Jump again and land with feet together. Repeat.

17. Crossovers
Similar to drill No. 1 except there is no lateral movement. Jump in the air and land with legs crossed. Jump in the air again and cross legs the other way.

18. Hop the Box
Stand in the middle of a taped box on the floor with four quadrants. Hop in and out from the center to the eight points, returning to the center each time.

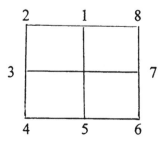

19. **Forward Lunges**

    Fall forward with one bent leg forward and the back leg fully extended. Push the front leg and return to the starting position. Repeat with the other leg forward.

20. **Depth Jumps**

    Jump off a 16-inch (40-cm) box, landing on one or both legs, and then jump high in the air, fully extending the legs.

21. **Depth Jumps—Side Movement**

    Same as drill No. 17 except on landing take one side step right or left and then sprint forward.

22. **Single and Double Leg Hops**

    From a standing position, drive one leg up and forward to gain distance. Land on the same foot or alternate foot. Pull arms to the side before landing and swing them upward and forward during takeoff. Repeat. Vary this by landing on both legs.

23. **Side Steps (Slide Board)**

    Using a slide board, step to the side as far as possible and then stride back.

24. **Shuttle Run**

    Run 10 feet (3 m) and touch the line, run 10 feet (3 m) back and touch the line. Rest for 30 seconds. Repeat.

ON-ICE DRILLS FOR QUICKNESS AND AGILITY

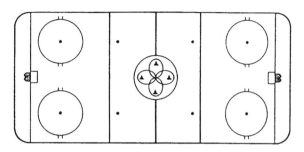

1   Players skate figure 8s backward around the pylons, with or without pucks.

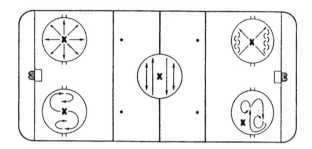

2   Players perform a different drill in each circle—stops and starts, figure 8s, speed-skate around the circle, etc.

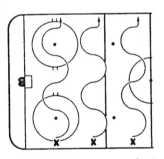

3   Players move in a wave across the ice, making 3 to 4 crossovers each way.

    Variation: The same drill but change the direction in response to a signal and do it the length of the ice.

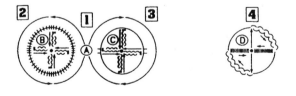

4 (1) Players skate a figure 8 backward.

(2) Players start in the middle, skate backward to the circle's edge, do crossovers for one-quarter circle, and skate forward to the dot. Have players repeat as many times as possible in time allowed.

(3) Players start in the middle of the circle and skate backward to the circle's edge and then forward to the dot. Have players repeat as many times as possible in time allowed.

(4) Players start in the middle and skate forward to the circle's edge, pivot, skate backward one-quarter circle, and then do stepovers back to the dot. Have players repeat as may times as possible in time allowed.

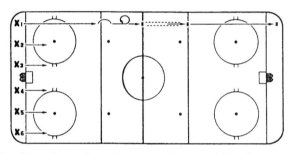

5 The players form lines behind the goal line for a race. On the whistle, the first players in each line skate full speed to the first blue line, dive on their stomachs, roll over like a log, then crawl on hands and knees fast to the far blue line, get up and skate full speed to the goal line at the far end.

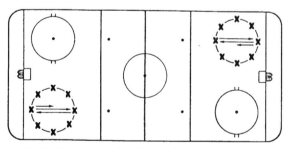

6 All the players stand in the circle facing outward (backs to the face-off dot). The "it" player touches another player and sprints back to his vacant spot. If the "it" player is touched before he gets back to his position, this player remains "it."

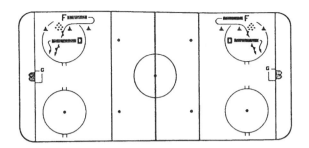

7 Place 3 pylons so that D has to do crossovers farther than F. On the whistle, both players move toward the goal. F returns, picks up the puck and goes 1-on-1 with D after the crossovers.

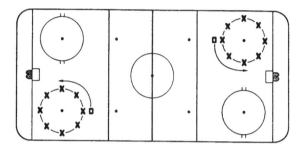

8 Players (10 to 12) stand on the perimeter of the face-off circle facing inward. A player designated as "it" skates around the outside and around the perimeter. While moving around the perimeter, the player tags another player, who chases the "it" player around the circle. The "it" sprints back to the vacated spot.

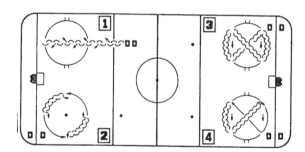

9 Position Ds in 4 different areas of the ice.

(1) Ds skate backward, opening up every other stride and a different way (left or right) each time.

(2) Skate the circle one-quarter forward, one-quarter backward, one-quarter forward, and finally one-quarter backward. Pivot a different way each time.

(3) Skate a figure 8 backward.

(4) Skate a figure 8 backward and forward, pivoting at the top and bottom of the 8.

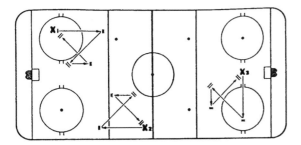

10 Players skate the pattern shown as fast as they can. Run 2 players at a time, then switch to a new set of 2.

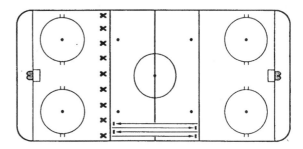

13 Have each group skate blue line to blue line, 2, 3, or 4 in turn.

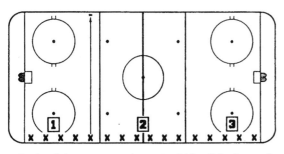

11 Each of the 3 groups skates 1 width of the ice or from the goal line to the center red line, in turn.
    Variation: Each of the 3 groups skates 2 widths of the ice or from the goal line to the center red line and back, in turn.

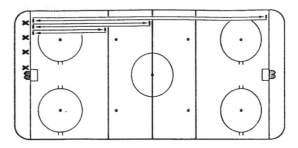

14 Each group skates from the near goal line to the far goal line and back, skates to the center red line and back, and skates to the near blue line and back.

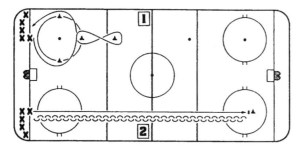

12 (1) The player skates around the circle into a small figure 8 and completes the circle. Time the player.
    (2) The player skates forward down the ice to the face-off dot (pylon), stops, and skates backward to the red line. Time the player.

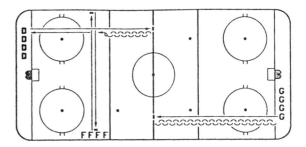

15 *Defense*: Skate forward to the red line, backward to the blue, and then turn and skate forward to the goal line. Do the drill 3 times, working on backward turns both ways.
    Forwards: Skate forward across the rink and back 3 times, touching the boards with sticks.
    Goaltenders: Skate forward to the center red line, drop to both knees with the goal stick and catcher in the proper position. Then skate backward to the goal line and do a double leg-pad slide to one side. Repeat drill doing the double leg-pad slide to the opposite side.

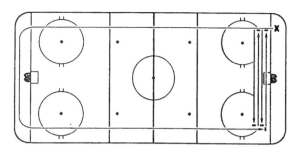

16 The players skate 1 lap of the ice on the perimeter and do stepovers across the ice twice.

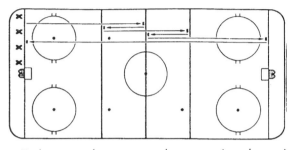

17 Each group does stops and starts, using the entire length of the ice, changing direction on the whistle. Have the groups work from 20 to 40 seconds.

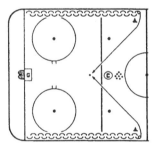

18 Position D as shown. The front player in each line skates backward around the pylon, pivots, and races for the puck. The player with the puck tries to score. The other player tries to check the D with the puck.

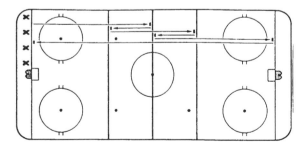

19 Each group skates forward from the goal line to the center red line, back to the near blue line, then to the far blue line, back to the center red line, then to the far goal line and all the way back.

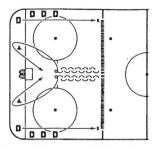

20 The front player in each line skates from the goal line to the blue line, cross-steps halfway across the blue line, skates backward to the hash marks of the circle, pivots to the outside, and skates to the corner. The player makes a sharp turn and returns to the front of the net.

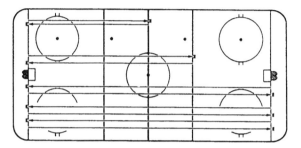

21 The players skate for speed at five distances:
   (1) center red line and back
   (2) far blue line and back
   (3) far boards (one length)
   (4) far boards and back (two lengths)
   (5) far boards and back twice (four lengths)

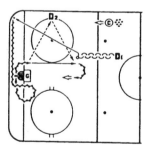

22 A puck is shot into a corner. Dl skates backward, pivots (a pylon can designate where to pivot), and skates to the corner. Dl gets the puck while doing a head-and-shoulder fake, skates behind the net and toward the far face-off circle. Coming out, D1 does a tight turn and returns behind the net. After stopping, D1 then starts again and passes to D2 near the boards. D1 skates out in front for the return pass from D2, does another tight turn, and shoots on goal. D1 then skates to D2's position on the boards and D2 goes to the blue line to repeat the drill.

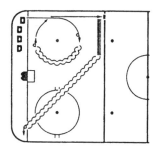

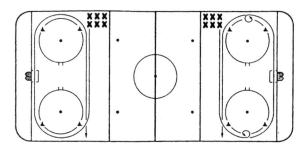

23 The Ds are in the corner. One at a time they skate the circle, always facing the far end of the ice. On reaching the blue line, they stop, do stepovers to the middle of the ice, then skate backward to the opposite corner. The next player goes when the one ahead passes upon completing the circle. When all the players have gone, they go the other way.

26 Players race around the course as shown. They go clockwise and counter-clockwise, forward and backward. *Variation*: Players do a 360-degree tight turn at the outside hash marks, being sure to turn clockwise at one set of hash marks and counter-clockwise at the marks on the other side.

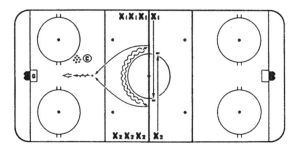

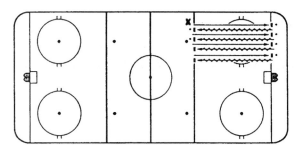

24 X1 and X2 start at the same time. They each skate to the farthest edge of the center-ice circle, stop, backward skate around half the circle, and, when they reach the center red line, they race for the puck set up inside the blue line.

27 Place pucks (5) on the blue line. Players start on the goal line, skate to the blue line, stop, pick up a puck, skate back to the goal line, stop, drop the puck, and repeat until all 5 pucks have been moved. The second group starts on the blue line and brings the 5 pucks back.

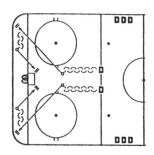

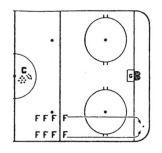

25 The players skate backward from the blue line and at a pylon or signal turn to the outside and skate forward to the corner and stop. They then skate backward a few strides, turn in the opposite direction to their first turn and skate to the net, and stop. Switch sides after each time through the drill.

28 The coach shoots a puck into the corner and 2 players race for the puck and attempt to score. The play continues until the coach blows the whistle, a goal is scored, or the goaltender freezes the puck.

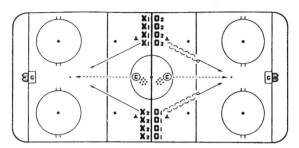

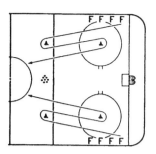

29   The coaches place pucks as shown. O1 and O2 at one
     end and X1 and X2 at the other end race for them.
     Variation: Players skate backward to the blue line, pivot,
     and race for the pucks.

32   The forwards start in opposite corners, skate around the
     pylons, and race for the puck. The first player to the
     puck takes a shot on goal while the other player tries to
     prevent it.

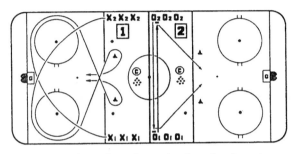

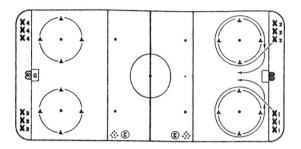

30   (1) X1 and X2 skate the circle, skate for the pylon, and
     do an outside-in turn and race for the puck.
     (2) O1 and O2 skate hard to the opposite side boards,
     touch the boards with their sticks, and race for the
     puck.

33   Position players and pylons as indicated in the diagram.
     X1 and X2 start the drill by skating the circle counter-
     clockwise and clockwise, respectively. As they come out
     of the circle, they race for a puck at the blue line (placed
     there by a coach), with the winner going in for a shot
     on goal. The other player can apply pressure or follow
     the play for a rebound.

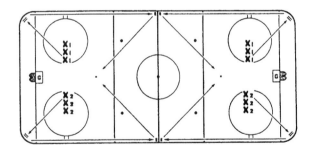

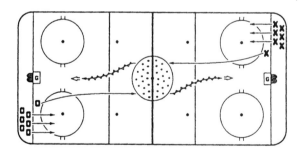

31   At the same time, 4 players skate to the corner, stop,
     skate to the blue line, stop, and then race for a puck
     placed at the blue line by the coach. The winner goes in
     for a shot on goal. The other players can apply pressure
     or follow the play for a rebound.

34   Pucks are spread out in the center-ice circle. On the
     whistle, each team sprints for the far goal line. On each
     rush, a different player picks up a puck, goes in, and
     shoots on the goaltender. The team that scores the most
     goals and finishes in the least amount of time wins the
     contest.

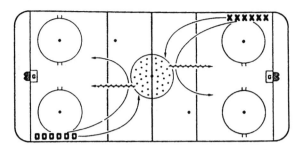

35 Divide the players into 2 teams. Pucks are spread out in the centre-ice circle. On the whistle, 2 players from each team go, pick up a puck, and try to score. They stay on the same puck until they do score. Once they have scored, they go back to center for another puck. The team that gets the most goals in 30 seconds gets 1 point for their team. The first team to reach 7 points wins. (Note: Players cannot be offside. Goaltenders cannot freeze the puck but must throw it to the corner.)

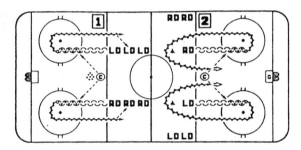

36 (1) D receives a pass from the coach while skating backward. D skates around the dot (or pylon) and skates forward, passing to the D next in line for a shot.

(2) After D skates out around the pylon in the neutral zone, D races back to the goal for a shot.

GOALTENDERS: ON-ICE QUICKNESS AND AGILITY DRILLS

Note: These are specific drills for quickness and agility for goalies. Some of the previous on- and off-ice drills can also be used for goalies.

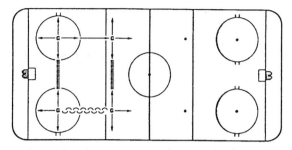

1 The goaltender moves in and out, and side to side, at each dot, backward and forward to the goal, and side-shuffles across ice to the next dot.

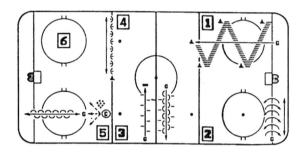

2 (1) Zigzag backward, stopping at the pylons.

(2) One foot is placed over the goal line.

(3) Knee drops. Skating forward, skating backward.

(4) Do cariocas. Cross right skate over left skate, then right skate behind left skate, etc.

(5) Skate forward, backward, react to thrown puck.

(6) Drop and recover. Knees, stomach, rear, back. *Variation*: Stop a puck on recovery.

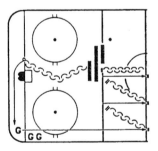

3 The goalie skates backward, forward, and sideways, stops, and shuffle-step right and left as shown.

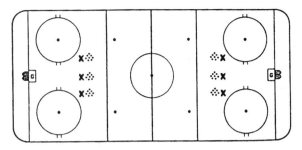

4   Players placed in a row shoot on the goaltender, 1 at a time. They shoot at the catcher, then the blocker, then the right skate and left skate, and finally at the pads. The player goes in for the rebound on the final shot.

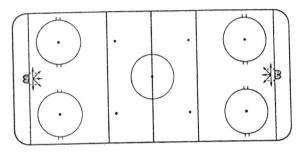

5   The goalie moves from side to side and in and out, returning to the middle each time.

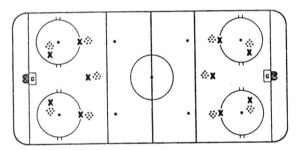

6   Players shoot on the goaltender from various angles on a signal from the coach.

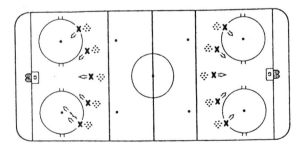

7   Players shoot on the goaltender going across the semicircle or alternate side to side.
     Variation: Each player has 2 pucks. The player shoots the first puck from a distance, then moves in on goal for a shot with the second puck.

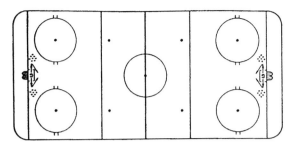

8   Pucks are placed on each side of the crease. The goalie, without a stick, moves from the middle of the crease, picks up a puck, returns and places it in the middle of the crease. Moves from side to side.

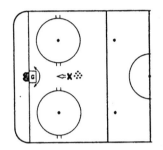

9   The goalie holds one post and the shooter shoots for the opposite side. The goalie must move across the net to block the shot. Shots should be low and high.

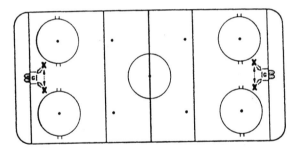

10   The player passes the puck across the crease. The goaltender does a double-pad save. Sometimes, the passer will shoot so the goaltender does not cheat on the drill.

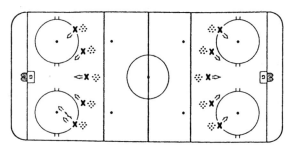

11 The goalie is down on one knee. Players shoot as the goalie recovers to a proper stance. Players can slap their sticks on the ice as the signal for the goalie to recover. Players shoot as the goalie regains his stance.

Variations: Goalie is down on both knees, on stomach, facing the shooters, or is facing the end boards.

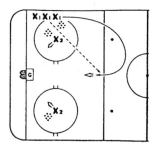

12 Position players as shown. X1 skates around the face-off dot (or pylon) and receives a pass from line X1. X1 shoots a slap shot or snap shot on goal from the blue line. X2 shoots a snap shot as soon as the first shot hits the goalie. X3 shoots a wrist shot as soon as the second shot fits the goalie. X1 goes to X2, X2 goes to X3, and X3 goes to the X1 line.

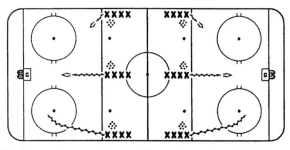

13 Place players as shown. Three players shoot with 3 seconds between each shot. The first player shoots inside the blue line, the second from the high slot, and the third pulls the goaltender.

14. Two players pass the puck to each other and shoot on goal.

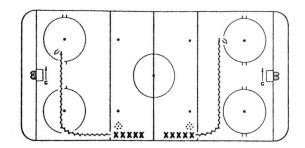

15 Players skate in from the boards and through the top of the face-off circles. The goaltender moves across the crease with the shooter. The shooter can shoot at any time.

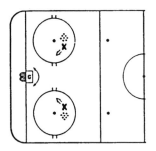

16 Two players alternate shooting from the circles. The goalie tries to stop the puck with and without a stick.

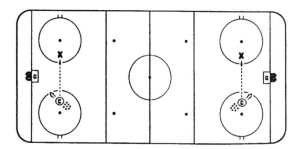

17 The coach either shoots or passes across for the shot. The goaltender reacts to the shot or the pass and then prepares for the next shot.

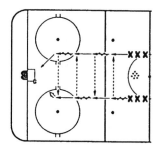

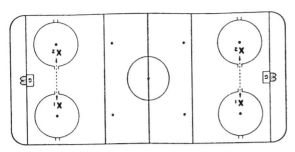

18 X1 and X2 pass back and forth with the goalie moving with the pass. X2 or X2 finally shoots.

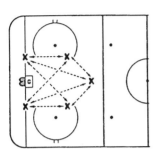

19 The players pass to each other to keep the goalie moving, and then one player shoots on goal.

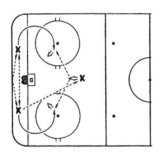

20 The players pass the puck to each other behind the goal and then pass to X in the high slot. The player in the slot can shoot or pass to one of the players down low, now in position off each post.

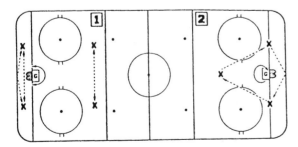

21 (1) The players pass the puck at the blue line or behind the net. The goalie must move according to the position of the puck.

(2) The players pass behind the net and to the player in the slot. The goalie sets up accordingly.

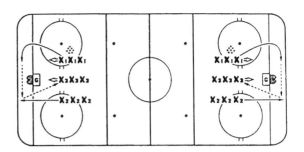

22 X1 shoots the puck off the glass, retrieves it, and passes to X2, who passes to X3 for the shot. X1 can also pass to X3 or come out from behind the goal.

23 Players shoot from the blue line and center line, and 2 players in front of the net try to deflect the puck or screen the goaltender.

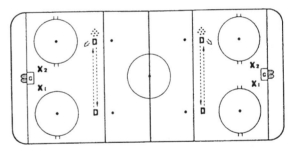

24 The Ds pass the puck back and forth and then shoot. X1 and X2 screen and/or deflect.

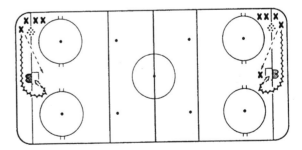

25 The player in the corner passes the first puck across the crease and attempts to pass or come out in front with the second puck.

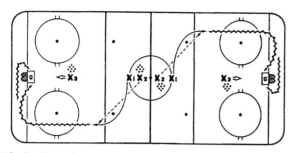

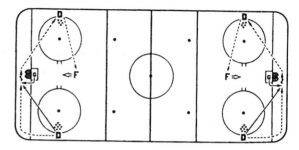

26 Position players as shown. X1 skates wide and takes a pass from X2 at the blue line. X1 then skates in on the short side and tries to jam the puck or go behind the net to try a wrap-around. After X1 has taken the shot, the goaltender must quickly recover to handle a shot from X3.

29 D rims the puck. D passes to D, who passes to F, who shoots. The goalie must stop the puck behind the goal and leave it there for D before returning quickly to the goal to get ready for the next shot.

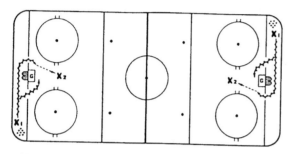

27 X1 comes out from the corner for a shot, or a pass to X2 for a shot. X1 can also go behind the goal, passing to X2 as X1 comes out the other side of the goal.

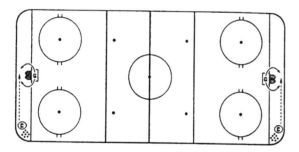

28 The goaltender moves side to side, in and out, and stops a puck behind the goal from one side, then the other.

GOALTENDERS: OFF-ICE QUICKNESS AND AGILITY DRILLS

1. **Jump**
   Goalie jumps back and forth with two feet at once, keeping arms in goaltending position.

2. **Jump**
   Goalie jumps back and forth, going from one to two feet.

3. **Jump**
   Goalie jumps sideways from one foot to the other.

4. **Butterfly Position and Up**

5. **Forward, Backward, and Sideways Running**

6. **Front Roll to Fast Stop**
   From initial stance, goalie performs front roll quick start and fast stop, and then moves sideways and sits down on chair.

7. **Front Roll and Fast Stop Variation**
   From initial stance, goalie performs front roll quick start and fast stop, and then moves sideways and sits down on chair. Coach hits tennis ball at goalie after front roll and fast stop.

8. **Dive to Crouch**
   Goalie dives forward and then comes back to a crouched position.

9. **Kip-up**
   Goalie does a front kip-up and then a back kip-up.

10. **Front Roll to Half-Splits Position**

11. **Cartwheel**

12. **Crouch and Jump**
    Goalie crouches and jumps as high as possible with arms stretched.

13. **Trampoline Work**
    Goalie does jumps, spins, forward and backward somersaults, and jumps with knees up.

Specific Catching Drills

1. **Catch Tennis Balls**
   Standing 5 feet (15 m) from the wall, with a tennis ball in each hand, goalie throws the balls alternately and together against the wall, and catches them on the rebound.

2. **Throw Tennis Balls**
   Working in a pair, goalies throw two tennis balls back and forth.

3. **Juggle**
   Goalie juggles two tennis balls.

4. **Hit the Tennis Ball**
   Goalie hits the tennis ball at the glove side and stick side.

5. **Medicine Ball**
   Working in a pair, goalies throw a medicine ball or volleyball back and forth.

6. **Butterfly Catch**
   Two goalies face each other in a butterfly position. A tennis ball is dropped between them and the two players attempt to catch the ball.

7. **Racquet**
   The goalie stands in front of a plywood board the size of a net, with both stick and catching glove. The instructor stands 15 feet (4.5 m) away and hits tennis balls with a racquet, high and low, trying to hit the plywood.

8. **High and Low**
   The goalie stands in front of a plywood board the size of a net, with both stick and catching glove. A screening player stands in front of goalie. The instructor stands 15 feet (4.5 m) away and hits tennis balls with a racquet, high and low, trying to hit the plywood.

CHAPTER 6

Flexibility Training

Flexibility exercises are important in ice hockey to ensure that the players have a full range of motion in movement patterns and to prevent injuries. Flexibility represents a prerequisite for the performance of skills with high amplitude (range of motion), and increases the ease with which fast movements can be performed. The success of performing such movements depends on the joint amplitude, or range of motion, which has to be greater than that required by the specific hockey skills.

Inadequate development of flexibility may lead to various deficiencies, such as:

- learning, or the perfection of various movements, is impaired;
- the player becomes injury prone; and
- the development of strength, speed, and coordination, is adversely affected.

Among the factors affecting flexibility are the form, type, and structure of a joint. Ligaments and tendons also affect flexibility; the more elastic they are, the higher the amplitude (range of motion) of a movement. Age and sex affect flexibility to the extent that younger individuals, and girls as opposed to boys, seem to be more flexible. Maximum flexibility appears to be reached at 15 to 16 years of age.

If a desired degree of flexibility is achieved, it does not mean that flexibility training should be neglected. On the contrary, from this point on, flexibility programs must have the objective of maintaining the achieved level.

METHODS USED TO DEVELOP FLEXIBILITY

Static slow stretch: Static stretch involves the athlete going through the range of motion slowly to the farthest point and holding this position for 5 to 10 seconds. This is repeated five or six times. Going through the movement slowly allows adequate time to rest the sensitivity of the stretch reflex, and a semi-permanent change in length of the muscle fibers and connective tissue can be gained. This is the safest method of flexibility training.

Dynamic ballistic stretching: This type of stretching involves a fast, strong, bouncing, rebounding, bobbing range of movement. This type of movement can cause muscle soreness and injury and is a controversial method.

Ballistic flexibility initiates the stretch reflex, and therefore muscular tension, making it more difficult to stretch the connective tissue. Dynamic flexibility movements are sport-specific, being used in sports such as karate, hurdling, and ballet, but are not recommended for most other sports.

Proprioceptive neuromuscular facilitation (PNF): Originally used as a physiotherapy procedure in rehabilitation, PNF is now accepted as an excellent method for developing flexibility. In this exercise, which requires a partner, the muscle is actively stretched to its end point, and then maximal isometric contraction is performed against the partner's resistance for five or six seconds. The muscle is then relaxed and stretched again to a new end point, and another isometric contraction follows. This procedure is usually repeated three times with each exercise (Holt, 1986).

Generally,

- Flexibility stretching training should be done daily and be included in both the warm-up and cool-down.
- Flexibility stretching training should include a short jog or skate before commencing the flexibility exercises.
- Stretching should progress from major joints to sport-specific stretching.
- Flexibility is also developed by playing or practicing the sport.
- Static stretching is the preferred method. Dynamic stretching is used for certain sports and should follow static stretching. PNF is an approved method of stretching, but must be done with a partner and be performed properly.
- Significant increases in flexibility can be achieved in 12 weeks. Flexibility can be maintained with two sessions per week. Flexibility is lost at a slower rate than it is gained.
- Children are most flexible in their early years, become less flexible up to adolescence, and then increase in flexibility until early adulthood. Generally, females tend to be more flexible than males.

Flexibility exercises must be incorporated in the warm-up part of a training plan, and be preceded by a general warm-up (jogging and calisthenics) lasting at least 10 minutes. The selection of exercises, as well as their complexity and difficulty, have to be related to the athlete's level of training. Each selected exercise has to be performed with one to 15 repetitions (or up to a maximum of 60 to 90 repetitions per practice). During the rest interval, relaxation exercises should be done. (To loosen the group of muscles that have performed, execute a light and short massage.) The amplitude (range of motion) of an exercise has to be increased progressively and carefully throughout the performance. At first, exercises are performed with amplitude that does not challenge the athlete, and then they are progressively increased up to one's limits. From this point on, each repetition should aim to reach this maximum limit and even increase.

For the ballistic method, there is a variety of exercises, flexions, extensions, and swings. For both the static and PNF methods, the athlete tries to position the joints so that the desired flexibility will be enhanced. The performer then statically maintains the position for six to 12 seconds, for a maximum of 100 to 120 seconds per training lesson for the chosen joints. Such time requirement can be built up progressively over a period of 10 to 18 months.

Flexibility in the periodization program should be achieved during the preparatory phase. The competitive phase is regarded as a maintenance period, when the energy and strain placed upon muscle groups will be directed toward specific training. In either case, however, flexibility has to be part of an everyday training program and should be performed toward the end of the warm-up.

STATIC SLOW STRETCH EXERCISES

The basic steps for this method are as follows:

1. The stretch should be slow and gradual until you feel the muscle pulling. However, the stretch should not be painful.
2. In the slow stretch, hold the stretch position for 5 to 10 seconds. Return to the start position and repeat five times.
3. Take a deep breath before you stretch, and breathe before you stretch, and breathe out as you stretch.
4. Do not use quick and jerky movements.

1 **Start Position (SP): Standing, feet apart.**
   Movement (M): Bend the body to the left and hold for 5 seconds. Bend the body to the right and hold for 5 seconds.

2 *(SP)*: **As above, arms above the head.**
   (M): Extended arms and upper body rotations from the left down and up through the right side and up above the head. Repeat in the opposite direction.

3 *(SP)*: **As above.**
   (M): Flex the hips, driving the right arm toward the foot of the left leg, left arm in an upward position. Return to the start position. Repeat the movement with the other arm toward the opposite leg. Return to the start position.

4 *(SP)*: **As above.**
   (M): Flex the upper body, touching the opposite leg with each hand. Bring the upper body to the horizontal, swinging the arms to the side and up. Return to the start position.

5 *(SP)*: **Sitting, arms extended above the head.**

(M): Flex the upper body forward and reach as far as possible with arms. Hold this position for 5 to 10 seconds. Return to the start position, arms still extended.

6 *(SP)*: **Lying on the back, feet and arms apart.**

(M): Raise the upper body, flex it over the legs, and touch the floor. Hold for 5 to 10 seconds and return to the start position.

7 *(SP)*: **Kneeling on both legs, arms relaxed beside the body.**

(M): Extend the right leg forward, accompanied by hip flexion toward left arm, touching the toes. Hold position for 5 to 10 seconds. Bring upper body and right leg back to the start position. Repeat movement on the left leg.

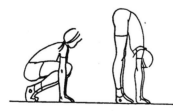

8 *(SP)*: **Flex the knees and hips, hands on the floor.**

(M): Extend the knees, maintaining the hands on the floor. Hold position for 5 to 10 seconds and return to the start position.

9 *(SP)*: **Sitting, arms above the head.**

(M): Flex the right leg with the knee pointing to the side, foot backward. Flex the hips, lowering the arms toward the feet. Raise the upper body and lower it toward the floor. Raise the body to the vertical and extend the leg back to the start position. Repeat, alternating each leg.

10 *(SP)*: **Kneeling on both legs, hips flexed, arms on the floor above the ahead.**

(M): Press the chest toward the floor and hold position for 5 to 10 seconds. Return to the start position.

11 *(SP)*: **Sitting, legs apart, holding a medicine ball in front of the chest.**

(M): Perform 4 complete, large rotations to the left. Repeat the same on the other side.

12 *(SP)*: **Standing in front of a wall, feet together, hands on the wall at chest level.**

(M): Bend ankles and knees toward the wall and hold for 5 to 10 seconds without lifting heels off the floor. Return to the starting position. *Note:* Adjust the distance between feet and wall so that it will be relatively difficult to reach the wall with the knees.

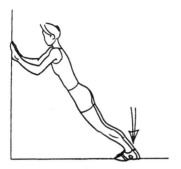

13 *(SP)*: **As above, with the feet as far away as possible, forming a diagonal line.**
(M): Bend the knees slightly to force the ankles to bend as much as possible without lifting the heels off the floor. Hold for 5 to 10 seconds and return to the start position.

14 *(SP)*: **Lying on stomach, arms flexed, placing the hands on the ground at shoulder level.**
(M): Extend the arms, arching the upper body while the hips are still on the ground. Hold this position for 5 to 10 seconds. Flex the arms and lower the body to the start position.

15 *(SP)*: **Kneeling on hands and knees.**
(M): Swing the right left and left arm upward, arching the back. Return to the start position. Repeat with the other limbs. Return to the start position.

FLEXIBILITY EXERCISES PERFORMED WITH A PARTNER

Note: A partner could be another athlete, parent, or instructor.

16 *(SP)*: **Partner A is sitting, Partner B stands behind him/her, placing hands on partner's back.**
(M): Partner B presses Partner A's upper body forward and down, holding for 6 seconds. Relax and return to the start position.

17 *(SP)*: **Partner A stands, arms above the head. Partner B stands behind, placing his/her right hand below shoulder level, left hand grasping partner's hands.**
(M): Partner B presses the upper back forward, pulling the arms backward, and holds for 6 seconds. Relax and return to the start position.

18 *(SP)*: **Partner A is lying on the stomach, arms above the head. Partner B stands with legs to both sides of Partner A's body, grasping the hands.**
(M): Partner B slowly raises the partner's arms, and holds for 6 seconds, then returns to the start position. Repeat, changing partners' roles.

19 *(SP)*: **Standing, Partner A three feet in front of Partner B.**

(M): Partner A raises left leg back and up, upper body vertical. Partner B catches the ankles with both hands. Partner B slowly presses A's leg upward. Hold in this position for 6 seconds. Lower the leg and return to the start position. Alternate leg action and partners' roles.

20 *(SP)*: **Partner A is lying on the back, arms above the head. Partner B stands at A's left side.**

(M): Partner A raises up the right leg. Partner B catches the ankle with both hands. Partner B applies a constant pressure downward against his/her partner's leg, and holds for 6 seconds. Partner A returns the right leg to the start position. Alternate legs and partners' roles.

CHAPTER 7

Recovery, Fatigue, Overtraining, and Detraining

Traditionally, coaches see part of their job as knowing how to better train their players. While many elements of training are often carried out well, a lot of coaches neglect to pay proper attention to recovery methods and techniques, yet the use of recovery techniques is as important as training. The more quickly players are able to recover after training or games, the more work can be done, and increased levels of training normally translate into a more effective game. Everyone involved in training should therefore change their view about rest and recovery.

Many methods and techniques can be used for recovery from the fatigue of training and games. The better you understand and employ these techniques, the better you can control fatigue, and in doing so you will prevent the undesirable effects of *overtraining*.

Most hockey players are exposed to a very demanding schedule of games, as well as traveling and training. This is why you should learn and use methods to overcome those things that restrict players' game effectiveness. To increase your training benefits, and players' game productivity, you should keep in mind the chain of events prior to and following a game:

- train as often as possible;
- unload, or have a mini-taper, prior to each game in order to eliminate physical and mental fatigue;
- play the game; and
- use recovery techniques to remove the fatigue encountered during the game.

The use of proper recovery techniques accelerates the rate of regeneration and restoration, and decreases the level of fatigue and frequency of injuries. Remember that when players are tired, their coordination is impaired and concentration levels decline, resulting in poor movement and skill control. Consequently, chances of injury are increased.

RECOVERY TECHNIQUES

The process of recovery or regeneration is multidimensional and depends on the following factors:

- The age of the player has been shown to affect the rate of recovery. Older players (>25 years) generally require longer periods of recuperation following training than their younger counterparts. Similarly, players who are younger than 18 will require longer periods of rest between workouts and following a series of games.
- Highly experienced players will recuperate faster because they have a much faster physiological adaptation and perhaps higher efficiencies of movement.
- Gender can affect the rate of recovery. Female players tend to have a slower rate of regeneration. This is primarily due to the endocrinological differences, in particular the lowered amount of the male hormone testosterone circulating within the female organism (Noackes, 1991; Nudel, 1989; Rowland, 1990; Vander et al., 1990).

Throughout training, the coach should avoid expressing any negative emotions or feelings such as fear of an opponent, fear of losing, indecisiveness, or a lack of will and determination, since these will place extra stress on the players. Players who carry such attitudes will affect others. If a player perceives such emotions as stressors, it will trigger the release of stress-related hormones. This in turn causes a variety of physiological problems that can inhibit growth and repair of muscle tissue, increase muscle tension, depress the inflammatory response, and affect timing and neuromuscular coordination. With this in mind, the coach should ensure that players do not become exhausted physically or psychologically during exhibition games or early in the regular season schedule.

The availability and replenishment of nutrients (vitamins and minerals) and the main fuels used in hockey may impact the recovery process.

When players compete in different countries, or across time differences exceeding three hours, these will have an affect on the circadian rhythms of the body. Some of the symptoms include malaise (lethargy, fatigue), appetite loss, tiredness during daylight hours, digestive disorders, and disturbed sleep.

When your team travels coast to coast or overseas we recommend the following:

For small time-zone shifts:

- If possible, preset sleep and wake cycles to the time of the destination.

- If possible, train and/or play in the morning after westward flights and in the evening after eastward flights.

- Travel in one direction when competing in different cities on extended road trips.

- Eat meals at regular times after arriving at the new destination.

- Have light meals before the flight. Eat a high-protein breakfast and a low-protein high-carbohydrate dinner following a time-zone advance.

- Avoid all alcoholic beverages before, during, and after the flight. Drink juices and water.

- Indulge in light social and physical activity (for two hours) after the flight.

- Intestinal gas expands at high altitudes, so it would be advisable to avoid any gas-producing foods (i.e., beans, and carbonated beverages).

For large time-zone shifts:

- Arrive at your destination at least one day early for each time zone crossed.

- For flights crossing over 10 time zones, westward flights should always be taken.

- Attempt to partially synchronize sleep and wake cycles and times of eating meals to the time of the destination.

- Indulge in light social and physical activity (for two hours) after the flight.

- Maintain regular sleeping times and eating times after arrival at the destination.

- Alter light and heavy meals (mostly light) three days before the flight. Eat a high-protein breakfast and a low-protein high-carbohydrate dinner following time-zone increases.

- Avoid all alcoholic beverages prior, during, and after the flight. Drink juices and water.

- Avoid any gas-producing foods (i.e., beans and carbonated beverages).

- Use eye-shades and try to nap on the flight.

- Stretch and move around the airplane every one or two hours.

For peak physiological and psychological regeneration of the human organism to occur, recovery techniques must be employed at specific times before, during, and after training or games. Ignoring the needs of adequate regeneration can have negative influences on players' training and playing capacity.

Recovery Methods and Techniques

Before utilizing various regeneration techniques, the coach should work in close cooperation with physicians and other medical personnel (i.e., physiotherapy and massage therapists). This can maximize the effectiveness of the players' regeneration through application of certain techniques, and also avoid any misconceptions.

Natural means of recovery:

- *Aerobic activity:* Following demanding training sessions, or difficult games and/or tournaments, have one or two light aerobic workouts. This will help players to eliminate waste products faster. Such sessions will replenish the energy stores faster than complete (passive) rest.

- *Stretch therapy:* Stretching should be used not only in the warm-up and following strength training, but also immediately after games. A stretched muscle is more flexible than a stiff muscle, improving the removal of waste products. Light continuous stretching alternated with massage will help the muscles to heal faster from micro-injuries. It is equally important for the coach to know that increased muscle elasticity also increases the muscles' resistance to damage (i.e., bruises and muscle pulls). Active stretching for 15 to 20 minutes before a game also ensures the players' readiness for the game. This becomes even more important for hockey players since they play in a cold environment, and especially considering that they stay inactive and immobile between shifts. Stretching is especially important for the tendons, which are highly stressed during the powerful actions typical of hockey. A strong and flexible tendon will always resist pulling and tearing better.

- *Complete rest:* Complete, or passive, rest is the main means of restoring players' working capacity. A player who has the desire to succeed in the game of hockey should rest for nine to 10 hours, most of it during the night, and go to sleep no later than 10:30 p.m.

Several methods can be employed to promote a relaxed sleep. Relaxation techniques—a massage or a warm bath before bedtime—all help. A dark, noiseless, and stress-free oxygenated (fresh air) room is necessary. Consider wearing eye-shades while sleeping to prevent any light reaching the eyes. Awake at the same time each morning.

A good night's sleep might be affected by:

- Physical disorders: restless-leg syndrome, sleep apnea, arthritis, chronic pain, asthma, and exercising within three hours of bedtime.
- Psychological difficulties: nightmares, depression, stress, anxiety disorders, emotional discussions or arguments before bed, chronic stress.
- Improper sleep environment: noise, temperature too high or too low, bed too hard or too soft, blankets too light or too heavy, snoring or restless bed partner, etc.
- Inadequate sleep habits: too much time spent in bed reading or watching TV, daytime naps (longer than one hour after 4:00 p.m.), irregular schedule, not eliminating bodily waste prior to bedtime.
- Substance overuse or misuse: nicotine, caffeine (i.e., coffee, tea, chocolate, and carbonated beverages that contain caffeine should be avoided after 7:00 p.m.), alcohol (which inhibits melatonin production), overuse of sleep medications, etc.

Physiotherapeutic Means of Recovery

Massage: This systematic manipulation of muscles will relax muscles and help remove toxic substances collected during training. Massage is useful 15 to 20 minutes before training, 10 minutes following the post-training shower, and after a hot bath or sauna. Whether done by a massage specialist or self-massage (you must learn the maneuvers), it has a highly regarded positive effect on players' mood state by reducing tension, anger, fatigue, depression, and anxiety. Via the specific techniques used, massage increases blood circulation, which brings more oxygen and nutrients to muscle cells, removes excessive swelling, and relieves muscle fatigue.

Heat therapy: Heat modalities come in several forms such as sauna, steam and hot baths, and moist heat pack. Steam baths and saunas have an effect on both the body and mind. Hot showers 97°F to 108°F (36°C to 42°C) for eight to 10 minutes relax muscles and improve blood circulation. The depth of heat penetration, such as the sauna, is about two inches, which stimulates perspiration that removes toxins from the body and improves sleep. If toxins are not

eliminated, fatigue will linger on, affecting the central nervous system stimulation. Heat therapy should not be applied immediately after training in cases of acute trauma or when a player has a fever.

Cold therapy: Cold applications such as ice massage using cups, cold packs, a bag filled with crushed ice placed around the injured limb, or cold whirlpool have an analgesic effect (feeling of less pain). The best results come from the use of cold therapy immediately following training, with an application time of 15 to 20 minutes. Do not use cold therapy when players have cold allergies, joint pain, nausea, or rheumatoid conditions.

Contrast baths: By alternating cold and hot therapy, players benefit from the "pumping" action within the muscle (vasodilation and vasoconstriction) that moves blood through the body faster, supplying nutrients and oxygen to the muscle cells. "Contrast baths" alternate cold water for one minute and hot water for five minutes, beginning and ending with cold, starting with the extremities and then the trunk of the body. They are best suited for superficial injuries, muscle relaxation, and removal of toxins from the body. As with all the other modalities, contrast baths can be used one to two hours after training or a game, at home or in the hotel room.

Sauna, cold whirlpool, dry sauna, and the traditional shower are often accessible to many players. By using them players will recover faster, be energized, and be ready for another training session or game.

RECOVERY FROM EXERCISE

It is necessary for the coach and players to be aware of the time that is required for the restoration of energy-releasing fuels like ATP/CP, intramuscular glycogen, and other metabolites at the cellular level. Under extenuating circumstances (i.e., severe glycogen depletion, dehydration, or disease), the restoration of these fuels and the clearance of their by-products could be hindered somewhat. Under normal training situations, however, the restoration of fuels and the removal of metabolic by-products require a certain length of time depending on the energy system used during training or games (i.e., aerobic, anaerobic lactic, or anaerobic alactic). Intimate knowledge of the restoration time of a given fuel is extremely important in order to properly calculate the rest interval between drills, sets, reps., etc. Table 7.1 indicates the restoration time necessary for each energy system.

TABLE 7.1: Recommended Times after Exhaustive Exercise

Recovery Process	Minimum	Maximum
Restoration of muscle phosphagen (ATP and CP)	2 min.	3–5 min.
Repayment of the alactacid O_2 debt	3 min.	5 min.
Restoration of myoglobin O_2	1 min.	2 min.
Repayment of the lactic acid O_2 debt	30 min.	1 hr.
Restoration of muscle glycogen		
a) After intermittent activity	2 hrs. to restore 40%	
	5 hrs. to restore 55%	
	25 hrs. to restore 100%	
b) After prolonged non-stop activity	10 hrs. to restore 60%	
	48 hrs. to restore 100%	
Removal of lactic acid from the muscles and blood	10 min. to remove 25%	
	25–30 min. to remove 50%	
	60–75 min. to remove 95%	

Restoration of Phosphagen (ATP/CP)

The restoration of ATP stores requires energy that is derived from the oxygen system through the metabolism of carbohydrates and fats.

The restoration of phosphagen is quite rapid, with 50% to 70% being restored during the first 20 to 30 seconds, and the remainder in three minutes. Although phosphagen restoration demands very little time, CP replenishment requires up to 10 minutes for full recovery. Generally speaking, it takes two minutes for 85%, four minutes for 90%, and eight minutes for 97% of phosphagen restoration.

Restoration of Intramuscular Glycogen Stores

Several factors (i.e., the manipulation of dietary nutrients, in particular carbohydrates) affect the rate of muscle glycogen recovery from exercise. Other factors include the intensity and duration (short versus long) of a training session or drills. In any case, before planning one's training options, the coach should consider that:

- Some intramuscular glycogen is restored within two hours following the cessation of exercise in the absence of any carbohydrates. The restoration is not, however, totally complete. Some restoration can even occur within 30 minutes.
- A high-carbohydrate diet is recommended for the complete restoration of muscle glycogen.
- The first five hours after the cessation of exercise has been shown to exhibit the most rapid restoration of muscle glycogen.
- Muscle glycogen stores are completely replenished within 24 hours through a normal diet.

Several factors influence the differences in muscle glycogen restoration. The amount of glycogen depleted during exercise will govern some of the replenishment requirements (i.e., the greater the exercise time, the greater the carbohydrate metabolized).

Systematic Removal of Lactic Acid (LA) from the Muscle

The removal of LA requires two phases: from the muscle and then from the blood. These will be influenced by what sort of activity is performed during the rest interval. If a player maintains light activity between drills, or performs 10 to 15 minutes of aerobics, light skating, or jogging after training, LA removal is twice as fast—one hour versus two hours for those who take a completely inactive rest.

Considering the extremely exhausting league games typical for most hockey teams, any method available to you should be used to speed up recovery. The faster a player recovers, the more energy will be available for the next game.

Permanent Means of Recovery

An effective training program requires the use of constant, permanent means of recovery. This recovery will facilitate a fast recuperation following training, and also maintain a continuous state of high physical and psychological capacity to achieve training objectives. Briefly, the permanent means of recovery should include:

- a rational alternation of work with regeneration phases
- an attempt to eliminate all social stressors
- a sound team atmosphere of calm, confident, and optimistic players
- a rational diet according to the phase of training
- active rest and involvement in pleasant, relaxing social activities
- permanent monitoring of each player's health status.

FATIGUE AND OVERTRAINING

Every time you expose your players to hard training, their bodies try to adjust to restore balance. Under normal conditions it takes no more than 24 hours for full restoration and energy fuel replenishment. When, however, players are under physical stress, such as constant high-intensity training and heavy game schedules, it can often be beyond their capabilities to adjust and restore to a balanced state. Failure to recover and regenerate results in fatigue. If a highly fatiguing schedule is maintained for a long time, it may result in overtraining. To avoid this, players and coaches should know the symptoms of fatigue for different types of training intensities (see Table 7.2).

TABLE 7.2: Symptoms of Fatigue for Four Different Types of Intensities

	Low-Intensity Training	Optimal-Intensity Training	Intensity Up to One's Limits	Intensity at or Slightly in Excess of One's Limits
Fatigue level	Low	High	Exhaustion	Exhaustion
Skin color	Slightly flushed	Flushed	Very flushed	Paleness for several days
Sweating	Light to medium	Heavy sweat in upper body	Heavy sweat in lower body	May sweat to a degree
Quality of Technical Movement	Controlled movements	Loss of precision, inconsistency, some technical faults	Poor coordination, technical uncertainty, many technical faults	Skill inconsistency, lack of power (24 hrs.), precision and accuracy impaired
Concentration	Normal, players react quickly to coach's remarks, maximum attention	Low ability to acquire technical elements, reduced span of attention	Low concentration span, nervousness, inconsistency	Mindlessness, unable to correct skills (24–28 hrs.), unable to concentrate on specific tasks
Training and Health Status	Performs all training tasks	Muscular weakness, lack of power, low working capacity	Muscle and joint soreness, headache and stomach upsets, vomiting sensation and feeling of malaise	Sleeping difficulties, muscle soreness, physical discomfort, high heart rate for up to and even longer than 24 hrs
Training Willingness	Eager to train	Desire for longer rest and recovery phase but still willing to train	Desire to stop training, need for complete rest	Lack of desire to train next day, carelessness, negative attitude to training requirements

For the coach and players to understand what the term "overtraining" means, a few terms must be defined:

- *Acute fatigue/muscular overstrain* is the result of a single training session. This form of fatigue is generally very short and lasts for one to two days or even less. It is usually accompanied by some muscle soreness, some sleep disturbance, and a heightened response to allergies.
- *Training intensity up to one's limits/muscular overstrain* is induced by several micro-cycles of high intensity. This form of fatigue could last longer than two days. Some of the symptoms include reluctance to work, disturbed sleep, lack of appetite, irrational use of energy, and emotional disturbances.
- *Over-reaching* is induced by one or more particularly intense micro-cycles, and/or is the result of too few regeneration periods. This form of fatigue is usually short term and will last for a few days or up to two weeks. There may or may not be some muscular overstrain associated with this state. The symptoms associated with this state are very similar to those found in "overload stimulus." Over-reaching is, however, a little more severe, with the addition of increased resting heart rate, premature fatigue, considerable drop in performance, and increased thirst (especially during the night).
- *Overtraining* is the result of successive over-reaching micro-cycles coupled with insufficient regeneration. This form of fatigue is more long term and could last from several weeks to several months. There are significant organic changes that occur during this phase of overtraining, mostly in the form of pronounced muscle weakness. This state may or may not also accompany some muscular overstrain.

There are three main areas that influence the state of overtraining. Although each system is independent of the others, they are all part of the makeup of the human body and are related.

Neuro-muscular fatigue is fatigue of the nervous system, and results from using only high-intensity training without alternating it with lower-intensity aerobic-type drills. This type of fatigue causes a drop in players' motivation, and results in poor reaction to speed/power drills, and a decrease in muscle force and the firing rate of muscle fibers.

Metabolic sources of fatigue/muscular overexertion could result in muscle damage, a feeling of discomfort, muscle soreness, and tendon damage. To force players beyond this state of fatigue may likely result in a higher rate of injuries.

The abuse of high-intensity training always results in increased levels of lactic acid in the blood and muscle (lactate fatigue). This could impair the mechanism of muscle contraction, resulting in a decreased ability to be fast and powerful. Lactic acid build-up also reduces the amount of oxygen able to reach the muscle cell, affecting players' ability to play for longer periods of time.

Neuro-endocrine fatigue results if the physical and/or mental stress is too high, exceeding players' capability to cope with it. This can cause increased resting heart rate, loss of appetite, disturbed sleep, an increased incidence of infection, decreased power output, weight loss, increased irritability, and a decrease in the quality, speed, and power of play.

A decrease in testosterone levels also affects players' overall force, as well as the ability to recover normally between training sessions and following games.

THE MONITORING, PREVENTION, AND TREATMENT OF OVERTRAINING

Most information available on fatigue and overtraining is post-fact, after athletes have experienced the negative effects of demanding training programs. Little is done, however, to prevent overtraining and avoid deterioration of performance prior to important games. The coach can often remedy this by planning training programs where work is constantly alternated with regeneration. Light aerobic-type training helps players to recover faster from fatigue, renew energy stores, and relax body and mind. Ideally, a game or a stressful high-intensity training session should not take place before the players have recovered from the fatigue of the last game or high-intensity training session. Individuals recover and respond to training at various rates, even though the training load may be identical. It is therefore up to the coach, and players, to utilize personal training diaries to obtain data and realize players' responses to training (please refer to the monitoring charts at the end of this chapter).

This practice should take place throughout the training year, providing constant feedback for the intensity and volume the coach plans during the annual plan.

Causes of Overtraining

Several factors can influence the rate of recovery and/or overtraining. These factors are almost always the result of a disparity among load, load tolerance, and regeneration. If players continue to train and/or play under very fatiguing conditions, they might be setting themselves up for overtraining (see Table 7.3). Adequate planning is therefore required as an effective means of reaching positive conclusions, especially if the coach and players are also using some methods of monitoring reactions to training.

TABLE 7.3: Activities that May Cause Overtraining

Training Faults	Player's Lifestyle	Social Environment	Health
• Overlooking recovery	• Insufficient hours of sleep	• Overwhelming family responsibilities	• Illness, high fever
• Higher demand than organism's capacity	• Unorganized diurnal program	• Frustration (family, peers)	• Nausea
• Abrupt increase of load in training following long pauses (rest, illness, etc.)	• Smoking, consumption of alcohol, coffee	• Professional dissatisfaction	• Stomach aches
• High volume of high-intensity stimuli	• Inadequate living facilities (space)	• Over-stressful professional activities	
	• Quarrel with peers	• Excessive emotional activities (TV, noisy music, etc.)	
	• Poor diet		
	• Overexciting and agitated life		

Detection of Overtraining

The outcome of overtraining is a decrease in working capacity and playing effectiveness. Insomnia, poor appetite, and profuse sweating during the night and day usually precede such symptoms. The coach can identify the symptoms of overtraining by observing the daily remarks made by players in their training diaries. For a more descriptive identification of fatigue, review the symptoms outlined in Table 7.4.

TABLE 7.4: Symptoms that Facilitate the Identification of Overtraining (Compiled based on data from Bompa [1969], Ozoline [1971], and Harre [1982])

Psychological	Motor and Physical	Functional
• Increased excitability	• Coordination – increment in muscle tension	• Insomnia
• Reduced concentration – irrational	– reappearance of mistake already corrected	• Lack of appetite

– very sensitive to criticism
  – tendency to isolate oneself from coach and teammates
	– inconsistency in performing rhythmical movements
	  – reduced capacity for differentiation and correcting technical faults
		• Digestive disturbances

– lack of initiative – depression		• Sweats very easily
– lack of confidence	• Physical preparation – decrease in level of speed, strength, and endurance	• Decrease in vital capacity

• Willpower
  – lack of fighting power
	– slower rate of recovery
	  – decrease in reaction time
		• Heart rate recovery longer than normal

– fear of games – prone to give up a tactical plan or desire to fight in a contest	• Prone to accidents and injuries	• Prone to skin and tissue infections

Simple Means and Methods to Monitor and Prevent Overtraining

Players should have an active role in the monitoring of recovery, such as a training diary, eating, stretching, saunas, contrast baths, relaxation techniques progressive muscle relaxation (PMR), breathing exercises, visualization.

Although there are numerous variables that the coach and players can monitor, practicality far exceeds any method that requires sophisticated and elaborate means of assessing players' reactions to training and league games. While some methods seem very simplistic, it is, however, the interpretation of them that can sometimes be more beneficial than going to a laboratory. In most instances, laboratory testing merely confirms in more detail what was determined by using simple monitoring charts and tests. Ideally, each player should complete monitoring charts each day, whereas the coach can employ simple methods to verify players' state of recovery following training:

- Observation of a player's level of fitness, expressed through the level of effectiveness in training or inadequate accomplishment of training objectives.

- Being aware of player's attitude. A conscientious and optimistic attitude during training camp, adequate relationships with teammates, and a generally positive reaction to the complexity of actions in training indicate that the load in training is proportional with the rate of recovery for that particular player.

Feedback can sometimes present itself in the simplest of ways, for example, by direct communication with the player. At the beginning of a training lesson ask him or her, "How do you feel today?" Responses such as "My legs feel heavy and stiff" or "I don't feel well" should be sufficient indication that the player has not adapted favorably from the previous day(s) training or game. Body language such as facial expressions, bending over to recover after an effort, a new or reoccurring training fault, and just looking into their eyes ("eyes are the window to a person's inner world") can provide effective means of feedback. It should also be of concern to the coach to become aware of any emotional problems the players might be experiencing, such as a quarrel with peers, girlfriends, boyfriends, or family, and stress from school and/or work. Steps should be implemented to assist players to remedy these problems so they do not become negative factors in overall performance and well-being.

- A player's health status, monitored by a team physician and subjectively sensed by the player, indicates the rate of recovery. An exhausted, unregenerated status may affect the normal functioning of the circulatory system.

- Noting indications of the recovery status, such as the player's training willingness, desire to surpass personal performances, appetite, state of sleep (poor sleep for more than two days in succession), and balanced emotions.

- Observing weight variations, with + or − 2 pounds (1 kg) (or > 3%) over a 24-hour period demonstrating a normal rate of recovery. Gains or losses over the above figure suggest either a light load in training (weight gain) or a load from which the player does not regenerate properly (weight loss).

- Measuring morning resting heart rate (HR), which is an important physiological indicator of the recovery status. A difference of more than eight beats per minute between the resting HR taken lying down and standing up represents a low rate of recovery, and consequently the training program should be altered.

- Muscle soreness enables the coach to plan the training loads for the following training lessons. Knowing how the player is responding to current training loads via residual soreness can be an effective tool in monitoring recovery (see Table 7.5).

TABLE 7.5: Classification of Muscle Soreness

Symptoms	Indication
Some discomfort when feeling muscle	Reduce training intensity for 2–3 days
Discomfort when walking Unable to squat without discomfort	Reduce training for 7 days
Severe pain	Reduce training for at least 2–3 weeks
Walking with difficulty	No games for 2–3 weeks

The intensity of training is more of a contributor to overtraining than the duration of training; therefore lessening the intensity of training (overly intensive drills) and/or maintaining the same volume will minimize the overtraining effect.

How to Use and Fill In Training Monitoring Charts

There are four charts, of which Charts 1 and 2 (Tables 7.6 and 7.7) are examples, and Charts 3 and 4 (Tables 7.8 and 7.9) are blank so the coach or player can photocopy them for his or her needs. At the top of each page there is a space for the name of the player and month of training. These charts should be placed either in the locker room or be part of each player's training log.

It is essential that the coach look at the charts of each player before the training session so that the training program may be changed according to the player's psychological state and level of fatigue. For instance, if the "heart rate" chart indicates a high level of fatigue, or the chart for the "length of sleep" shows just four hours of restless sleep, then the daily program must be made easier, with no high intensity (which normally increases the level of fatigue).

The heart rate chart is very useful for monitoring players' reaction to the previous day's training program.

Before a player uses the chart, he or she should know that the base heart rate (BHR) is a measure of the heart rate taken in the morning before stepping out of bed. The heart rate is taken over a 10-second period and then multiplied by six to give a value in beats per minute (b/m). Take a blank chart and place a dot representing the BHR in the lower third of the chart (Table 7.8) and write the value of the heart rate in the space provided. Then complete, upward and downward, all the spaces of the chart. As the player continues to take the BHR daily, he or she repeatedly places dots on the chart and links them together with a line to form a curve.

The BHR illustrates the player's physiological state and reaction to training. Under normal conditions the curve does not have too many deflections. The dynamics of the curve could change, however, according to the phase of training, as well as the way the player is adapting to the training program. The BHR curve will drop progressively as the player adapts to training. The better the adaptation, the lower the curve.

The BHR also reacts to the intensity of training in the previous day. Where the BHR increases by six to eight b/m in one day (Table 7.6) over the standard curve, it could mean that the player did not tolerate the training well, or he or she did not observe a typical athletic lifestyle. In such a case the coach should find out the actual reason for such a change from the player. In either case, the planned training program has to be changed so that it does not add to an already high level of fatigue. When the curve decreases to its standard levels, the normal program can resume.

Whereas the BHR can be used to monitor training for the short term, the body weight (BW) chart can be employed for the long term. A well-trained player whose diet is correlated to the volume and intensity of training should have a steady BW.

BW can have some fluctuations, especially during the transition phase where some players gain weight. During the preparatory phase, however, it quickly drops to normal levels. If, on the other hand, the coach plans a very changeable training program of volume and intensity beyond a player's threshold of tolerance for a longer time, it can result in a high level of fatigue. When fatigue is acute, it is often com-plemented by a loss of appetite, and as a result the player starts to lose weight.

BW loss does not occur abruptly; on the contrary, it is a long-term process (see Table 7.6). If the curve of BW drops constantly, this can signal a critical level of fatigue, and even possible overtraining. In such a case, the player should be examined by a physician, his or her diet checked by a nutritionist, and the training load decreased until the player fully recovers.

The charts that monitor psychological traits and appetite have a high correlation between them. When a player experiences a high degree of fatigue, sleeping patterns are disturbed while appetite decreases. These in turn correlate with an increase in tiredness sensation, and a decrease in training and competitive willingness if overtraining is experienced.

The proposed simple and practical charts for monitoring training are very useful for the serious player. Filling them in every day and having a coach examine them before every training session can prevent cases of fatigue and promote optimal levels of health. Spending a minute a day may help a player to avoid overtraining!

TABLE 7.6: Training Monitoring—Chart 1

NAME _____   MONTH _____

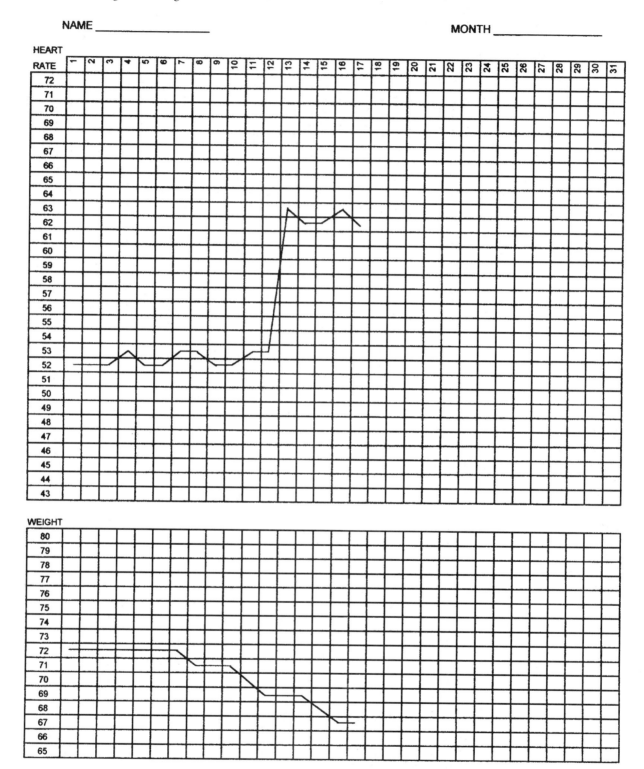

TABLE 7.7: Training Monitoring—Chart 2

NAME_____   MONTH_____

LENGTH OF SLEEP	1	2	3	4	5	6	7	8	9	10	11	12	13	14	15	16	17	18	19	20	21	22	23	24	25	26	27	28	29	30	31
12 + Hours																															
11																															
10																															
9																															
8																															
7																															
6																															
5																															
4																															
No sleep at all																															

QUALITY OF SLEEP

Very deep																															
Normal																															
Restless																															
Bad with Breaks																															
Not at All																															

TIREDNESS SENSATION

Very Rested																															
Normal																															
Tired																															
Very Tired																															
Painful Tiredness																															

TRAINING WILLINGNESS

Very Good																															
Good																															
Poor																															
Unwilling																															
Did Not Train																															

APPETITE

Very Good																															
Good																															
Poor																															
Eat Because Should																															
Did Not Eat																															

COMPETITIVE WILLINGNESS

High Indeed																															
Average																															
Low																															
Not at All																															

MUSCLE SORENESS

No Pain																															
Little Pain																															
Moderate Pain																															
Severe Pain																															

TABLE 7.8: Training Monitoring—Chart 3 (Blank)

NAME _____   MONTH _____

HEART RATE	1	2	3	4	5	6	7	8	9	10	11	12	13	14	15	16	17	18	19	20	21	22	23	24	25	26	27	28	29	30	31
72																															
71																															
70																															
69																															
68																															
67																															
66																															
65																															
64																															
63																															
62																															
61																															
60																															
59																															
58																															
57																															
56																															
55																															
54																															
53																															
52																															
51																															
50																															
49																															
48																															
47																															
46																															
45																															
44																															
43																															

WEIGHT																															
80																															
79																															
78																															
77																															
76																															
75																															
74																															
73																															
72																															
71																															
70																															
69																															
68																															
67																															
66																															
65																															

TABLE 7.9: Training Monitoring—Chart 4 (Blank)

NAME_____   MONTH_____

LENGTH OF SLEEP	1	2	3	4	5	6	7	8	9	10	11	12	13	14	15	16	17	18	19	20	21	22	23	24	25	26	27	28	29	30	31
12 + Hours																															
11																															
10																															
9																															
8																															
7																															
6																															
5																															
4																															
No sleep at all																															

QUALITY OF SLEEP																															
Very deep																															
Normal																															
Restless																															
Bad with Breaks																															
Not at All																															

TIREDNESS SENSATION																															
Very Rested																															
Normal																															
Tired																															
Very Tired																															
Painful Tiredness																															

TRAINING WILLINGNESS																															
Very Good																															
Good																															
Poor																															
Unwilling																															
Did Not Train																															

APPETITE																															
Very Good																															
Good																															
Poor																															
Eat Because Should																															
Did Not Eat																															

COMPETITIVE WILLINGNESS																															
High Indeed																															
Average																															
Low																															
Not at All																															

MUSCLE SORENESS																															
No Pain																															
Little Pain																															
Moderate Pain																															
Severe Pain																															

Treatment of Overtraining

When the overtraining state is identified, training has to be reduced or terminated immediately, irrespective of the causes. If the state of overtraining is very severe, in addition to complete training abstinence the player should be sheltered from negative social stress. A physician and training specialist must be consulted immediately to determine the causes. In the case of a mild overtraining state, when training has only to be reduced, the coach should not expose the player to any testing or games. Consequently, high-intensity training should be completely eliminated from both training and lifestyle. Active rest (mild exercise) has to be considered even for a player who is in a severe overtraining state, since an abrupt interruption of training may be harmful to a player accustomed to extensive physical involvement.

Specific regeneration techniques should be utilized to enhance the rate of recovery. Dietary modification might also be called for during this time period—the increase and/or manipulation of some nutrients can influence the regeneration process. For example, the addition of carbohydrates along with proteins and essential fats has been shown to elevate nighttime melatonin levels, which in turn can provide the player with optimal rest. In all cases, strict adherence to the various forms of regeneration will be fundamental to bringing the player out of this undesirable state of training.

In the case of "sympathetic overtraining," caused by continuous and constant high intensity, and overstressing the emotions of hockey players in too many games, regeneration techniques like those outlined in Table 7.10 should be used. The player should also see a physician, a sport medicine specialist, and a nutritionist to ask for professional advice.

TABLE 7.10: Techniques Employed for the Treatment of Overtraining

Special Diet
- stimulate appetite through alkaline food (milk, fruit, fresh vegetables)
- avoid stimulatory substances (coffee), small quantities of alcohol permitted
- increase quantities of vitamins (B group)

Physiotherapy
- outdoor swimming
- bathing 15 to 20 minutes at a temperature of 95°F to 97°F (35°C to 37°C) (but no sauna)
- cold showers and brisk toweling in the morning
- massage
- light and rhythmical exercises

DETRAINING

Detraining, or the players' loss of work output, occurs in two circumstances in hockey.

- *Detraining during league games:* The extremely long competitive phase (league games) in hockey, where training is often neglected, is bound to have some negative effects on players' work output. This strongly applies to younger players who are far from having a strong fitness base. While technical and tactical training has an anaerobic and aerobic benefit, off-ice strength training is very neglected.

  The lack of strength training maintenance results in protein degradation, where muscles progressively lose their contraction force; every time the muscles' contraction force decreases, so do speed, power skating, and quickness in changing direction. You should always remember that any loss of strength affects speed, one of the most important qualities sought in hockey.

- *Detraining during the transition phase:* As already mentioned, a longer transition than four to five weeks will always result in loss of fitness. While many players are fond of golf, which is important for mental relaxation and enjoyment, this game has very negligible fitness effects on a sport where speed/power are determinant physical abilities.

  If a hockey player indulges in a long transition of six to eight weeks, fitness loss will be in both the strength and endurance areas. The rate of strength loss per day can be roughly 3% to 4% in the first week, while endurance capacity decreases by 7% in the first seven to 12 days. The degeneration of fitness capacity will be more severe as the transition phase progresses beyond the acceptable four- to five-week period. In addition, if fitness training is grossly neglected during transition, one will need to spend some four to five weeks of the new preparation phase to gain back what could have been maintained without too much effort. In a sport where physical preparation is very important, this loss of four to five weeks will affect the rate of fitness improvement from year to year, decreasing players' ability to meet their fitness expectations.

Speed and agility are affected less by detraining than other factors such as strength and muscular endurance. Technique is important in both speed and agility, and small losses can be reversed quickly. Speed and agility require a high level of nerve-cell adaptation, and loss of either speed or agility may initially be related to the susceptibility of the nervous system to detraining.

Flexibility is lost at one-third the rate at which it is gained. It is recommended that a maintenance program of two to three times per week should be included in a year-round program. Flexibility exercises lasting 10 minutes per day, if possible, should be part of the players' daily regimen throughout the year.

Cardiovascular endurance Maximum Oxygen Uptake (MVO_2) is visibly affected by long transition phases. Studies have shown a drop of 6% in MVO_2 after two to four weeks of inactivity (Coyle et al., 1984), and even greater declines of 15% after a three-month cessation for male and female track athletes.

It appears that in comparison with strength, power, and speed and agility, maintenance of cardiovascular endurance is more difficult when regular training is stopped. Studies show that the cardiovascular-endurance training must be performed three times per week, as anything less will result in declines of MVO_2 values.

CHAPTER 8

Injuries: Prevention and Recovery

Hockey is a highly dynamic and aggressive contact sport that exposes its players to injuries. The incidence of injury often depends on the nature and character of both players and coach.

Injuries, or repeated injury, are more common among players who are inclined to take risks but lack the ability to cope with stress associated with these risks, or those who experience a high level of fatigue and the eventual lack of movement control as a result. Some players are also prone to injuries when they are exposed to life's stressful events, such as death of family members, divorce, a change of schools, etc., or have a high anxiety level.

Some of these causes of injuries could easily be averted if the coach has a good rapport with the players and is in close and constant communication with them. As a result, the coach would be informed about the players' concerns and problems, and how these might affect their playing abilities. Early detection of problems could be an effective damage-control technique.

A coach's attitude, training philosophy, and aggressive style could also lead to injuries. If the coach's philosophy is "no pain, no gain," or "you have to be tough," or "you have to play with pain," this could be interpreted by some players as having to play through an injury. Players must be able to distinguish between pain and injury as early as possible in their playing career. This is an educational concern, and both the coach and parents should explain to the players the difference between being committed—even "tough"—and acknowledging an injury.

When an injury occurs, no matter how simple, the coach and parents should immediately look for professional assistance. Whether it is a simple or severe injury, the coach and parents should be very supportive throughout the ordeal. If an injury keeps the player away from the game, then his or her parents, and especially the coach, should be positive and supportive. Strong support from the team is equally important so that healing will be certain and the player will look forward to rejoining the team on the ice.

Although any injury should be handled by professionals, such as certified physiotherapist personnel, the coach should also know that in most cases an injured player goes through four phases:

- Phase 1: Denial. The player tells himself or herself that everything will be okay, and that the next day he or she will be able to train again.
- Phase 2: Anger. The next day arrives and the player realizes that the injury persists, and optimism and hope are replaced with anger. The player often tends to be anxious and lonely, even attempting to isolate himself or herself.
- Phase 3: Disbelief. As the injury continues and the player cannot rejoin the team, anger is replaced by disbelief, and the player may fall into a state of depression.
- Phase 4: Acceptance. The player accepts the fact that he or she is injured and with treatment and rehabilitation is on the road to recovery. Throughout this phase, the coach and the team should make the injured player feel part of the team, especially when the team wins. If this is overlooked the injured player will feel he or she is an outsider and unwanted, and as a result experience a high level of anxiety and depression.

COMMON HOCKEY INJURIES

Hockey players are exposed to several types of injuries, and although first aid and the management and treatment of them have to be performed by qualified personnel, the coach should have some basic knowledge of some injuries and their treatment.

Contusions

A contusion, more commonly called a bruise, is produced by a blow from another player that causes the skin and muscles to be compressed against the hard bone underneath. A hard blow usually results in swelling and bleeding into the tissues, caused by the rupture of blood vessels (capillaries). The color of the bruise can often indicate its severity. Bluish-purple indicates superficial damage, and the discoloration will last for a few days. This area is painful when touched or during movement. Dark-blue indicates a hard hit, with damage to the muscle that will be quite painful for a few days, and the discoloration will remain for two to three weeks.

If a contusion is exposed to repeated blows, small calcium deposits may accumulate in the area, often impairing some physical movement. This is why any bruise, especially if severe, has to be protected from further injury.

Treatment: First aid and contusion-management techniques. Consider ice, compression, and rest, if necessary. Swelling, which produces increased pressure in the area, may cause more pain and sometimes, depending on the area of the bruise, may impair some movement. To speed up recovery, swelling has to be controlled and eliminated with cold therapy. Ice treatment for 20 minutes is often uncomfortable, with a sensation of cold following by burning and even numbness. The benefits could, however, be control of the swelling, a decrease of pain, and reduction of the swelling. Ice treatment should be applied to the area for two to three days.

Groin Strain

A groin strain is often the result of lack of groin flexibility. A groin strain is the outcome of groin muscles overextending, the hip rotating externally, or the groin muscles contracting forcefully. A groin muscle strain is always associated with discomfort and moderate to severe pain. A chronic strain, on the other hand, may even cause some bleeding in the groin muscles.

Treatment: Depending on the degree of groin strain, treatment performed by specialized personnel considers ice, compression, ultrasound, pain-free progressive-resistive strengthening exercises, and pain-free stretching exercises.

Prevention: To avoid groin strain, players should have a very good stretching and strength training program throughout the year, especially during the preparatory phase. Flexibility exercises should include hip and hamstring flexions, outside leg rotations, and hip flexions with the legs as far apart as possible.

Strength training should not only address groin and hip muscles, but also the abdominals, which often are poorly trained. Weak abdominals, especially the obliques, increase the chance of groin injuries because the obliques work with the opposite leg adductors (bringing the leg inward)—left obliques with right adductors and right obliques with left adductors.

Knee Injuries

The knee ligaments are injured when they are not able to resist tension from either abnormal movement, hyperextension of the knee, or abnormal force applied against the side of the knee. The most common injuries occur with the anterior crucial ligament, posterior crucial ligament, medial and collateral ligaments, the meniscus, and the patellar tendon, which is the continuation of the quadriceps tendon. Inflammation and pain are commonly associated with knee injuries.

Treatment: When a knee injury occurs, the player should immediately be referred to a sports injury clinic. Except for cases of surgery, the treatment of knee injuries could take the form of stretching to the degree of tolerance, and strengthening exercises performed by a certified physiotherapist.

Prevention: As in most cases, injury prevention techniques refer to stretching exercises to the full range of motion, and exercises aimed at strengthening the ligaments and tendons of the knee joint. You should always remember that ligaments and tendons are trainable, as are the muscles. Most training programs, however, disregard the need to train ligaments and tendons over a longer period of time with light and progressive loads. In many cases, strength training for younger players is either conducted by individuals with questionable qualifications, or simply follows the program for elite, junior, or professional teams.

As part of a team's injury prevention method for knee injuries, a coach should consider our suggested program for the age group in which you are interested. Our programs address long-term progressive development of the muscles, ligaments, and tendons. In addition, every proposed program has an anatomical adaptation phase that is an injury prevention training strategy.

Lower-Back Injuries

All athletes, hockey players being no exception, are fearful of lower-back injuries because they can be quite disabling. The lumbar spine (lower back) consists of five vertebrae. The vertebrae are large bones designed to absorb body weight. Between the vertebrae are the intervertebral discs, which act as shock absorbers for the spine. The vertebrae are connected by a series of paired joints that help to control flexion, extension, and rotation of the vertebrae, and also aid in weight bearing. In addition, there are numerous ligaments that add stability to the lumbar spine, and muscles that are concerned with movements of the vertebral column.

Back strain due to stress of the back being in incorrect positions during a game, or when exercises are being performed incorrectly, is responsible for the majority of lower-back injuries.

Treatment: For any complaint from a player, the coach should ensure that he or she is taken to a sports medicine clinic to assess the degree of the injury and the corresponding treatment. For lower-degree injuries such as strain, pain, and muscle spasm, qualified personnel use modalities for reducing the pain of muscle spasm, stretching to improve lower back flexibility, and training to strengthen the abdominal muscles to improve posture and especially to stabilize the trunk region.

Prevention: Any back injuries can be attributed to a weak abdominal musculature. The abdominal muscles protect the lower back by helping to stabilize the spinal column and by balancing intradiscal pressures, so remember to train the abdominal muscles. In addition, your players should strengthen the buttocks and intervertebral muscles.

A good comprehensive flexibility program is also very important so that the trunk in general, and the lower back in particular, will improve the range of motion for trunk rotation, flexion (bending), extension (arching), and overall shoulder flexibility.

Abdominal Injuries

As a high-intensity contact sport, hockey also exposes the players to abdominal muscle injuries caused, in most cases, by a sudden twisting movement, a blow, or being hit by a puck traveling at high speed.

The abdominal muscles, such as rectus abdominis, the internal and external obliques, and the transverse abdominis, are between the groin area and the lower ribs. Here are the most frequent injuries:

Contusions can be produced by either a collision with another player or by being struck by the puck. A contusion may be superficial, affecting the skin, or much deeper, affecting the musculature. If a contusion is at the rectus abdominis muscle level, it may cause a hematoma (a localized collection of blood), causing pain and tightness in the injured region.

Treatment: A cold pack or ice bag, and a compression elastic wrap, should be applied to the affected area immediately. If the contusion is larger or deeper, you should immediately consult medical personnel.

Abdominal muscle strain can be experienced as a result of sudden twisting of the trunk or an uncontrolled fall, which can tear the abdominal muscles. These types of injuries can result in pain and hematoma formation, which may disable the player.

Treatment: This may consist of full rest or performance of pain-free exercises or on-ice activities.

Prevention: The best prevention for both contusions and strains is excellent conditioning, which strengthens all of the abdominal muscles. For this reason, every program suggested in this book has at least one exercise that addresses the abdominal muscles. Since hockey so often involves trunk rotation, which is produced by the obliques muscles, you should not overlook the strengthening of these two sets of muscles. Please observe that one of our exercises with medicine balls closely imitates shooting the puck.

RECOVERY FROM INJURIES

Any committed hockey player can attest to the wear and tear, fatigue, and muscle soreness that can result from particularly strenuous training and games. Of the many methods employed for recovery from injuries, we will refer only to some that are easily available for players. Rehabilitation programs should include the following therapies.

Flexibility

Flexibility is defined as the ability of a joint to move easily through its entire range of motion. A high degree of flexibility is known to decrease the incidence of injuries, minimize muscular soreness, promote circulation and relaxation, and improve coordination by allowing increased freedom and ease of movement.

Unfortunately, most players either never stretch before or after their workouts, or they stretch incorrectly. This can only be detrimental to their training. If players take the time to stretch before and after each workout, there will be less likelihood of injury. The muscles will also receive the benefit of being strengthened through a greater range of motion, which can lead to greater strength gains.

Static stretching is a slow, gentle stretch that is held for at least 15 to 20 seconds. The joint is taken to the end of its range of motion, and then gentle pressure is applied to stretch the muscle further. The stretch is held at the point of tightness and should never reach the point of pain.

Cold Therapy

The therapeutic value of cold therapy is often overlooked. The most common forms of cold therapy include ice packs, ice baths, cryogel packs, and ice massage. The body responds to cold therapy in many ways. One response is a decrease in swelling.

The key to managing injuries in the acute phase (24 to 48 hours post-injury) is to limit the amount of soft-tissue swelling, because this creates most of the cellular damage through local tissue hypoxia (deficiency of oxygen) and the release of chemical mediators. The application of cold controls swelling in the following ways:

- It decreases circulation to the injured site by constricting blood vessels in and around the site, which causes blood to become more viscous, or resistant to flow.
- It decreases local fluid accumulation and promotes the absorption of excess fluid.

Cold therapy can also cause a decrease in hemorrhaging. It is thought that the application of cold reflexively controls the bleeding of blood vessels.

A third benefit of cold therapy can be a decrease in muscle spasm and pain.

Method of application: The recommended length of time for cold therapy is 20 minutes. Depending on the severity of the injury, it can be applied as often as every hour until swelling is controlled. Cold therapy should be used under the supervision of a physiotherapist or physician. To avoid frostbite or cold burns, simply place a tissue or thin cloth between the skin and the ice pack.

Cold application is highly recommended following intense training sessions. This will prevent excessive fluid accumulation and muscle soreness that might result from lactic acid build-up or microtearing of the muscle tissue. By treating minor discomforts as they occur, the player can better prevent injury and continue with his or her strenuous training.

Heat Therapy

Heat therapy, like cold therapy, is an inexpensive yet effective method of treating injuries. It is administered through the use of moist heat packs, hot compresses, whirlpools, hydrotherapy, electric heating pads, and contrast baths.

The body responds to heat therapy in many ways:

- decreased joint stiffness
- decreased muscle spasm: heat is thought to relieve muscle spasm
- decreased pain: heat also reduces the conduction velocity of the nerve fibers that are responsible for carrying pain messages to the central nervous system
- increased blood flow: heat causes vasodilation and a subsequent increase in the flow of nutrients, antibodies, and oxygen to the tissues, all of which aid in tissue healing.
- hastened resolution of inflammatory infiltrates, edema, and excessive fluid accumulation.

Method of application: A heat therapy session should last no longer than 20 minutes. The main concern when using heat therapy is the avoidance of burns. When using moist heat packs or a heating pad, make sure that there is sufficient toweling between the heat source and the skin. The temperature of whirlpool baths must be closely monitored and should not exceed 108ºF (41ºC).

Contrast baths use both hot and cold therapies. The injured limb is kept in hot water for one minute, and then in cold water for 30 seconds. This cycle can be repeated for 15 to 20 minutes. The purpose of the contrast bath is to increase local circulation within the injured limb through alternating vasodilation with vasoconstriction. It is probably most useful in the treatment of chronic musculoskeletal injuries that need increased blood flow.

Caution: *Take the above precautions to avoid the possibility of burns. Use heat cautiously, or not at all, on subjects with dermatological conditions, open or infected wounds, impaired skin sensation, or gross edema. Do not apply heat to areas affected by circulatory disease.*

Heat or Ice?

The effects of heat and cold are quite similar, although the mechanisms are different. The current practice is to use cold therapy on acute soft-tissue injuries and overuse injuries. It is the safest choice when the main concern is to control swelling and bleeding in the injured tissue. The use of heat is advised once the swelling has subsided and the soft tissues and joints are stiff. By increasing the temperature of the collagen, it is easier to stretch the connective tissue and adhesions.

Rule of thumb: Always use cold therapy before heat therapy. Other modalities for treatment of injuries include ultrasound, massage, and electrical muscle stimulation, administered by specialists in these fields. Massage, however, can be learned by some players and self-massage performed, or they can work in pairs. A massage therapist can teach some of the more mature and interested players the basic, simpler techniques, and they can use them regularly before, and especially after, training and/or games. This will help the players to relax and feel good, and also to constantly control muscle tightness and foster muscle relaxation and elasticity.

Once injured, will a player always be susceptible to reinjury?

Reinjury generally occurs because most players do not aggressively rehabilitate their injuries. If soft-tissue injuries are left to recover on their own, they might not regain normal elasticity and tensile strength. Given the amount of force and stress imposed on the tissues during training and games, reinjury is common in untreated tissue.

What is the lesson to be learned from this? Take any and every injury seriously and consult a medical professional or physiotherapist for the best way to rehabilitate players' injuries.

CHAPTER 9

Evaluating Fitness

The true measure of the fitness of a hockey player can only be determined through some type of monitoring or testing. The monitoring process should be done at least twice and ideally three times per year: at the beginning of the preparation period, before training camp, and midway through the competitive season. Although this is the ideal, most teams usually perform tests before training camp and at the end of the season. Other tests, such as 1RM to calculate the load in strength training during the preparatory phase, have to be tested in each macro-cycle.

Testing at the end of the season indicates a hockey player's present fitness. A training program can then be designed to develop total fitness with an emphasis on the player's weaker components. The testing provides feedback on the training state and progress made.

Testing procedures can be on-ice, off-ice (field tests), and in a laboratory setting. The on-ice tests are hockey-specific and measure both fitness and skill (e.g., skating ability). The off-ice tests measure fitness and are more easily administered than on-ice or laboratory tests. Laboratory testing, although more accurate in measuring certain physical parameters, is usually expensive and not very practical unless at the professional or elite level.

The coach and the player should realize that results of physiological testing alone cannot predict athletic success, nor should they ever be used as the sole criterion in selecting players.

An effective program should test variables that relate to the sport, should be valid (measures what it claims to measure), reliable (produce consistent results), as hockey-specific as possible, and should be administered properly.

LABORATORY TESTS VERSUS FIELD TESTS

The coach must decide whether laboratory tests or field tests are more appropriate for the team. A laboratory test is one in which the environment is controlled, and the testing is normally performed in a sports science laboratory (although some equipment is portable), and by some fitness-testing organizations.

The coach or assistant usually performs the field test in a simulated sports situation in the facility where the training takes place. For example, measuring a hockey player's anaerobic power while skating is a field test, whereas testing a player's anaerobic power on a stationary bicycle ergometer is a laboratory test.

The advantages of field tests are that they are hockey-specific and related to performance, relatively inexpensive, simpler to score and administer, and can be done in the regular training facilities. Norms may be available, but if not, team-specific norms can be developed.

Laboratory tests are more precise, reliable, and valid than field tests. They are very specific in terms of the factors measured, but are not as sport-specific as field tests. One of the biggest problems for amateur organizations is that the testing equipment is expensive and trained personnel are needed to administer the tests, so the costs may be prohibitive.

A third type of tests could be classified as lab-like tests. These modified lab tests are not usually as accurate as the highly controlled laboratory tests, but can be administered with minimal training by the coaches and their assistants, and in most cases involve minimal cost.

Quality Interpretation

For most tests we are presenting test results. These scores will allow you to compare your players' scores against these test results. To make a quality interpretation, you should consider that:

- a score over 80 percentile = excellent
- from 60 to 79 percentile = good
- from 40 to 59 percentile = average
- from 20 to 39 percentile = weak, and
- below 20 percentile = very weak

MEASURING AEROBIC POWER (MVO$_2$)
Field Tests

The Cooper 12-minute run and the half-mile run are the most common field tests to measure aerobic power.

Twelve-Minute Run

Aerobic fitness is assessed by the distance covered in 12 minutes around a 400-meter track.

Method: The players work in pairs; one player takes the test and the other records the total distance covered. A whistle is blown at the end of 12 minutes and the number of laps covered (to the nearest lap) is recorded. The players need to warm up before starting.

Equipment: A stopwatch, recording sheets, pens, clipboards, and use of a 437-yard (400-m) track.

Note: Although the 12-minute run is used by many to test the aerobic capacity, our suggestion to you is to replace this test with a hockey-specific test such as the "Figure 8—40 Laps" test (see Figure 9.4).

TABLE 9.1: Twelve-Minute Run Scores (in meters) (from Larivière, Godbout, and Lamontague, 1997; reprinted by permission of the Canadian Hockey Association)

Percentile	Age/Level						
	12	13	14	15	16	Midget	Junior
90	2400	2440	2520	2500	2620	3300	3320
80	2240	2300	2320	2440	2480	3160	3180
70	2120	2200	2240	2340	2420	3080	3100
60	2040	2100	2120	2260	2360	3000	3020
50	1980	2040	2040	2160	2260	2920	2940
40	1880	1960	2000	2000	2200	2800	2840
30	1780	1860	1920	1940	2100	2720	2740
20	1660	1740	1820	1840	1880	2640	2660
10	1480	1460	1640	1660	1700	2480	2560

(For conversion chart, see page 199.)

Half-Mile (800-m) Run

In this test of aerobic fitness, a player runs a half-mile (800-m) distance in his or her best time possible.

Method: Players work in pairs; one player runs the distance and the other records the time called out by the timer as the player completes the distance.

Equipment: A stopwatch, pens, recording sheets, clipboards, and a measured half-mile (800-m) distance.

TABLE 9.2: Half-Mile (800-m) Run Scores (in minutes)

Percentile	Age				
	12	13/14	15/16	17/18	19+
90	5:45	5:25	5:10	4:45	4:25
80	5:50	5:30	5:15	4:50	4:30
70	5:55	5:35	5:20	4:55	4:35
60	6:00	5:40	5:25	5:00	4:40
50	6:05	5:45	5:3 0	5:05	4:45
40	6:10	5:5 0	5:3 5	5:10	4:50
30	6:15	5:55	5:40	5:15	4:55
20	6:20	6:00	5:46	5:20	5:00
10	6:25	6:05	5:50	5:25	5:05

Laboratory Tests

An open-circuit metabolic unit measures aerobic capacity. The maximum oxygen a player can consume (MVO_2) is calculated along with other measurements such as blood pressure and electrocardiogram activity. The treadmill is the most common apparatus for determining MVO_2, and a variety of tests including Balke, Bruce, Naughton, and Ellestad are used. The treadmill allows the application of precise exercise intensities, using walking and running at increasing intensities without a rest period between stages.

The bicycle ergometer is also quite popular for increasing the exercise intensity and measuring MVO_2. The bicycle ergometer should include indicators of frictional resistance and revolutions per minute. Oxygen consumption is either measured directly or estimated with a bicycle ergometer, using a predictive equation.

The Forest Service Step Test is a lab-like test that uses recovery heart rates after bench stepping for five minutes to the count of a metronome. The recovery heart rates then give a predicted MVO_2 value, obtained by referring to a table.

Maximum oxygen uptake is usually measured in ml/kg/min. or in some cases in liters/min.

MEASURING ANAEROBIC POWER (ALACTIC)

The short-burst anaerobic alactic system can be measured with quick power bursts of under 10 seconds.

Field Test

55-Yard (50-m) Sprint

Method: The player sprints 55 yards (50 m) from a standing start. Time is recorded to the nearest tenth of a second.

Equipment: Two or more stopwatches, clipboards, pens, recording sheet, 55-yard (50-m) straight track, and four pylons to indicate start and finish line.

TABLE 9.3: 55-Yard (50-m) Scores (in seconds)

Percentile	Age				
	12	13/14	15/16	17/18	19+
90	7.5	7.0	6.5	6,3	6.0
80	7.6	7.1	6.7	6.4	6.1
70	7.8	7.2	6.8	6.5	6.2
60	7.9	7.3	6.9	6.6	6.3
50	8.0	7.4	7.0	6.7	6.4
40	8.1	7.6	7.1	6.8	6.5
30	8.2	7.8	7.2	6.9	6.6
20	8.3	7.9	7.3	7.0	6.7
10	8.4	8.0	7.4	7.1	6.8

Laboratory Tests

The Margaria Staircase Test is used for measuring lower-body anaerobic power. A player must run up a series of stairs as quickly as possible, stepping on every third stair. A timing device on the third and ninth step will activate to measure the elapsed time between these two points.

The Wingate Anaerobic Test requires the player to pedal on a stationary bike at a maximum rate against a high constant resistance; the highest five-second output is measured.

Muscle biopsies, where a small amount of muscle tissue is analyzed for the amount of enzymes, ATP, and CP, is also a laboratory procedure for measuring alactic power. A medical doctor must perform this procedure.

MEASURING ANAEROBIC LACTIC POWER

Anaerobic lactic power can be measured with intense exercise lasting from 30 to 90 seconds. The power aspect of the lactic system is usually measured with all-out activity in approximately 30 to 40 seconds, while capacity is usually measured with all-out exercise in approximately 90 seconds.

Field Test
437-Yard (400-m) Run

Method: A player runs 437 yards (400 m) as fast as possible from a standing start. Time is measured to the nearest tenth of a second.

Equipment: Two to four stopwatches (to test two to four players at one time), clipboards, pens, recording sheets, and a 437-yard (400-m) track.

TABLE 9.4: 437-Yard (400-m) Run Times (in seconds)

	Age				
Percentile	12	13/14	15/16	17/18	19+
90	65	69	57	54	52
80	68	63	59	56	54
70	70	65	61	58	56
60	72	68	63	60	58
50	74	70	65	62	60
40	76	71	67	64	62
30	78	72	69	66	64
20	80	74	71	68	66
10	82	76	73	70	68

Laboratory Test

The Wingate Anaerobic Test is used to test the anaerobic lactate system. The total work accomplished in 30 seconds is used, instead of measuring peak power in five seconds as with the alactic power test.

MEASURING STRENGTH AND MUSCULAR ENDURANCE

Strength is the ability to exert or apply a force, and muscular endurance is the ability to sustain repeated muscular contractions.

Measuring strength and muscular endurance is usually related to specific muscle groups, such as arms and legs, and in some cases strength can vary in the different muscle groups. It is, therefore, important to measure strength and muscular endurance in the major muscle groups used in the specific sport.

Strength Field Tests
Maximum One Repetition (1RM)

Method: For a given weight, a number of trials are given to determine the maximum weight that can be lifted just once (1RM). Exercises such as bench press, standing press, curl, and leg press are the most common maximum-strength tests. The exercises that are to be used should be included in the training program, and extreme caution should be used if the player has had no experience with the designated lift or lifts.

Equipment: Designated barbells or weight machines used in the specific exercise, two spotters, recording sheets, pens, and a weight room or gymnasium.

TABLE 9.5: Optimum Strength Values for IRM

Body Weight lb.	Bench Press Male	Female	Standing Press Male	Female	Curl Male	Female	Leg Press Male	Female
80	80	56	53	37	40	28	160	112
100	100	70	67	47	50	35	200	140
120	120	84	80	56	60	42	240	168
140	140	98	93	65	70	49	280	196
160	160	112	107	75	80	56	320	224
180	180	126	120	84	90	63	360	252
200	200	140	133	93	100	70	400	280
220	220	154	147	103	110	77	440	308
240	240	168	160	112	120	84	480	336

(For conversion chart, see page 199.)

Chin-ups, or Pull-ups (Upper Body)

Method: With palms of the hands facing the body, the player seizes the bar and pulls his or her body off the ground until the chin reaches above the bar. The player must keep the legs straight, with no motion of raising the knees or kicking the legs. The maximum number is performed, with only complete chin-ups counted.

Equipment: Wooden or metal bar 1½ inch (3.75 cm) in diameter, pens, clipboard, and a recording sheet.

TABLE 9.6: Strength Ratings Estimated from Number of Pull-ups

	Number of Pull-ups		
Age	Low	Average	High
9–10	0	1	6
11	0	2	6
12	0	2	7
13	1	3	8
14	2	4	10
15	3	6	12
16	4	7	12
17+	5	7	13

Flexed-arm Hang (Females)

Method: This test is specifically for females and is similar to the chin-up exercise, except the female player does one pull-up with the elbows flexed and, with chin above the bar, holds the position for as long as possible. This "held" position is timed until the chin touches the bar, is tilted backward to avoid the bar, or descends below the bar.

Equipment: Stopwatches, clipboard, pens, recording paper, 1½ inch (3.75 cm) metal or wooden bar set approximately at the height of the player.

TABLE 9.7: Strength Rating for Females in the Flexed-arm Hang

	Hang Time in Seconds		
Age	Low	Average	High
9–10	3	9	30
11	3	10	30
12	3	9	26
13	3	8	25
14	3	9	28
15	4	9	27
16	3	7	23
17+	3	8	26

Laboratory Tests

No one test is accepted as standard for measuring total body strength. There is a high degree of specificity of major muscle groups, and a high level of strength in one muscle group does not always correlate to high levels of strength in other muscle groups. Total body strength seems to be best represented by strength tests in three areas: upper body, lower body, and trunk. Devices to measure strength include spring-type, pressure, and electrical devices. In the past, spring-type dynamometers, specifically the cable tensiometer, have been most commonly used. The pressure and electrical devices coupled with microcomputers are becoming more prevalent, being able to provide detailed analyses of strength and power curves throughout a full range of motion.

MEASURING LEG POWER
Field Test
Standing Long Jump

Method: The player stands behind the starting (drawn/taped) line on the floor. The legs are bent, while the arms are swung backwards. At the second or third forward swing of the arms, the player jumps forward, bringing the knees upward and extending them down for maximum distance. Both feet should be together on landing and knees bent to absorb the shock. Best score is considered between the starting line and the closest point the legs or body touch on a gymnastics mat or the ground. Best of two or three trials is recorded.

TABLE 9.8: Standing Long Jump Scores (in cm) (from Larivière, Godbout, and Lamontague, 1997; reprinted by permission of the Canadian Hockey Association)

	Age/Level						
Percentile	12	13	14	15	16	Midget	Junior
90	183	198	223	230	230	245	255
80	173	185	213	220	223	237	236
70	168	177	205	213	216	231	239
60	164	172	198	219	212	227	235
50	162	170	193	206	208	223	232
40	158	167	188	202	205	218	229
30	154	163	182	196	201	214	224
20	148	157	174	190	195	207	211
10	139	148	161	182	184	198	206

(For conversion chart, see page 199)

MEASURING MUSCULAR ENDURANCE
Field Tests
Pushups

Method: The body is in the prone position, with the hands beneath the shoulders and the toes pointed. The arms are straightened with full extension, and then flexed until the nose touches the floor, with the back kept straight. The maximum number is done in succession. Only complete pushups, with the arms fully extended, are counted. The players work in pairs, with one counting and the other performing the pushup.

Equipment: Mats, clipboards, pens, and a scoring sheet.

TABLE 9.9: Muscular Endurance Ratings from the Number of Pushups Executed

Age and Sex	Low	Average	High
Under 14			
Males	Under 15	15–30	Over 30
Females	Under 10	10–20	Over 20
Over 14			
Males	Under 20	20–40	Over 40
Females	Under 10	10–30	Over 30

Situps

Method: The player assumes a prone position with the hands placed behind the neck. The knees are bent at 90º. The heels are on the floor, the ankles held by a partner. The player sits up and touches the elbows to the knees, then returns the upper body to the floor. Each time the elbows touch the knees counts as one situp. The number of situps performed in one minute is the score.

Equipment: Stopwatch, mats, clipboards, pens, and a recording sheet.

TABLE 9.10: Muscular Endurance Ratings from the Number of Situps Executed

Age and Sex	Low	Average	High
Under 14			
Males	Under 15	15–30	Over 30
Females	Under 10	10–20	Over 20
Over 14			
Males	Under 30	30–50	Over 50
Females	Under 25	25–45	Over 45

MEASURING FLEXIBILITY

Field Test

Method: A common test measures the flexibility of the trunk and hamstrings. The player sits with the legs flat and toes upward. After the player has pre-stretched a couple of times, he or she reaches forward, with one hand on top of the other, as far forward as possible toward the toes.

With a ruler (in inches), measure the distance between the toes and the outstretched hands with the number 6 at the toes.

Equipment: 12- or 18-inch (30.5- or 46-cm) ruler, mats, recording sheet, pens, and clipboards.

TABLE 9.11: Flexibility Ratings (in inches)

	Low	Average	High
Males	< 3	2 to +2	3+
Females	< 1	2 to 4	5+

(For conversion chart, see page 199.)

Laboratory Test

Trunk flexion is tested with the Wells–Dillan sit-and-reach apparatus, or by a protractor device called a "goniometer," or a more accurate device called the "height on flexiometer."

MEASURING BODY FAT AND LEAN BODY WEIGHT

When assessing body composition, the total body weight is divided into lean body weight and fat weight. "Lean weight" refers to the total body weight of the muscle, skin, bone, organs, and all other non-fat tissue. Lean weight is determined in the laboratory, using Archimedes' principle and an underwater weighing technique to determine the density of the body.

Body fat can be determined in the field by using skinfold calipers. Measurements are taken, with folds of the skin being held firmly between the thumb and index finger. The calipers are placed as closely as possible to the thumb and the index finger. Measurements are usually taken at the triceps, biceps, sub-scapula (below the shoulder blade), and abdomen.

TABLE 9.12: Classification of Body Fat (from thickness of skinfolds for male and female players)

Male Players	Skinfold Thickness (mm)				
Classification	Body Fat	Triceps	Scapular	Abdomen	Sum
Lean	<7%	<7	<8	<10	<25
Acceptable	7–15%	7–13	8–15	10–20	25–48
Overly fat	>15%	>13	>15	>20	>48
Female Players	**Skinfold Thickness (mm)**				
Classification	Body Fat	Triceps	Scapular	Abdomen	Sum
Lean	<12%	<9	<7	<7	<23
Acceptable	12–25%	9–17	7–14	7–15	23–46
Overly fat	>25%	>17	>14	>15	>46

ON-ICE TESTS
Anaerobic Power

Skating Test

Measures the capacity of the player to execute highly intensive work over a short period of time.

Method: The player is required to skate 12 repeats of a 20-yard (18-m) course. The player starts at the goal line, skates forward 20 yards (18 m), stops at the pylon and returns to the goal line. The player repeats this circuit six times for a total of 12 times 20 yards (18 m). The time is recorded for the total distance. A demonstration should precede the test. The player must come to a full stop at each end of the course.

Equipment: Measuring tape, stopwatch, and four pylons. Players wear full equipment and carry a hockey stick.

FIGURE 9.1: Skating Anaerobic Power Test (from Larivière, G., Godbout, P., and Lamontague M., *Physical Fitness and Technical Skill Appraisal of Ice Hockey Players* (Ottawa: Canadian Hockey Association, 1997), 55–56. Reprinted by permission.)

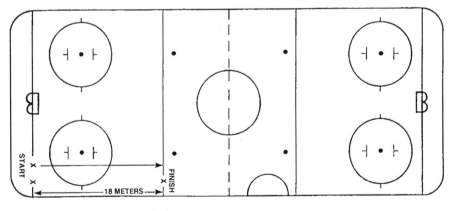

X Pylons

TABLE 9.13:

MEASURE = Skating Anaerobic Power   TEST = 12 times 20 yards (18 m)
UNIT   = Seconds

(from Larivière, G., Godbout, P., and Lamontague M., *Physical Fitness and Technical Skill Appraisal of Ice Hockey Players* (Ottawa: Canadian Hockey Association, 1997), 101. Reprinted by permission.)

Percentile	12	13	14	15	16	Bantam	Midget	Junior	Percentile
95	51.8	50.0	47.3	46.5	46.3	47.9	46.7	45.9	95
90	53.2	51.2	48.5	48.0	47.4	48.8	47.9	47.0	90
85	54.1	52.0	49.6	48.8	48.4	49.4	48.8	47.6	85
80	55.0	52.7	50.3	49.3	49.0	49.9	49.5	47.9	80
75	55.7	53.5	51.1	49.9	49.7	50.4	49.8	48.2	75
70	56.4	54.0	51.5	50.4	50.3	50.8	50.2	48.5	70
65	57.0	54.5	52.0	51.0	50.9	51.1	50.5	48.8	65
60	57.5	55.0	52.5	51.7	51.9	51.3	50.7	49.2	60
55	58.0	55.6	53.0	52.3	52.2	51.9	50.9	49.5	55
50	58.5	56.2	53.5	53.0	52.8	52.3	51.1	49.8	50
45	59.1	57.0	54.1	53.6	53.1	52.8	51.4	49.9	45
40	59.8	57.5	54.6	54.2	53.7	53.1	$1.6	50.1	40
35	60.4	58.4	55.6	54.9	54.0	53.5	51.8	50.5	35
30	61.0	59.4	56.3	55.6	54.3	53.9	52.1	50.8	30
25	61.9	60.2	57.0	56.3	54.7	54.4	52.4	51.1	25
20	63.1	61.2	58.0	57.2	55.5	55.1	52.8	51.7	20
15	64.5	62.7	59.3	58.4	56.3	56.0	53.4	52.3	15
10	66.2	64.4	61.0	59.9	57.5	57.8	53.9	53.1	10
5	70.1	67.0	64.3	62.2	61.8	60.1	54.7	54.3	5
Mean	59.6	57.7	54.8	54.5	53.8	53.2	51.3	50.1	Mean
S.D.	6.4	6.5	5.8	5.4	4.9	3.1	2.7	2.9	S.D.

Sprint

Blue to Blue

Method: Player sprints from one blue line to the other blue line. A starter is at one line and a timer at the other. Time is recorded to the nearest tenth of a second. Repeat three times and take the average.

All players should first be tested as a group before starting the second trial, to allow adequate recovery time. The standard distance from one blue line to the other is 60 feet (18 m). If the distance is not 60 feet (18 m), then measure the exact distance and use it as the course.

Equipment: A stopwatch, two pylons, measuring tape, and a clipboard.

Anaerobic Alactic Quickness Skating Test

Method: Player starts at the blue line, skates to the center line, stops, returns to the blue line, stops, and skates past the center line. Record the time from the start until the player crosses the center line.

TABLE 9.14: Blue to Blue Test Results (in seconds)

Percentile	Age			
	14/15	16/17	College	Pro
90	3.0	2.9	2.7	2.5
80	3.1	3.0	2.8	2.6
70	3.2	3.1	2.9	2.7
60	3.3	3.2	3.0	2.8
50	3.4	3.3	3.1	2.9
40	3.5	3.4	3.2	3.0
30	3.6	3.5	3.3	3.1
20	3.7	3.6	3.4	3.2
10	3.8	3.7	3.5	3.3

Equipment: Stopwatch and clipboard.

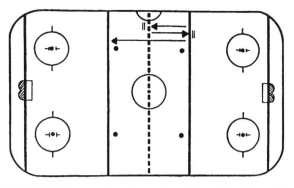

FIGURE 9.2: On-ice Quickness Test. (from MacAdam, D. and Reynolds, J., *Hockey Fitness* (Champaign, IL: Leisure Press, 1988), 118. Reprinted by permission.

ANAEROBIC CAPACITY (LACTATE)

Speed Test

Method: Divide the distance between the blue lines into five equal segments, using pylons. The players work in pairs. One player skates from blue line to blue line as quickly as possible. The other records the distance skated in 60 seconds. Record the distance in tenths of a lap; one lap equals the distance from blue line to blue line and back. Record the total distance in laps or in tenths of a lap. The timer can also call out elapsed times at 15, 30, 45, and 60 seconds, and accumulated distance can be recorded. This can provide information on drop-off times and the player's anaerobic capacity for a 60-second shift on the ice during a game.

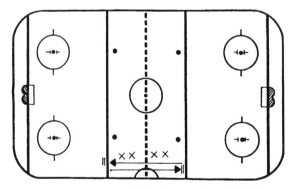

FIGURE 9.3: On-ice Speed Test/On-ice Quickness Test. (from MacAdam, D. and Reynolds, J., *Hockey Fitness* (Champaign, IL: Leisure Press, 1988), 116. Reprinted by permission.)

Aerobic Capacity Test

Figure 8 – 40 Laps

Method: The aerobic skate involves skating at a constant pace for 40 laps in a figure-8 pattern in as fast a time as pos-

sible. Players count their own laps or have a partner count for them. The nets are placed even with the hash marks. The distance between the nets should be 160 feet (49 m).

Equipment: A stopwatch, clipboard, and measuring tape.

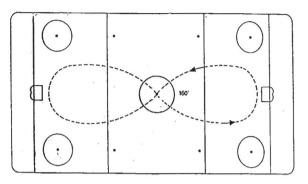

FIGURE 9.4: The Format of the Aerobic Capacity Test (from Rhodes, T. and Twist, P., *The Physiology of Ice Hockey* (Vancouver: University of British Columbia Press), 127. Reprinted by permission.)

Twelve-minute Skate

Method: The players skate continuously for 12 minutes and total distance for each is recorded to the nearest 1/8 of a lap. The players try to cover as much distance as possible in 12 minutes. Players work in two groups; one group skates as the other records distances.

Equipment: A stopwatch, 10 clipboards, and pens.

TABLE 9.15: Aerobic Skate Test Results (in minutes) (from Rhodes, T. and Twist, P., *The Physiology of Ice Hockey* (Vancouver: University of British Columbia Press, 1990), 127. Reprinted by permission.)

| Percentile | Age | | | |
	14/15	16/17	College	Pro
90	11:00	11:30	10:50	10:00
80	11:15	11:45	11:00	10:15
70	11:30	12:00	11:10	10:30
60	11:40	12:15	11:20	10:40
50	11:50	12:30	11:30	10:50
40	12:05	12:45	11:40	11:05
30	12:20	13:00	11:55	11:20
20	12:35	13:15	12:10	11:35
10	12:50	13:30	12:25	11:50

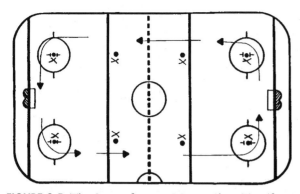

FIGURE 9.5: The Set-up for a 12-Minute Skate Test (from MacAdam, D. and Reynolds, J., *Hockey Fitness* (Champaign, IL: Leisure Press, 1988), 118. Reprinted by permission.)

Agility and Quickness

Method: Set up the course as illustrated in Figure 9.7. The player starts behind the start line, with stick and puck also behind the line. (Note that this test can be performed with or without a puck.) The player should first practice skating the course, and verbal instructions are useful during the test. The player skates forward from the starting line to the red line, straight back to the first pylon, and proceeds to weave through the pylons to the red line, and back. After rounding the last pylon on the way back, the player skates straight to the red line, stops, and then returns to the finish line. The time is recorded. If the player loses the puck, or skates the course incorrectly, the drill must be re-run.

Equipment: Stopwatch, measuring tape, four pylons, pucks, and clipboard. The players wear full equipment for this test.

EVALUATING GOALTENDERS

Although goaltenders can be involved in many elements of training and fitness evaluation designed for hockey players (mostly movement time, agility, speed and power training, and tests), they also have to be tested in some position-specific tests, such as measuring movement time.

Arm and Leg Movement Time Test

Method: The goalie stands in the basic stance (A), with the skate blades parallel, just outside of the outermost point midway between the two goal posts. At the coach's signal, the goalie, as quickly as possible, moves towards the right, touching the post with the right leg pad (B), and returns to the starting point (A). Perform the same action to the left (C), and return to the starting point. As quickly as possible, he or she skates to touch the upper right corner of the goal (D) with the right glove, and returns to the starting point. The goalie performs the same to the left, touching the upper left corner of the goal (E) with blocker, then skates back to the starting point.

A complete test consists of five cycles (left-handers may perform the test starting with the left post of the goal).

The coach/tester should observe that a cycle is complete and the player crosses the red goal line with both blades at the end of the cycle.

FIGURE 9.6: Skating Agility with or without the Puck (from Larivière, G., Godbout, P., and Lamontague M., *Physical Fitness and Technical Skill Appraisal of Ice Hockey Players* (Ottawa: Canadian Hockey Association, 1997), 57–58. Reprinted by permission.)

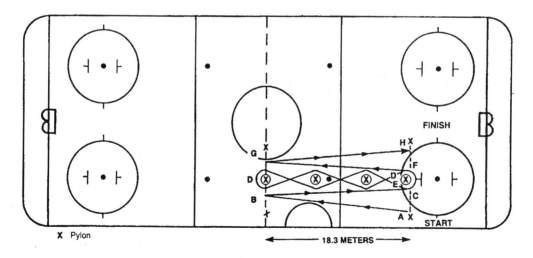

X Pylon

← 18.3 METERS →

TABLE 9.16: MEASURE = Skating Agility   TEST = Skating Agility without the Puck   UNIT = Seconds
(from Larivière, G., Godbout, P., and Lamontague M., *Physical Fitness and Technical Skill Appraisal of Ice Hockey Players* (Ottawa: Canadian Hockey Association, 1997), 99. Reprinted by permission.)

| Percentile | Players (Age) | | | | | Elite players (Categories) | | | Percentile |
	12	13	14	15	16	Bantam	Midget	Junior	
95	25.2	24.3	23.8	23.4	23.1	23.8	23.0	22.9	95
90	26.1	25.1	24.2	23.8	23.6	24.2	23.5	23.3	90
85	26.7	25.5	24.5	24.0	24.0	24.4	23.9	23.5	85
80	27.0	25.9	24.8	24.3	24.4	24.5	24.2	23.6	80
75	27.2	26.2	25.1	24.5	24.6	24.6	24.3	23.7	75
70	27.5	26.5	25.4	24.8	24.8	24.7	24.4	23.9	70
65	27.8	26.8	25.6	25.0	25.0	24.8	24.5	24.0	65
60	28.0	27.0	24.8	25.1	25.1	25.0	24.6	24.1	60
55	28.3	27.1	26.0	25.3	25.3	25.2	24.9	24.2	55
50	29.6	27.3	26.2	25.5	25.5	25.3	24.9	24.3	50
45	28.9	27.6	26.4	25.7	25.7	25.4	25.0	24,4	45
40	29.2	28.0	26.7	25.9	25.9	25.5	25.2	24.5	40
35	29.5	28.2	27.0	26.1	26.0	25.7	25.4	24.6	35
30	29.9	28.6	27.2	26.4	26.3	25.9	25.6	24.7	30
25	30.2	29.1	2.6	26.7	26.6	26.2	25.7	24.8	25
20	30.7	29.6	28.1	27.0	26.9	26.6	25.9	24.9	20
15	31.4	30.1	28.7	27.5	27.3	27.3	26.1	25.0	15
10	32.3	30.9	29.6	28.1	27.9	28.0	26.7	25.4	10
5	34.0	32.5	31.7	29.0	28.9	29.4	27.8	26.3	5
Mean	29.0	28.1	26.6	25.9	26.0	25.5	25.2	24.5	Mean
S.D.	3.7	3.5	3.8	3.4	2.9	1.7	1.5	1.2	S.D.

TABLE 9.17: MEASURE = Skating Agility   TEST = Skating Agility with the Puck   UNIT = Seconds
(from Larivière, G., Godbout, P., and Lamontague M., *Physical Fitness and Technical Skill Appraisal of Ice Hockey Players* (Ottawa: Canadian Hockey Association, 1997), 99. Reprinted by permission.)

| Percentile | Players (Age) | | | | | Elite players (Categories) | | | Percentile |
	12	13	14	15	16	Bantam	Midget	Junior	
95	27.0	25.9	25.0	24.3	24.0	24.6	23.8	23.5	95
90	28.0	26.6	25.6	24.8	24.7	25.0	24.2	23.8	90
85	28.6	27.2	26.1	25.2	25.3	25.2	24.5	24.0	85
80	29.1	27.7	26.5	25.6	25.7	25.4	24.6	24.1	80
75	29.5	28.0	26.7	25.9	26.0	25.6	24.8	24.2	75
70	29.9	28.3	27.0	26.2	26.3	25.8	25.9	24.3	70
65	30.2	28.8	27.1	26.6	26.6	26.0	25.1	24.4	65
60	30.7	29.3	27.6	26.9	26.8	26.2	25.3	24.6	60
55	31.1	29.7	27.9	27.2	27.0	26.3	25.4	24.7	55
50	31.4	30.0	28.2	27.5	27.2	26.4	25.5	2CS	50
45	31.8	30.3	28.5	27.8	27.4	26.5	25.7	24,9	45
40	32.2	30.7	28.9	28.2	27.7	26.6	25.9	25.2	40
35	32.7	31.2	29.5	28.4	28.0	26.8	26.2	25.2	35
30	33.2	31.8	29.9	28.8	28.3	27.0	26.5	25.3	30
25	34.0	32.5	30.4	29.1	28.7	27.3	26.7	25.4	25
20	34.8	33.3	31.0	29.5	29.2	27.7	26.9	25.6	20
15	35.8	34.3	32.0	30.0	29.8	28.2	27.1	25.8	15
10	37.2	35.5	33.1	31.1	30.9	28.9	27.6	26.1	10
5	39.8	37.6	35.7	33.4	32.5	30.0	28.5	27.6	5
Mean	32.4	30.1	29.1	28.1	27.4	26.6	25.9	25.1	Mean
S.D.	5.2	5.0	3.8	3.0	4.3	2.0	1.3	1.3	S.D.

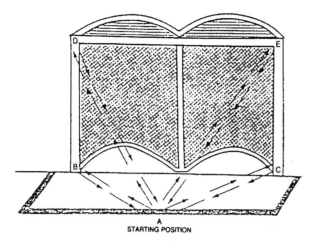

FIGURE 9.7: The Arm and Leg Speed of Movement Test (from Larivière, G., Godbout, P., and Lamontague M., *Physical Fitness and Technical Skill Appraisal of Ice Hockey Players* (Ottawa: Canadian Hockey Association, 1997), 70, 71. Reprinted by permission.)

TABLE 9.18: Goaltender Arm and Leg Speed of Movement (in seconds) (from Larivière, G., Godbout, P., and Lamontague M., *Physical Fitness and Technical Skill Appraisal of Ice Hockey Players* (Ottawa: Canadian Hockey Association, 1997), 107. Reprinted by permission.)

Percentile	Pee Wee	Bantam	Midget
90	54.6	48.6	43.7
80	57.8	51.9	47.0
70	60.1	54.3	49.3
60	62.1	56.3	51.4
50	63.9	58.2	53.2
40	65.8	60.1	55.1
30	67.8	62.1	57.2
20	70.1	64.5	59.5
10	73.3	67.8	62.8

Lateral Movement Agility Test

Method: The goalie positions him or herself beside one of the goal posts, with a leg pad and hip leaning against it, as shown in Figure 9.8 (position A). The test is started when the goalie moves rapidly to the opposite goal post, touching it with the leg pad and hip (position B). The goalie then returns across the front of the net and around behind it, touching the mark on the boards behind the goal with a leg pad (position C). The goalie skates back to the front of the goal and touches the farthest goal post (position B) with a leg and hip. The goalie then repeats the same cycle in the opposite direction. The goalie must complete 10 full cycles, five in each direction. The total test time is measured in seconds.

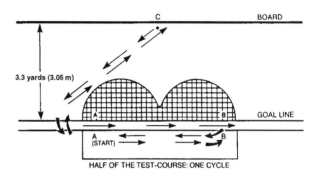

FIGURE 9.8: Lateral Movement Agility Test (from Larivière, G., Godbout, P., and Lamontague M., *Physical Fitness and Technical Skill Appraisal of Ice Hockey Players* (Ottawa: Canadian Hockey Association, 1997). Reprinted by permission.)

TESTING PROTOCOLS

Professional		Junior	
O$_2$:	Figure 8–40 laps	O$_2$:	Figure 8–40 laps
LA:	Skating anaerobic power test	LA:	Skating anaerobic power test
Alactic:	Blue line to blue line test	Alactic:	Blue line to blue line test
Agility:	Skating agility test	Agility:	Skating agility test
Leg power:	Standing long jump	Leg power:	Standing long jump
MxS:	Reverse leg press, bench press	MxS:	Reverse leg press, bench press
Midget (16–17 years old)		**Pee Wee and Bantam (13–15 years old)**	
O$_2$:	Figure 8–40 laps	O$_2$:	Figure 8–40 laps
LA:	Skating anaerobic power test	Alactic:	Blue line to blue line test
Alactic:	Blue line to blue line test	Leg power:	Standing long jump
Agility:	Skating agility test	MxS:	Hang and hold
Leg power:	Standing long jump	Agility:	Skating agility test
MxS:	Reverse leg press, bench press		

CHAPTER 10

Nutrition

The hockey player's diet is an essential link in the physical year-round training program. The energy used to move the muscles and restore energy during recovery is directly related to nutrition, as well as to the development of the cardiorespiratory and muscular systems. The hockey player involved in a rigorous training regimen has to pay special attention and understand how, what, and when to eat properly.

THE HOCKEY PLAYER'S DIET

The average person consumes between 1200 and 1500 calories per day through food intake. The hockey player who trains daily, however, may require between 2000 and 5000 calories per day, depending on the training intensity and characteristics such as age, size and weight, etc.

An optimal diet for an athlete would include approximately 60% to 65% carbohydrates, 25% fats, and 15% protein.

The four basic food groups supply the carbohydrates, fats, and proteins:

1. milk and cheese
2. meat and fish
3. fruits and vegetables
4. breads and cereals

Vitamins, minerals, and water are also essential for a well-balanced diet.

The carbohydrates in the diet that are broken down to simple sugars, primarily glucose, are stored in the muscle and liver as glycogen, and are the key to supplying energy for athletic performance. The major problem for today's hockey player is to have a 60% to 65% carbohydrate diet and limit the amount of fat to 25% along with 15% protein. High-carbohydrate diets produce more stored glycogen and have an effect on performance, especially in endurance activities lasting more than one hour that deplete these glycogen stores. In short-burst power activities, on- and off-ice, the glycogen stores are usually not fully depleted. Today's so-called junk foods (hamburgers, hot dogs, french fries, etc.) contain high fat levels, and it is important for the hockey player to limit intake of these foods and concentrate on those rich in carbohydrates.

The common prescription of three meals per day may be suitable for the average person. However, the hockey player, who may need twice as many calories, can eat five or six meals per day and planned nutritional snacks.

As well as the daily meals, the hockey player must eat a well-planned pre- and post-competition meal, along with some additional fluid and nutrition during the event.

Carbohydrates

Carbohydrates are made up of carbon, hydrogen, and oxygen, and are commonly known as starches and sugars. Carbohydrates, the main source of energy in intense exercise, supply the cells with glucose and glycogen, which are then converted to energy. Carbohydrates are found in three groups that vary in complexity and the size of the molecules: simple sugars, or monosaccharides; disaccharides, which are two linked monosaccharides; and polysaccharides, or complex carbohydrates.

Monosaccharides, or simple sugars, are often listed on food labels as glucose, fructose, or dextrose. Linking two monosaccharides such as fructose and glucose, which forms common table sugar, makes disaccharides. The joining of two monosaccharides also forms other simple sugars, such as maltose and lactose.

Polysaccharides can be of two types: starch and fiber. This complex carbohydrate is formed by a large number of simple sugar groups. These types of starches are found in grains and cereals, and in vegetables such as potatoes and corn.

Most food products contain mixtures of all three types of carbohydrates, and it is important for the hockey player and coach to read and understand the labels on food products to ascertain the carbohydrate value.

For the carbohydrates to be used as fuel for energy, they must be broken down to simple sugars by digestive enzymes before leaving the stomach to enter the small intestine to be absorbed by the blood. Only glucose can be used directly by the cells, and the blood carries the remaining simple sugars to the liver, where they are converted to glucose. When glucose enters a cell, some is used directly, while the rest is stored as glycogen for future use. Any glucose that remains after the glycogen stores are filled is stored as fat.

Glycogen stored in one muscle cell cannot be used by another cell. The liver has the only cells in the body that can convert glycogen back to glucose, which can then be re-released into the bloodstream.

Insulin is important for carrying glucose to the cells, and is released by the pancreas when there is an elevated amount of glucose in the blood.

Some specific foods that are rich in carbohydrates are:

- Pasta such as spaghetti and macaroni.
- Cereals such as bran and oat bran. These cereals are also a good supply of fiber.
- Vegetables such as potatoes, corn, and legumes.
- Muffins, bagels, and pizza. Whole-grains muffins (bran, oatmeal, corn) are better than white flour muffins, donuts, etc.
- Whole grain and dark breads. Whole grain breads have more nutritional value than white grain breads.
- Fruit and fruit juices such as orange, banana, and apple.

Fats

Along with carbohydrates, fats supply the majority of energy for the body; proteins supply very small amounts. Fats are stored as triglycerides in specialized cells in the body called "adipose tissue." Fats contain large amounts of carbon and hydrogen, and relatively small amounts of oxygen. Fats do not supply energy as quickly as carbohydrates, but more energy can be stored as fat. Fats are more important as a fuel source in prolonged activity that lasts more than an hour, while carbohydrates are used primarily in intense exercise of a shorter duration.

There are two types of fat sources: saturated and unsaturated. It is believed that saturated fat from animals, as well as coconut and palm oil, are related to the incidence of atherosclerosis and cardiovascular disease, and excessive amounts should be avoided. Unsaturated fats from vegetable oils and plants are considered better for hockey players. As only 25% of the total diet should be made up of fats, hockey players should take care not to exceed this limit.

Here are some recommendations regarding fats that should and should not be included in a hockey player's diet:

- Use olive oil, canola, safflower, and sunflower oils for cooking;
- Cut back or eliminate hamburgers, hot dogs, sausage, butter, and cheese;
- Use low-fat cheese, margarine, yogurt, peanut butter, and salad oils; and
- Read labels to find low-fat foods.

The major problem with the fat content in the hockey player's diet is that it is difficult to maintain the desired 25% level. Most hockey players tend to have a higher proportion of fat in their diet, to the detriment of the larger (60%) proportion that should be carbohydrates.

Protein

Protein, which should make up 15% of a hockey player's diet, is essential to the body for physical growth and repair of damaged tissue. Also, the enzymes that control the chemical reactions in the body are made up of proteins. Proteins are composed of chains of smaller substances called "amino acids," which are made up of carbon, hydrogen, oxygen, nitrogen, and, in some cases, sulfur atoms. The nitrogen content makes the protein different from carbohydrates and fat. There are 20 different amino acids, eight of which are called "essential" because the liver cannot make them from carbohydrates, fats, and protein. Three of these essential amino acids—namely, valine, iolencine, and leucine—are essential to energy production (Brooks, 1987).

The daily requirement of protein for the average person is one gram per kilogram (g/kg) of body weight. An athlete, while training, requires 1.4 to 2.0 g/kg (Clark, 1990). Amino acids can be found in the protein of both animals and plants. Animal proteins have a greater distribution of amino acids compared to plants, and are considered a better source. The average person with a normal diet usually consumes more than 2.0 g /kg of protein per day.

Taking in an excessive amount of protein—more than 15% of the total diet—is not recommended. With excessive amounts of protein the body removes the nitrogen and converts the remaining amino acid to fat or carbohydrates; therefore, excess protein cannot be stored. Excess amounts of protein have been known to cause dehydration and constipation because the kidneys must use water to wash out the nitrogen (urea) and other waste products resulting from protein metabolism.

Since a well-balanced diet produces more than enough protein for the hockey player in training, and because the body cannot store excessive protein, the protein supplements on the market, many of which make unsubstantiated claims, are unnecessary. A diet with a normal amount of protein is quite adequate for protein needs.

Some recommended sources of protein are:

- lean beef
- chicken and turkey
- fish, especially salmon, tuna, sardines, swordfish
- peanut butter
- beans, lentils, legumes, tofu
- milk, eggs, cottage cheese

Vitamins

Vitamins are essential to the body as parts of enzymes and coenzymes involved in the metabolism of carbohydrates and fats, but they are not a direct source of energy themselves. Vitamins are also involved in the formation of red blood cells and bone. Vitamins are not manufactured and must be ingested from the food in the diet. Some vitamins are water-soluble (C and B complex) and cannot be stored, so the excess is passed in the urine. Other vitamins are fat-soluble (A, D, E, and K) and are absorbed with the fat in the stomach and small intestines. Excessive amounts are stored in the liver and fatty tissue, and are not excreted in the urine.

These fat-soluble vitamins are required in small amounts and do not need to be supplied each day, but deficiencies can lead to serious illness or death. Excessive amounts, on the other hand, can be toxic.

With a diet comprising all essential vitamins, additional supplementation is unnecessary, and in many cases can be toxic or have side effects. The well-balanced diet can supply an ample amount of the required vitamins for the healthy hockey player.

Water-soluble Vitamins

Vitamin C (ascorbic acid): Vitamin C has been advocated as effective in the prevention of the common cold, although the research is inconclusive on this topic.

It has also been hypothesized that vitamin C can be helpful for the athlete who is constantly under training stress. There is evidence that vitamin C is important in collagen synthesis, which is involved in strengthening existing and developing new connective tissue. Excess vitamin C is excreted in the urine, and the value of megadoses is not supported by conclusive research.

Sources of vitamin C:

- orange, tomato, apple, cranberry juice
- broccoli
- brussel sprouts
- tomatoes
- cantaloupe
- green peppers

B Vitamins (Thiamine B_1 Riboflavin B_2 and Niacin, plus others): Thiamine (B_1), riboflavin (B_2), and niacin are important in the release of energy from food, assist in the function of the nervous system, and are a factor in the healing of skin.

Sources of B vitamins:

Thiamine	lean beef, pork, poultry, and fish enriched bread
Riboflavin	green leafy vegetables milk, eggs peas, beans lean beef fish whole grain cereals, enriched breads
Niacin	lean beef, pork, poultry, and fish enriched bread, whole grain cereals peanut butter

Fat-soluble Vitamins

Vitamin A: This vitamin is essential for healthy eyes and protects against night blindness. It is also important for healthy skin and keeps mucous membranes firm and resistant to infections.

Sources of vitamin A:

- peaches, apricots
- broccoli, spinach
- cantaloupe
- carrots
- sweet potatoes

Vitamin D: This vitamin helps build calcium and phosphorous in bones, and assists the body in absorbing calcium.

Sources of vitamin D:

- sunlight
- milk
- eggs
- fish
- cod liver oil

Vitamin E: There have been some claims that vitamin E is related to better athletic performance, especially in aerobic endurance events at high altitude (Kobayashi, 1974). Vitamin E does assist with tissue growth and red cell wall integrity. There is no research on humans to substantiate that excess supplementation of this vitamin is related to improved athletic performance.

Sources of vitamin E:

- green leafy vegetables
- wheat germ
- vegetable oil
- cereals
- margarine, shortening

Vitamin K: This vitamin is important for the clotting or coagulation of blood in cuts or any incision in the skin.

Sources of vitamin K:

- milk
- green leafy vegetables
- cabbage
- cereals
- meats

Minerals

Minerals are inorganic compounds found in small amounts throughout the body, and are essential to body function.

The minerals include the so-called electrolytes, namely, sodium, potassium, and chloride; the minerals involved in bone metabolism, including calcium, phosphorus, and magnesium; and zinc and iron.

The Electrolytes—Sodium, Potassium, and Chloride

A great deal has been written about sport drinks as a means to replace electrolytes during and after exercise. Electrolytes are charged molecules. Most molecules are neutral, with an equal number of positive protons and negative electrons. When electrolytes are consumed in the food we eat—mostly found in fruits, vegetables, and grains—they combine with either the extracellular (outside) or the intercellular (inside) fluids (mostly water) in the body, but not in equal concentrations. Sodium (Na^+) and potassium (K^+) are found in the largest concentrations. Sodium is found in the extracellular fluids, and potassium is found in the intracellular fluid, as shown in Figure 10.1. The balance of the concentrations of sodium and potassium inside and outside the cell is critical to life functions, especially muscle contraction.

During exercise, water moves from the extracellular fluid through the membrane into the muscle cells. This fluid is replaced in the extracellular compartment by water from the blood plasma. This movement of water across the membrane causes a difference in concentrations of the electrolytes on the inside and outside of the cell. If excess salt (NaCI) is taken into the body, the concentration of sodium becomes greater on the outside of the cell, and water is drawn across the membrane from the inside of the cell to equalize the concentrations. This movement of water out of the cell alters the chemical reaction that produces energy (water is important for this process) and impairs muscle contraction.

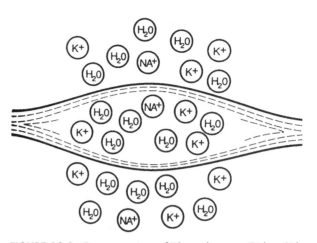

FIGURE 10.1: Concentration of Electrolytes on Either Side of the Membrane of the Cell Must Be Balanced

A similar situation occurs when water is lost through sweating, which also disturbs the electrolyte balance. When water is lost from extracellular space and the sodium concentration is allowed to increase, water again moves from inside the cell to outside to balance the concentrations.

The electrolyte balance in the body can be kept at a normal level by the food we eat. An increase in the consumption of fruits and vegetables is the best way to replenish the electrolytes, as well as drinking as much water as is comfortable. A regular, normal salting of food is also acceptable, but excessive amounts are not necessary. Salt tablets must be consumed with at least 1 pint (.5 L) of water per tablet, and this method is not recommended. Electrolyte sport drinks are useful as they replace both electrolytes and water, although the cost may be a deterrent.

Potassium (K^+) imbalance in the blood is also a problem with exercise. The rising concentration of potassium in the blood, called "hyperkalemia," is caused by potassium being released from the muscle cell and a loss of fluid from the plasma.

The best method of replacing potassium is through a proper diet; fruits, vegetables, and lean meats are the main providers. Sport drinks also include potassium.

Some food sources of sodium and potassium:

- bananas, apples, apricots, oranges, tomatoes
- broccoli, potatoes, squash, carrots, green beans
- kidney beans
- whole wheat bread
- chicken
- spaghetti with meat sauce
- raisins

Calcium, Phosphorus, and Magnesium

Calcium, phosphorus, and magnesium are important in the makeup and formation of bones and teeth.

Of the three minerals, *calcium* is the most abundant in the body. As well as being found in bones and teeth (99% of the total amount), a small portion plays a role in muscle contraction, the transmission of nerve impulses, and the breakdown of glycogen (Williams, 1985).

A calcium deficiency can lead to a decrease in bone density called "osteoporosis." Females with a smaller bone mass than men seem to be more susceptible. Stress fractures and muscle cramping are possibly affected by calcium deficiency (Neilson, 1986; Williams, 1985). It has also been postulated that a calcium deficiency may have a more severe effect on females who are amenorrheic, a condition where their menstrual periods have been suppressed.

Calcium can be found in dairy products and plant foods, although the absorption from dairy products is superior. Taking excess calcium is not recommended and may lead to kidney stone formation.

Some sources of calcium:

- milk
- cheese
- green leafy vegetables
- egg yolk

Phosphorus, found in bones and teeth, is part of the energy-producing ATP (adenosine triphosphate) and CP (creatine phosphate). Deficiencies of this mineral seem rare.

Some sources of phosphorus:

- poultry
- fish
- milk
- meat
- eggs
- cereal
- grains

Magnesium is also involved in the chemical reactions related to the release of energy, muscle contraction, and the transmission of nerve impulses. As with phosphorus, deficiencies are not common.

Some sources of magnesium:

- nuts
- whole wheat bread
- green leafy vegetables

Deficiencies of calcium, phosphorus, and magnesium can be made up by adapting the diet to include more of the foods mentioned above, and supplements are not recommended.

Iron

Iron is one mineral to which hard-training athletes, especially females, must pay attention. Iron is found in the red blood cells and is responsible for the oxygen-carrying capacity of the blood. It is an important constituent of hemoglobin, which carries oxygen within the cell, and cytochromes, which are involved in the aerobic system.

Endurance athletes have been found to have lowered levels of iron after heavy training. When iron is at extremely low levels, athletes become anemic (experience reduced hemoglobin in the blood), or, more commonly, may suffer from suboptimal hemoglobin, a condition not as extreme as anemia.

Adolescents and women in their menstrual cycles are the most susceptible to iron losses, and they must take care to have the required level of iron in their diets. The athlete can consider iron supplements, but they should be taken only when prescribed by a doctor, as overdoses can be toxic.

Iron is found in:

- green leafy vegetables
- egg yolk
- liver, kidney, heart
- nuts
- dried beans
- red meat
- enriched bread and cereals

Zinc and Chromium

Research is inconclusive on the minerals zinc and chromium, but some recent work has been done on the importance of chromium in athletic performance. These minerals are found in trace amounts in the body and can be found in:

- fish
- fats
- eggs
- vegetable oils
- oatmeal
- wheat germ
- bran
- calf's liver
- nuts
- green leafy vegetables

WATER

Water is the most essential nutrient in the body. It is located in both the extracellular and intracellular parts of the body and makes up over half the body weight—over 70% of muscle weight and 80% percent of blood.

Water replacement is essential before, during, and after exercise, as over 2% of body weight can be lost through sweating. Also, water should be consumed regularly, with eight glasses or more being the daily minimum. During training or competition, hockey players should drink water frequently; 3 to 6 ounces (85 to 170 mL) at a time, at least every 10 to 15 minutes. Stomach cramps usually result from consuming too much water at one time rather than from drinking water that is too cold. A range of 45°F to 55°F (7°C to 11°C) is ideal temperature for water, as it has been shown that drinking water in this range empties the stomach faster (Bowers, Foss, and Fox, 1988).

Lack of water in the body causes a reaction in muscular strength; lower plasma and blood volumes; lower oxygen consumption; a decrease in work performance times; depletion of liver glycogen stores; and an increase in the amount of electrolytes lost from the body.

Water can be taken alone, but it is also found in most foods, especially in:

- watermelon
- oranges
- carrots
- pineapple
- apples
- potatoes
- lettuce
- celery
- pickles
- broccoli

PRE-GAME NUTRITION

What and when the hockey player eats before a game is important. It should be mentioned here that an ideal pre-game meal does not compensate and provide the fuel for energy if the player's diet has been lacking up to this time.

The main purpose of the pre-game meal is to help provide the fuel for energy by digesting foods that can be stored as glycogen. The meal also settles the stomach and removes the feeling of hunger, as well as preventing hypoglycemia (low blood sugar), which can interfere with performance. The following guidelines should be followed for the pre-event meal.

1. The meal should be high in carbohydrates such as pasta, potatoes, and enriched bread, low in fats, and offer protein from small portions of lean meat, fish, or chicken. Avoid gas-forming, greasy, and spicy foods.

2. A normal-sized meal should be eaten at least three to four hours before the game. Smaller meals or snacks can be eaten two to three hours before the game, and liquid meals can be ingested one to two hours before. It is important that the stomach and small intestine be emptied before the competition begins. Some players now eat a large meal five to six hours before competition, and then have a small nutritious snack about one to two hours before. The time of the meal is more important before intense exercise than before low-intensity endurance exercise. Meals should be eaten a longer time before intense exercise takes place.

3. Avoid glucose and sugary food less than one hour before competition. Sugary foods stimulate secretion of insulin, and the amount of glucose in the blood is actually decreased. This in turn puts a greater dependence on glycogen in the muscle and therefore depletes the stores sooner, contributing to fatigue.

4. Drink plenty of fluids. Water and/or juices should be consumed regularly both before the game day and on the day of the event—four to eight glasses, two to three hours before the game, and one or two glasses half an hour before the game.

5. Eat food with which you are familiar and enjoy. Do not experiment with new foods on game day, but rather try these foods on training days. Discomfort, or a poor-tasting meal, may upset the preparation for a game.

Some players may prefer liquid meals. There are several available now, including brand names such as Nutriment, Ensure, Ensure Plus, and Sustacal. These meals are easily digested and assist energy intake, as well as providing fluids. Do not use liquid meals for the first time on competition day. Many players prefer to have a full pre-game meal.

NUTRITION DURING THE GAME

Water should be consumed at regular intervals (10 to 15 minutes) throughout competition. Personal water bottles should be provided for all hockey players, and they should consume small quantities whenever possible.

When hockey training lasts longer than two hours, the replacement of carbohydrates is necessary. Blood glucose levels with this type of activity may drop to a level where the deficiency affects performance. The most popular means of supplying the added fuel necessary seem to be sports drinks or a combination of glucose and water. The liquid should have a pleasant taste and should contain 2.5% to 10% carbohydrates, and electrolytes such as sodium and potassium.

NUTRITION AFTER TRAINING AND GAMES

One of the areas most neglected by hockey players is when and what type of foods and liquids should be consumed after training and competition. The timing and what is ingested are very important in the recovery process.

Fluids

Fluids should be replaced as quickly as possible after competition. Water is the natural choice, as up to, and sometimes more than, 2% of body weight is lost due to sweating, and must be replaced as quickly as possible. Fruit juices and sport drinks are ideal as they also replace carbohydrates, electrolytes, and vitamins. Watery-type foods such as grapes, watermelons, oranges, and soups are also effective.

Alcohol

Alcohol consumption is not recommended as a means of fluid replacements as it has a dehydrating effect on the body. If hockey players feel they would like alcohol (a couple of beers) after a competition, then advise them to drink a couple of glasses of water before or along with the alcoholic drinks. Alcohol is also low in carbohydrates, and there is no truth to the theory that alcoholic calories are stored as glycogen.

Carbohydrates

It is becoming increasingly clear that it is important not only to replace carbohydrates after training and games, but also to replace them within a certain time after the activity.

It is recommended that the replacement of carbohydrates starts within one hour of a game and not longer than four hours afterward. The recommended amount is 10 grams per kilogram of body weight within the first two hours after a game, followed with the same amount two hours later. This amount would range between 75 to 100 grams of carbohydrates taken twice in the first four hours. Bananas and juices are an ideal immediate source after the competition, and the typical pasta meal of spaghetti or macaroni serves to replace the carbohydrates. It is therefore recommended that hockey players eat a high-carbohydrate meal within two to four hours after the game.

Electrolytes

Electrolytes such as sodium and potassium can be replaced easily by fruit juices and sport drinks, as mentioned previously. Bananas are also a convenient and easily eaten food after a game. The use of salt tablets and other pill-form replacements after games is unnecessary and not recommended.

Along with eating the proper foods after competition, it is important to rest to allow the body to restore the glycogen to its pre-event levels. Active players need between eight and 10 hours of sleep per night.

CAFFEINE

Mention should be made of the effects of caffeine, found commonly in coffee and tea, before and after competition and training. Some players rely on coffee before competition to pick them up, whereas others avoid it because it makes them jittery and causes discomfort.

Caffeine appears to have a short-term stimulating effect on the nervous system, which may account for the fact that some players feel it makes physical effort easier. The effect does not last, however, and should not be a reason for a player to consume caffeine. Some research has shown that certain larger amounts of caffeine allow fatty acids to be mobilized and can enhance an athlete's endurance (Bowers and Fox, 1992).

It is interesting to note that the International Olympic Committee bans caffeine in large doses. Twelve milligrams of caffeine per milliliter of urine is enough for disqualification, but this amount would require the consumption of approximately eight cups of coffee, 16 cola drinks, or 24 Anacin tablets.

ANABOLIC–ANDROGENIC STEROIDS

The only reason for mentioning steroids is the fact that many athletes, especially in the strength and power sports such as hockey, football, and track and field, have heard about them and may be tempted to use them.

The first point to mention about steroids is that the International Olympic Federation and most sports' governing bodies ban them. They are associated with adverse side effects on the liver, cardiovascular system, and reproductive system, as well as affecting behavior.

Steroids are a derivative of the male sex hormone testosterone, secreted by the testes. The term "anabolic" refers to the building of tissue, and "androgenic" refers to the development of the male secondary sexual characteristics, which can also occur as side effects in females who use these substances.

The use of anabolic–androgenic steroids can increase body weight and muscular strength when associated with training. They do not increase aerobic power or capacity.

Coaches should look for signs that their players might be using steroids, such as an unnatural rapid gain of weight and strength, and changes in personality such as over-aggressiveness and mood shifts. It is important for coaches to stress that proper training methods are the best way to increase strength and weight. Also, as well as being banned, steroids have serious negative side effects which can greatly affect the players in their daily and future lives.

Androstenedione (Andro)

Some mention should be made of the steroid androstenedione, as it has been used by a number of top athletes in professional sports such as baseball and has not as yet been banned in some sports. Research is very scarce on this topic, but it is known that andro is the crudest of the steroids and thus most likely to have the most diverse side effects if taken in large doses (Gwartney and Stout, 1999). Some information on the topic is summarized in the *Strength and Conditioning Journal*, February 1999 Androstenedione

- Is a weak androgenic (muscle building) hormone. It is not found in the food we eat and is classified as a dietary supplement, legally sold in the United States and illegal in Canada. It is sold in a pill form.
- Is banned by most amateur and some professional sports' governing bodies.
- Has, to date, no studies to support that andro supplementation has a positive effect on lean mass, strength, or performance.
- Has side effects for females include deepening of the voice, increased facial hair, enlargement of the Adams apple, decreased breast size, and enlargement of the genitals. Side effects for males include emotional outbursts, acne, early puberty, growth stunting, and hair loss or balding. Feminizing traits such as breast development and decreased testes size will occur when excess andro is converted to estrogen. In older athletes, increased androgen levels may also accelerate male pattern balding, benign or cancerous growth of the prostate gland, liver disease, and undesirable changes in blood lipids.

It is not recommended to allow athletes to use this agent under any circumstances.

CREATINE

Another nutritional substance on the market today is creatine. *The Strength and Conditioning Journal*, February 1999, also reports extensively on the effects of the usage of creatine, summarized as follows (Plisk and Kreider, 1999):

- Found naturally in meat, fish, and poultry, it is involved in the formation of phosphocreatine, which is important in the formation of ATP in the phasphogen or ATP CP system. (See Chapter 4, The Energy Systems.)
- Sold in a powder form and at present is not a banned substance by amateur and professional sports' governing bodies.
- Ergonenic (improved performance) benefits of creatine supplementation have not been found in all studies.
- Some studies have shown short-term creatine supplementation to improve the following:
  Maximal strength/power (5% to15%) and work performed during sets of maximal effort (5% to 15%).
  Single-effort sprint performance (1% to 5%) and work performance during repetitive sprints (5% to 15%).
- Weight gain is a reported side effect of creatine supplementation.
- More research is needed on the long-term side effects of this substance.

The authors of this book wish to state that *we do not support the use of the aforementioned substances*. The negative side effects on the long-term well being of the athletes have not been studied fully and their use should not be supported by coaches or trainers. A well-balanced diet with plenty of rest and sleep while training is the correct and legal method to improve athletic performance.

SMOKING

Smoking affects athletic performance by reducing the oxygen-carrying capacity of the blood and increasing airway resistance for the taking of oxygen into the lungs.

Oxygen combines with hemoglobin to be carried by the blood to the cells. When a person smokes, a by-product of the smoke is carbon monoxide (CO). Carbon monoxide has more than 200 times the affinity for combining with hemoglobin as oxygen does. If both oxygen and carbon monoxide are present, carbon monoxide combines much quicker with the hemoglobin. As a result, the oxygen-carrying capacity of the blood is reduced by as much as 10% for a heavy smoker.

The increased airway resistance caused by smoking can result in shortness of breath. The resistance causes the respiratory muscles to work harder to consume more oxygen. This added cost of ventilation could rob the working muscles of a percentage of their potential oxygen supply. During all-out exercise, this could lead to reduced performance, and during submaximal exercise an increase in anaerobic metabolism may cause early fatigue.

For hockey players who choose to smoke, abstaining for 24 hours before a game can lower the oxygen cost of ventilation by as much as 25%, but is still 60% higher than for non-smokers (Bowers, Foss, and Fox, 1988).

In addition to the effect smoking has on athletic performance, it also causes a greater risk of coronary heart disease and lung cancer.

CHAPTER 11

Mental Training

While much of this book is focused on the physical preparation of the hockey player, some mention should be made of mental training, as it is difficult to separate the two.

The motivation, perseverance, and mental toughness required to do the physical training, as well as the mental skills such as relaxation, positive self-talk, energizing, visualization, and focusing (concentration) that allow the hockey player to perform at his or her best, are essential to a player. Players and coaches can work together to develop these skills, which should be included throughout a player's training period (periodization). These mental skills, carefully planned and implemented throughout the year, develop what is classically named the "ideal performance state."

THE BASIC MENTAL TRAINING SKILLS

Relaxation, Autogenic, Visualization/Imagery Relaxation, Positive Self-talk, Energizing (Arousal), Visualization/ Imagery, Concentration/Focusing

Relaxation

Relaxation techniques are important for both players and coaches. These techniques can help relieve stress before a game, and also allow players and coaches to get a restful sleep before games.

The five common methods of relaxation training that are useful for players and coaches are:

- breath relaxation
- progressive muscular relaxation (PMR)
- autogenic training
- biofeedback
- imagery relaxation

Breath Relaxation

Orlick (1986b) describes a very simple method of relaxation training that is used by many players before, during, and after a game. The procedure involves taking a deep breath followed by a long, slow exhalation. At the same time, the player mentally focuses on relaxing, and relaxes the muscles. This procedure is repeated several times. It is the simplest and most often used method of relaxation, and can be practiced before any stressful situation.

Progressive Muscular Relaxation

Edmund Jacobson developed progressive muscular relaxation (PMR) in the 1930s. Its basic premise is that it is impossible to be nervous or tense when the muscles are completely relaxed. While this premise is not supported by research, PMR is effective in reducing muscle tension, which is essential for optimal sport performance. Its value, however, is in the recovery from, rather than the preparation for, a game. PMR is based on the principle of neuromuscular relaxation, where players are taught to tense the muscles and then relax them. Sixteen muscle groups are used initially, followed by seven, then four, and then the entire body is tensed and then relaxed. PMR is taught by a trained instructor and should be practiced three or four times per week, with effective results taking about six weeks of training. One hour per day is necessary at the beginning, but once the relaxation procedure is well learned, relaxation can be achieved in a few minutes (Nideffer, 1981).

Research supports that this method is effective in eliciting relaxation and, when used with other arousal and cognitive methods, can be associated with improved performance (Greenspan and Feltz, 1989; Onestak, 1991).

The PMR method involves the following steps:

1. Select a quiet environment where there will be no distractions.

2. Make sure the players are dressed in warm, dry clothing.

3. The players should be well spaced from each other.

4. The players lie on their backs on a mat, with their arms at their sides and the palms of their hands facing slightly upwards. The calves of the legs are slightly touching, and the body is straight, with weight equally distributed. The eyes are lightly closed.

5. Muscles are contracted for five seconds and then relaxed.

6. Practice contracting and then relaxing one muscle group at a time. Feel the muscles relax. The muscles may feel warm, tingle, or feel heavy. Concentrate on tensing and relaxing one muscle group only.

7. Practice breathing control. Do not breathe when contracting muscles. Breathe out when you relax the muscle.

8. The exercises begin at the toes and progress to the head.

9. Use the following progression and, with the limbs, start with the left, then the right:

- Curl toes backward (do not move ankles).
- Curl toes curl under.
- Do ankle bends—feet back to shins.
- Do ankle stretches—point your feet.
- Press knees together.
- Thighs.
- Buttocks.

Take eight even breaths between each exercise. Check to see if muscles are relaxed. If not, repeat the exercises.

Take 12 easy breaths. The ankles, legs, and buttocks should be totally relaxed.

- Stomach.
- Back—pull shoulder blades together. Press shoulders into mat.
- Raise your shoulders. Pull shoulders toward the feet and reach fingers as far down the thighs as possible.

Check body and legs to determine if they are relaxed. Count 12 small, even breaths.

- Pull the jaw down toward the neck.
- Press your head into the mat. Do not arch.
- Jut your jaw forward.
- Clench your teeth.

Take eight even breaths.

- Spread lips as far apart as possible.
- Press your tongue against the roof of your mouth. Make your tongue as big as possible.
- Pull cheeks up and eyebrows down. Compress your eyes to the back of your head.
- Wrinkle your forehead. Eyes are closed.

Take 12 small, even breaths. Check whole body for heaviness.

Take 12 slow breaths.

Finish by moving each part of your body, starting from the toes up. Sit, kneel, stretch, and then stand. (Adapted from Coaching Association of Canada, 1992c.)

Autogenic Training

Autogenic (self-generated) training includes a system of standard exercises designed to return the mind and body to homeostasis. The basis of the exercises is passive concentration, or self-hypnosis, and beneficial effects can occur without noticeable physical sensations. Players begin with three to five standard exercises repeated for 30 to 60 seconds. The player then activates and repeats another set of exercises. After about six months of daily practice, the player typically repeats commands for:

1. Heaviness: "My right arm is heavy—my left arm is heavy—both arms are heavy—my right leg is heavy—my left leg is heavy—both legs are heavy."
2. Warmth: "My right arm is warm—my left arm is warm—both arms are warm—my right leg is warm—my left leg is warm—both legs are warm."
3. Heartbeat: "My heartbeat is calm and regular."
4. Respiration: "My breathing is calm and regular."
5. Solar plexus: "My solar plexus is warm."
6. Forehead: "My forehead is cool."

The player maintains a passive concentration and visualizes the statement as if it is written, says the command subvocal, and feels the area of the body where the statement is directed. Autogenic training is used primarily in the recovery time between games.

Visualization/Imagery Relaxation

Imagery relaxation involves the player visualizing an environment or setting that is very pleasing and relaxing, such as waves on a beach or a picturesque mountain. The place must conjure up a peaceful, relaxing feeling. The image must be vivid and usually in color. The players must practice this visualization in a quiet place, and as well as seeing the scene, they must hear the sounds (e.g., waves lapping) and smell the air, for the image to be successful for relaxation. More information on visualization techniques is provided later in this chapter.

Positive Self-talk

Talking to oneself in a positive manner is a confidence booster for players, and there is some evidence of its effectiveness. Rushall and colleagues (1988) did a study with elite cross-country skiers using three types of self-talk. One method included task-like terms such as "uphill," "quick," and "grip"; another included positive self-assertive statements such as "feel strong" and "feel great"; and the third included emotional mood words such as "drive" and "blast." All three methods used showed a 3% increase in performance as opposed to the control group who used no self-talk and showed no increase in performance times.

Positive self-talk is an important way for players to gain assurance that they can accomplish what they want to do. Players should be reminded of their strengths and their past successes.

As important as positive self-talk is, the opposite—negative self-talk—can be very destructive to a player before and during a game. Players are more likely to engage in negative self-talk when they are stressed. Some types of negative thoughts for players include worrying about performance, self-criticism, self-blame, predicting losing, a preoccupation with physical stress, dislike of teammates, and dislike of the coach.

The player must first recognize that he or she has negative thoughts that can affect performance. Martens (1987) described some steps that can be used to try to eliminate negative thoughts:

1. A coach should talk with the player and assess whether the negative thoughts are disruptive for performance.
2. A coach should try to identify the causes of the player's negative thoughts.
3. A player should be able to stop—or park—the negative thoughts immediately.
4. A player should develop positive self-talk thoughts to replace the negative ones.
5. A player should practice these self-talk skills in training, and then in games.

Ellis and Grieger (1977) described irrational beliefs that many players have, and suggested ways of counteracting their beliefs.

Belief:

1. I must not make errors or do poorly.

2. I am right to blame people who act unfairly or are not kind to me.

3. A bad experience in my past will always determine my behavior and feelings.

4. People and events should be the way I want them to be.

5. I must be loved and approved by every important person in my life.

Counteraction:

1. Playing well is satisfying, but I am going to make some errors.

2. Even though I feel I have been treated unfairly, I should not blame others for my performance.

3. A bad experience in my past should not affect my behavior today. I can change things by working hard.

4. People are going to act the way they want, not the way I want them to.

5. It is nice to have the approval of everyone, but I can still work and enjoy myself without it.

The old adage of controlling what you can control, and not worrying about what you cannot control, definitely applies to self-talk. Self-talk should be confined to the positive and to the task at hand. Players and coaches should identify both the positive and the negative self-talk they use, and work to eliminate the negative.

Energizing (Arousal)

"Energizing" (frequently called arousal) refers to the psychological conditioning that a player has about having reserve energy to call upon. It is a positive feeling that leads to confidence and an ability to cope with and control a situation. Things the player does and thinks while preparing for games affect energizing.

Botterill (1986) lists a number of ways to energize:

1. *Exercise*: A good warm-up or physical exercise on a game day can be energizing as long as it is not so demanding on the energy system as to create fatigue. A short exercise session of about 15 to 20 minutes gets the body and the circulation moving, and creates a positive feeling in the body.
2. *Stretching*: A good program of stretching the major muscle groups and holding the stretch for 15 to 20 seconds, energizes the body and also reduces tension.
3. *Read-and-react drills*: Working the skills of the game using simple read-and-react drills with hand-eye and foot-eye coordination can energize the player.
4. *Tense and relax muscles*: Alternate tensing and relaxing different muscle groups.
5. *Showers and massage*: Temperature contrasts and physical massage can both energize and relax the player.
6. *Music*: Music can be relaxing or energizing. Energizing music is usually upbeat, rock-type music, but different types of music affect people differently. Some teams have a team theme song that has an energizing effect on the players.
7. *Videotapes*: Videotapes of positive highlights of team successes, accompanied by upbeat music, can have an energizing effect on players. The videos should not be longer than 10 minutes to keep the players' attention.
8. *Pep talks*: The coach or a respected member of the team can give an inspirational talk to the players to energize them. The pep talk should be used selectively, in situations when it appears the players are not energized. This can be when the opponent is taken lightly or the players appear fatigued. The pep talk should be short and delivered with enthusiasm and meaning.
9. *Verbal interaction with the players and coaches*: Positive statements among players and coaches such as "Here we go!", "Let's get it done!" "Show time!" and "Let's do

it!" are examples of positive interactions that help players energize.

10. *Energize by thinking*:
    • Visualizing and imagining. Develop a positive image in your mind about performing successfully and overcoming all obstacles.
    • Focus on positive cues and activities or rituals. Focus on cue words and phrases such as "Blast off!" "Intensity!" and "Power to spare!" Use positive mental rehearsal of the skills.
    • Park negative thoughts and concentrate on positive thoughts.

11. *Take energy from your environment*: Focus on energy from spectators, teammates, the sun and wind, etc.

12. *Energy from faith*: Some players energize from their faith and beliefs in religion or related ways of life. Lectures in the areas of positive thinking and motivation have been known to energize players.

13. *Goal setting*: Positive goal setting by players and teams are methods of energizing if the goals are attainable and are both short- and long-term.

Inverted U

The "inverted U" refers to the point where being over-energized can be detrimental to performance. Players must be energized to perform well, and this level must be reached. Being over-energized can result in the player being psyched out instead of psyched up. The inverted U, as illustrated in Figure 11.1, is familiar to most coaches, and what is important to note is that the arousal level varies with the type of talk being performed. Also, each player has a different arousal or energizing level. Martens (1987) noted that most players reach their peak performance when their psychic energy is high and their stress level is low. Coaches must, therefore, try to teach players that while psychic energy is important, they must also keep their stress levels low by using various means of relaxation and focusing skills.

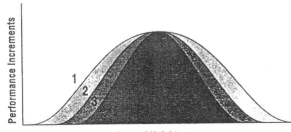

FIGURE 11.1: The Inverted U Principle of Arousal with Various Types of Tasks

Task #1: Requiring direct simple expression of force, few accuracy requirements.

Task #2: Requiring force, plus accuracy to a moderate degree.

Task #3: Requiring extreme accuracy.

It should be mentioned here that some experts in the 1990s have been critical of the inverted U theory, as they feel it is far too simplistic to account for the complex relationship between arousal and performance (Weinberg, 1990).

Energizing is a skill that must be practiced regularly to be effective. The players should learn to be self-energized, and psychologists and coaches can assist with this process.

Visualization/Imagery

A number of terms have been used to describe the process of visualizing a performance, including "imagery," "mental rehearsal," "visual motor behavior rehearsal (VMBR)," "cognitive behavior modification," and "success visualization."

"Visualization" refers to a process where a player sees himself or herself experiencing a movement or skill. This visualization can also involve any or all senses, including the kinesthetic sense of body position.

In a survey done with top athletes, 98% of them reported doing some type of visualization practice before competing (Nideffer, 1985). Visualization is used to help players learn motor skills, rehearse strategies and reactions in games, see success (visualize best performance), become familiar with the game site and possible distractions, and generally mentally prepare for games.

Sports psychologists have identified two types of visualization—*internal* and *external*. Internal visualization refers to seeing the movement or skill performed through your own eyes. External visualization refers to seeing documentation of your performance done with a camera or video machine. The research done in this area has shown the internal method to be superior to the external, but both methods can and should be used.

Does visualization help to perfect skills and plan strategy moves in a sport? A number of research studies support the premise that it does. Associated with these studies is the concept that visualization, coupled with relaxation training, is even more effective (Suedfeld and Bruno, 1990).

Kolonay (1977) and Lane (1980) studied the effectiveness of basketball free-throw success with visualization, relaxation, and a combination of the two. The combination method was the most successful. Davis (1990) noted that there was a significant relationship between performance in professional hockey and visualization. Research in the field supports the position that visualization in a sports setting is effective.

It is important for both coaches and players to realize that visualization is a learned skill, as are physical skills, and improvement can be attained through practice. Cox (1994) suggests some steps to develop general visualization skills:

1. Find a quiet place where you will not be disturbed, assume a comfortable position, and relax completely.
2. Practice imagery by visualizing a circle that fills the visual field. Make the circle turn a deep blue. Repeat the process several times, imagining a different color each time. Allow the images to disappear. Relax and observe the spontaneous imagery that arises.
3. Create the image of a simple three-dimensional glass. Fill it with a colorful liquid and then add ice cubes and a straw. Write a descriptive caption underneath.
4. Select a variety of scenes and develop them with rich detail. Include sport-related images such as a swimming pool, tennis courts, and a beautiful golf course. Practice visualizing people, including strangers, in each of these scenes.
5. Imagine yourself in a sport setting of keen interest to you. Visualize and feel yourself successfully participating in the scene. Relax and enjoy your success.
6. End the session by breathing deeply, opening your eyes, and adjusting to the external environment.

Martens (1987) used three main steps to develop visualization skills specifically for sport:

1. Sensory awareness.
2. Vividness.
3. Control ability.

Sensory awareness refers to the player becoming more aware of what he or she feels, sees, and hears when performing a sport skill alone or in a team situation. The past experience of being more aware of body position, timing, movement patterns and so on in these situations helps the player to better visualize these movements in the future.

Vividness allows the player to develop distinct images and feel all the senses—sound, smell, touch—as well as visual. The vividness exercise allows the player to visualize the images more exactly in a setting that mimics the actual sport situation.

Control ability refers to the manipulation of the images to produce a successful sport movement or strategy. The player visualizes the movement done correctly with a successful outcome.

To practice visualization away from the game setting, the player should be in a relaxed state in a pleasant environment. It is important that the players have a set routine for practicing the visualization skills and be motivated to train. Visualization can also be used when the player is injured or unable to practice because of weather, facility problems, etc.

Visualization can be used to evoke concentration and, more commonly, to rehearse game-specific situations such as a one-on-one in ice hockey. It can also be used to overcome anxiety related to a certain facility or venue.

When mentally rehearsing for the development of a skill, players can use visualization in three ways:

1. To practice the performance.
2. To pre-play the performance.
3. To replay the performance.

In practicing the performance, the players mentally practice a skill they have performed in the past. Pre-play visualization occurs immediately before the skill is performed, as a diver would do immediately before the dive. Replay visualization is done immediately following a skill, when a player mentally reviews the motions performed. Golfers tend to mentally review the swing after the ball has been hit.

It is important for the coach to sell the idea of visualization training to the player. As mentioned earlier, most high-level players engage in some form of visualization training. Very few players, however, practice visualization skills in a systematic way throughout their training. In the discussion of periodization of the mental-training program that follows, a systematic program is suggested.

Coaches can also use visualization. Coaches commonly use visualizing reactions to certain situations that occur in an athletic contest. Visualization coupled with relaxation can also help the coach to alleviate stress during the competitive season.

Concentration/Focusing

The ability to focus, or concentrate, during a game with pressures and distractions often separates the top players from those with a similar level of physical skill. Certain cues become important, and the player must be able to discriminate between the relevant and the irrelevant ones.

"Centering" refers to focusing on one point, or directing your thoughts internally for a moment to mentally check and adjust your breathing and level of muscle tension. The concept comes from the martial arts and refers to a feeling of being calm, relaxed, receptive, and clear (Nideffer, 1992). The point that is consciously attended to is the center of gravity, which is located just below and behind the navel.

To be centered is to have the knees slightly bent, muscles loose, and breathing slower and slightly deeper than normal. The feet are apart with one slightly ahead of the other. The body is in a balanced position and able to move in any direction. Players and coaches are familiar with centering that involves lowering the center of gravity, frequently called "the ready position."

TABLE 11.1: Positive and Negative Physical and Psychological Feelings Associated with Centering

Physical Feelings		Psychological Feelings	
Positive	Negative	Positive	Negative
Loose	Tight	Controlled	Beaten
Relaxed	Tense	Confident	Scared
Solid	Shaky	Powerful	Weak
Balanced	Unsteady	Commanding	Dominated
Strong	Weak	Calm	Upset
Light	Heavy	Tranquil	Panicked
Energetic	Tired	Peaceful	Worried
Effortless	Hard	Easy	Rushed
Fluid	Choppy	Clear	Confused
Smooth	Awkward	Focused	Overloaded

Centering is a combination of a physical positioning and a psychological feeling. Nideffer (1992) lists some cue words associated with centering, as illustrated in Table 11.1. These cue words relate to both positive and negative physiological feelings that can affect the ability of the player to be centered.

When a player is centered, he or she is ideally physically positioned for the particular performance setting. Becoming physically centered requires attention to breathing and refocusing. The player should feel confident and in control when in the centered position.

Dimensions of Attention

Nideffer (1976) described two types of attention to be applied to a sport situation, as shown in Figure11.2.

FIGURE 11.2: Two-dimensional Model for Attention in Sport

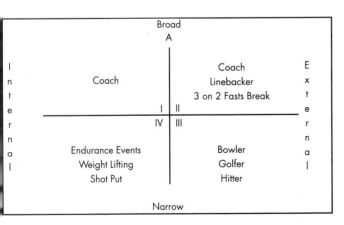

FIGURE 11.3: Internal and External Attention Focuses Shown as Dichotomous Rather than Continuous (from Martens, R., *Coaches' Guide to Sport Psychology* (Champaign, IL: Human Kinetic Publishers, 1987), 141. Reprinted by permission.)

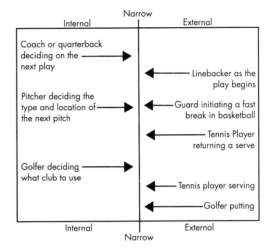

The "width of attention" refers to whether we have a narrow focus or a broad focus of attention in a sport. A quarterback in football must have a broad focus of attention to spot the various pass receivers, whereas a baseball player must have a narrow focus when concentrating on hitting the ball.

The coach and player should analyze the attention demands of hockey and determine the cues and their order. Keep the number of cues to a minimum.

Martens (1987) outlines some guidelines for improving concentration skills:

1. Analyze the sport to determine whether the attention should be broad or narrow and internal or external.
2. External attention should focus on a few discernible cues the player can learn and to which he or she can respond.
3. Internal attention should concentrate on positive and constructive thoughts
4. Concentrate on the forms and execution of the skill, not the outcome.
5. When learning skills, minimize distractions at the beginning but later add game-like distractions.

Refocusing

Players should develop a plan to refocus when events do not go as planned and unexpected distractions occur. Develop a "what if" list, so that every type of distraction and an appropriate response is thought out beforehand. If a distraction occurs before the execution of a skill, then shift focus, relax, and then refocus. Players should always concentrate only on what can be controlled, and not on events that are out of their control such as facility problems and late starts to games. Players should be able to "park" any negative distraction and refocus.

THE IDEAL PERFORMANCE STATE

The psychological study of how players feel when they give their best performances has received attention from Maslow (1965), Ravizza (1977), Csikszentmihalyi (1979), and Loehr (1983).

Loehr asked athletes to describe their internal feelings and experiences when they performed well and when they performed poorly. Athletes described their psychological feelings when they had high energy and positive feelings as alert, lively, energetic, stimulated, vigorous, enthused, and high in team spirit. When their high energy was accompanied by negative feelings, they described themselves as fearful, nervous, anxious, angry, frustrated, upset, and vengeful. Low energy accompanied by pleasant feelings was described as tired, weary, exhausted, and low in desire. Low energy accompanied by negative thoughts produced feelings such as bored, disinterested, annoyed, irritated, and lacking motivation. Obviously athletes wish to have high energy and positive thoughts, and these characteristics are prevalent when they perform their best.

Loehr draws the following conclusions from his research:

1. An ideal performance exists for every athlete.
2. An athlete's performance is directly related to how he or she feels. When an athlete feels right, he or she can perform right.
3. The components of the ideal performance state are the same for all athletes in all sports.

Loehr concluded from analysis of hundreds of reports from top athletes that the following distinct feelings are present when an athlete performs optimally:

- physically relaxed—looseness of muscles
- mentally calm—feeling of inner calmness
- low anxiety—feeling of lack of pressure
- optimistic—feeling positive with no negative thoughts
- effortless—mind and body working in harmony
- automatic—performed without thought, played by instinct
- focused—attending to the relevant aspects of play and blocking out the irrelevant

- self-confident—calm, poised, inner belief in oneself
- in control—in total control of the situation
- alert—heightened awareness, ability to read the situation
- energized—most important are feelings of joy, challenge, determination, power, and intensity.

THE PERIODIZATION OF MENTAL TRAINING

The integration of mental training with components of the physical, technical, and tactical training in the annual plan is not carried out well by most coaches. Mental skills, like physical skills, must be practiced for improvement and should be integrated into the various phases of the annual plan. Mental preparation is improved by using the five basic mental skills of relaxation, positive self-talk, energization, visualization, and concentration (Bacon, 1989).

Not all players respond in the same manner to mental training. According to a study by Seabourne, Weinberg, Jackson, and Suinn (1985), subjects who were able to choose the mental skills they felt comfortable with improved as much as those who had programs designed for them.

Another point is that the need for coaches to establish periodization for mental training is essential, and many of the books on psychological preparation do not relate the material to the training schedule or training phases (Bacon, 1990).

Psychological preparation can be divided into the following categories: basic mental skills, sport-specific mental skills, and individual game strategies. As was pointed out in the discussion of periodization, the annual plan is divided into pregame (general and specific), game, and transitional phases.

General Preparation

In the general preparation phase, an initial measuring of mental skills using assessment tools such as the test of attentional and interpersonal styles, or TAIS (Nideffer, 1976), the competitive reflections form (Orlick, 1986b), or the self-assessment questionnaires (Suinn, 1986) is necessary. After this, the acquisition of various mental skills can take six to eight weeks of practicing three to five times a week for 15 to 30 minutes a day. Williams (1986) suggests that relaxation skills should be taught first, followed by positive self-talk, energizing, visualization, and concentration.

FIGURE 11.4: The Five Basic Mental Skills and Their Related Techniques

---

Relaxation

The ability to relax the body and/or mind to an appropriate level:

- centering
- progressive relaxation training (PRT)
- autogenic training
- meditation
- breath control
- biofeedback
- stress management

Positive Self-talk

The ability to stay positive and eliminate inappropriate negative thoughts or feelings:

- positive thinking
- positive affirmations
- stopping negative thoughts
- positive thought control
- rational emotive therapy
- stress inoculation training (SIT) (relaxation + positive self-talk)
- cue words

Energization

The ability to raise physical and/or mental activation to an appropriate level:

- music
- psychic energy management
- self-regulation
- energy control
- energizing cue words
- rapid tensing and relaxing of muscles
- physical exertion
- quick, deep breaths
- visualizing energizing scenes

Visualization

The ability to imagine (see, feel, etc.) scenes to enhance effectiveness:

- imagery
- mental rehearsal
- mental practice
- visual-motor behavior rehearsal (VMBR)
- self-hypnosis (relaxation + visualization + positive suggestions)

Concentration

The ability to focus on the appropriate thing while blocking out irrelevant distractions:

- centering
- meditation
- focusing
- attention control training (ACT)

Specific Preparation

In the specific-preparation phase, the emphasis shifts to applying the mental skills to specific requirements of the sport in simulations during practice. In the pre-competitive phase, the player applies these learned skills to actual games, both in the preparation and actual performance in exhibition or non-league games.

Pre-competitive

In the pre-competitive phase, the player should work on both psychological and physical preparation. Psychological preparation should be concerned with pre-game routines including concentration, relaxation, energizing, and visualization skills in progressively more challenging situations in exhibition or non-league play. The preparation should also include the physical logistics of pre-game meals, stretching and warm-up, getting equipment ready, getting to the game site, talking with the coaches, etc.

Competitive

During league games the player refines the various mental skills, preparing for peaking during the playoffs. Visualization to prepare for opponents, relaxation and positive self-talk to manage stress, and concentration skills during the games are developed.

After a game is over, there should be some type of analysis of the performance of the team and the players. It is always a question whether coaches should talk about the performance immediately after the contest or wait until the next training session. Most coaches say a few words after the game and reserve the more detailed analysis for the next training session. Some coaches prefer to wait until the next day for comments, when they have had time to analyze the performance, usually with the aid of video. Comments on work effort can usually be made immediately following the game.

Post-game analysis usually falls into four categories, especially in team sports, which are i) played well and won, ii) played poorly and won, iii) played well and lost, and iv) played poorly and lost.

Taper

In the tapering (unloading) phase before the final game, mental skills can play a role in lowering stress, enhancing confidence, and focusing on the talk at hand (Bacon, 1990).

TABLE 11.2: Summary of Objectives for Mental Preparation in the Annual Plan (Coaching Association of Canada, 1994)

Phase	Mental Training Objectives
General	1. Evaluation of mental skills
	2. Learn basic mental skills in a quiet setting
Specific Preparatory	1. Adapt and practice mental skills in sport-specific situations
	2. Use mental skills to help attain training objectives
	3. Maintain basic mental skills
Pre-Competitive	1. Develop and practice focus plan
	2. Use focus plan in simulations
	3. Maintain basic mental skills
Competitive	1. Evaluate and refine focus plan
	2. Use mental skills to prepare for specific opponents and games
	3. Use mental skills for stress management
Unloading	1. Use mental skills to aid regeneration and lower stress
Transition	1. Recreational activities to maintain fitness and prevent staleness

A well-thought-out mental training plan developed in conjunction with the various phases of the annual physical training schedule can greatly assist the player to perform at his or her maximum potential. The mental training objectives are summarized in Table 11.2.

Sports psychologist T. Orlick (1986b) suggests that the coaches meet with the players early in the training to begin to develop mental-training preparation plans and begin to practice the various mental training skills. He suggests three early mental preparation meetings, with the first meeting coming early in training, the next three days later, and the third two weeks later. The goals of the three meetings should be:

1. To develop a pre-game plan.
2. To develop a game focus plan.
3. To develop a refocus plan to deal with distractions and keep focused.
4. To develop a communication plan to facilitate team harmony and open discussion of problems.

The first meeting might include a discussion of the importance of mental preparation and training for it; setting goals; and reflecting on previous games, that is,

the mental state for best performance and worst performance, and so on. The second meeting would develop the pre-game, game, and refocusing mental preparation plans, and include a discussion of team harmony. The third meeting would set out the plans for practicing the mental preparation skills and incorporating them into the yearly, monthly, and weekly plans (discussed below). Like physical skills, the mental preparation skills must be practiced, and focusing, imagery, and relaxation should be used in training, as well as in games.

For further information on psychological preparation, coaches and players can consult the following:

Martens, R., *Coaches' Guide to Sport Psychology* (1987)
Nideffer, R., *Psyched to Win* (1992)
—*Players' Guide to Mental Training* (1985)
Orlick, T., *Psyching for Sport: Mental Training for Athletes* (1986a)
—*Coaches' Training Manual* (1986b)
—*In Pursuit of Excellence* (1990)
Singer, R., *Handbook of Sport Psychology* (1993)
Vernacchia, R., R. McGuire, and D. Cook, *Coaching Mental Excellence* (1996)

THE PERIODIZATION OF STRESS

The intensity of training and game situations are the major causes of stress for a player. Other factors, such as crowds, peers, family, and pressures from the coach, also must be considered. The amount of stress varies throughout the training year, as shown in Figure 11.5. Stress is the lowest in the preparation period, although testing and the selection period can raise stress levels. Stress levels go up and down during the competitive period with alternate game and development micro-cycles. Regeneration from highly stressful games and the unloading prior to games are both important factors in the planning process relative to stress levels (Bompa, 1994).

FIGURE 11.5: Stress Cure during the Mono-cycle. (from Bompa, T., *Theory and Methodology of Training* (Dubuque, IA: Kendall/Hunt, 1994), 176. Reprinted by permission.)

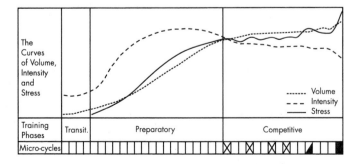

CHAPTER 12

Growth Characteristics and Training Implications

In sports that involve children, special attention should be paid to growth characteristics to determine what systematic training method, if any, should be used at various growth stages. An understanding of both growth and maturation is essential. Growth refers to changes in body size such as height and weight, while maturation is the genetically determined process where the various parts of the body (organs, and cardio and circulatory systems) gradually reach their full development.

A thorough understanding of the growth stages that boys and girls go through will better equip the coach with the knowledge to train and assist in the development of the young athlete. Improper training at various age groups can lead to serious developmental problems, injuries, and high dropout rates in the sport.

Over the past decade, outstanding performances have been achieved in a variety of sports. Several sport scientists and coaches claim that those athletes who were exposed as children and youths to a well-organized and systematic training program usually accomplish the best performances. Coaches who are impatient and pressure children to achieve quick results usually fail because the athletes often quit before attaining athletic maturation. We are more likely to produce healthy and outstanding athletes by employing correct principles of training, and by dividing the training of children and youth into systematic stages with clearly defined objectives.

It is essential for anyone involved in children's sports to incorporate periodization principles into the training of children and youth. Figure 12.1 shows that all athletes, regardless of their high-performance potential, should participate in a generalized phase and a specialized phase of training. Within the generalized phase, athletes are gradually introduced to sport-specific training (initiation) and their athletic talents are progressively formed (athletic formation). The primary purpose of the generalized phase is to build the foundation upon which complex physical abilities can be effectively developed, resulting in a smooth transition to the specialized phase.

There are two stages within the specialized phase, namely, specialization and high performance. During the specialization stage, athletes choose which sport or event to participate in and which position in the chosen sport or event they would like to play. Once athletes have specialized, the intensity and volume of training can increase progressively, resulting in high performance.

Although Figure 12.1 outlines ages associated with each stage, it is important to understand that this model can shift considerably depending on the sport. For example, in sports such as women's gymnastics and diving, the age at each stage may be reduced by two to four years. It is also critical to understand that the rate at which children and youth grow and develop is highly varied, and the individual maturation differences of each athlete must be considered. The training and competitive programs must, therefore, be adjusted accordingly. Familiarity with some of the physical, mental, and social characteristics of athletes in the initiation, athletic formation, and specialization stages of development will allow better establishment of training guidelines that will enhance athlete development, ultimately resulting in high performance.

Growth characteristics presented here will be divided into the categories of physical, mental, and psycho-social, along with suggested guidelines for training.

FIGURE 12.1: The Periodization of Long-term Training

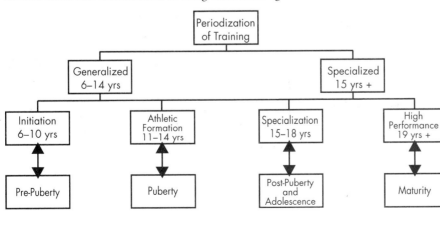

INITIATION STAGE—6 TO 10 YEARS

As demonstrated in Figure 12.1, children in this stage of development should participate in low-intensity training programs. Most young children are not capable of coping with the physical and psychological demands of high-intensity training or high-intensity organized competitions. Training programs for these young athletes must focus on overall athletic development and not sport-specific performance. The following guidelines will help in designing training programs that are suitable for young athletes.

General Training Guidelines for 6 to 10 Years

- Emphasize overall multilateral development. Introduce children to specific drills and exercises that will help them learn skills that are fundamental for their chosen sport and other sports. Multilateral skills should include running, sprinting, jumping, catching, throwing, batting, balancing, and rolling. It is also important to encourage children to learn the skills of activities such as cycling, swimming, and skiing.
- Provide every child with enough time to adequately develop skills, and equal playing time for games and activities.
- Positively reinforce children who are committed and self-disciplined. Reinforce improvements in skill development.
- Encourage children to develop flexibility, coordination, and balance.
- Encourage children to develop various physical abilities in low-intensity environments. For example, swimming is a terrific environment for developing the cardiorespiratory system while minimizing the stresses on joints, ligaments, and connective tissues.
- Select a suitable number of repetitions for each skill, and encourage children to perform each technique correctly.
- Modify the equipment and playing environment to a suitable level. For example, children who do not have the strength to shoot a normal-sized puck using the correct technique should use a smaller and lighter puck.
- Design drills, games, and activities so that children are provided with opportunities for maximum active participation.
- Promote experiential learning by providing children with opportunities to design their drills, games, and activities. Encourage them to be creative and use their imagination.
- Simplify the rules so that children understand the game. If they cannot understand the rules of the game, they may not develop feelings of self-control, which will likely affect their self-esteem and desire to continue participating.
- Children should participate in games that introduce them to basic tactics and strategies. For example, if children have developed basic individual skills such as skating and puck handling, they will likely be ready to successfully play a modified game of hockey. During the game the young athletes could be introduced to situations that demonstrate the importance of teamwork and position play.
- Encourage children to participate in drills that develop concentration and attention control. This will certainly help them prepare for greater demands of training and competition that take place in the later stages of development.
- Emphasize the importance of ethics and fair play.
- Provide opportunities for boys and girls to participate together.
- Make sure that sports are fun for all children.
- Parents should find time for children to play. Children who don't play don't develop imagination.

DEVELOPMENT STAGE—11 TO 14 YEARS (BEGINNING OF PUBERTY)

The first phase of puberty begins around the ages of 11 to 12 for girls and 13 to 14 for boys, and lasts for about two years. The activity of growth and sexual hormones starts increasing one to two years before puberty. The increase in the secretion of testosterone during puberty contributes to the increase in muscle mass in both boys and girls.

Considering the information presented in Table 12.1, it is appropriate to moderately increase the intensity of training during the next stage of development. Although the majority of athletes are still quite vulnerable to injuries and emotional damage, their bodies and capacities are rapidly growing and developing. It is, however, important to understand that the variances in performance may be the result of differences in growth and development. Some athletes may be experiencing a rapid growth spurt, which can explain why they lack coordination during particular drills. As a result, the emphasis should still be on the development of skills and physical abilities and not on performance and winning. The following guidelines will help in designing training programs that are appropriate for athletes between 11 and 14 years of age.

TABLE 12.1: Characteristics of Athlete's Development During Adolescence

Physical

- Following the growth spurt, adolescents continue to grow slowly. In some cases they will reach adult capacity in size. As a result, the awkwardness that was characteristic during early adolescence gradually corrects itself and, consequently, there is improvement in complex coordination.
- The bone ossification process nears completion toward the end of adolescence.
- The cardiorespiratory system is approaching, and in some cases reaches, maturity. Adolescents are capable of training the anaerobic lactic acid system.
- Females generally have less muscular strength than their male counterparts, but muscle mass occurs in both sexes.

Mental

- The brain has reached full size, although it continues to mature neurologically. Complex and abstract thinking abilities are improving.
- Adolescents are analytical. They often develop strong opinions.
- Mental capacities such as cognitive thinking, memory, divergent thinking, convergent thinking, and evaluation become highly functional.

Social-Psychological

- The adolescent is searching for a stable self-image, which is still based primarily on successes and failures.
- Adolescents have a better understanding of their emotions and, generally, are relatively better at identifying and coping with training stress.
- Adolescents need to be recognized and accepted by their peers.
- Decision-making and leadership skills are becoming more developed.
- Adolescents continually seek independence.
- Relationships with the opposite sex become increasingly important.

General Training Guidelines for 11 to 14 Years

- Athletes should participate in a variety of exercises from both hockey and other sports that will help them improve their general athletic skills and prepare them for competition in ice hockey. The volume and intensity of training should be progressively increased.
- Design drills that introduce athletes to fundamental tactics and strategies, and reinforce skill development.
- Athletes should be refining and automating the basic skills they learned during the prior stage of development (6 to 10 years), and learning skills that are a little more complex.

- Place emphasis on improving flexibility, coordination, and balance.
- Emphasize ethics and fair play during training sessions and games.
- Provide all children with opportunities to participate at a challenging level.
- Avoid placing young athletes in potentially humiliating situations.
- Introduce the athletes to exercises that develop general strength. The foundation for future strength and power gains should begin in this stage of development. Place emphasis on developing the core sections of the body, in particular the hips, lower back, and abdomen, as well as muscles at the extremities – shoulder joints, arms, and legs. The equipment needs are minimal since most exercises should involve body weight and light equipment such as medicine balls, rubber (surgical) tubing, wall pulleys, and dumbbells. Low-resistance, high-repetition weight training will also enhance general strength development.
- Continue the development of aerobic capacity. A solid endurance base will enable athletes to cope more effectively with the demands of training and competition during the specialization stage of development.
- Introduce athletes to moderate anaerobic training. This will help them adapt to high-intensity anaerobic training that takes on greater importance, in most sports, during the specialization stage of development. Athletes should not compete in events that place excessive stress on the anaerobic alactic acid energy system. They are usually better suited for short sprints that involve the anaerobic alactic energy system. Also, endurance training of longer distances at slower speeds, such as 880- to 1650-yards (800- to 1500-m) runs, is more suitable for this age than training that challenges the lactic acid system.
- To improve concentration and attention control, introduce athletes to more complex drills.
- Encourage athletes to develop strategies for self-regulation and visualization. Formalized mental training should be introduced.
- Introduce athletes to a variety of fun competitive situations that allow them to experience the application of various techniques and tactics. While young athletes like to compete, it is important to de-emphasize winning. Structure competitions to reinforce skill development.
- Provide time for play and socializing with peers.

SPECIALIZATION STAGE: ADOLESCENCE— 14 TO 18 YEARS

For girls, adolescence begins around age 13 to 14, while for boys it begins around age 14 or 15, and usually ends between the ages of 20 to 25. It is characterized by a slowing of the growth process, and can vary from individual to individual.

The majority of athletes in this stage of development are capable of tolerating greater training and competition demands. The most significant changes in training take place during this stage. Athletes who have been participating in a well-rounded program, with a great emphasis placed on total development, will now start performing more exercises and drills aimed specifically at high-performance development. Closely monitor the volume and intensity of training to ensure that athletes improve dramatically with very few, if any, injuries. The following guidelines will help in designing training programs that are suitable for players specializing in hockey.

General Training Guidelines for the Specialization Stage

- Closely monitor the development of athletes during this stage. They will be developing strategies for coping with the increased physical and psychological demands of training and competition. They are also quite vulnerable to experiencing physical and psychological difficulties from overtraining.
- Athletes should be progressively improving the dominant general physical abilities for hockey such as power, anaerobic capacity, specific coordination, and dynamic flexibility.
- The volume of training for specific exercises and drills must increase to facilitate a performance improvement. The body must adapt to specific training load increments to prepare effectively for competition; therefore, now is the time to stress specificity.
- Increase intensity of training more rapidly than volume, although volume must still be increased progressively. Athletes should be prepared to perform a particular skill, exercise, or drill, with the appropriate rhythm and speed. Training should closely simulate the actions that take place during a game. Although fatigue is a normal outcome of high-intensity training, it is important that athletes do not reach the state of exhaustion.
- Involve athletes in the decision-making process whenever possible.

- Multilateral training must still be emphasized, particularly during the pre-season. It is more important, however, to emphasize specificity, and to utilize training methods and techniques that will develop a high level of sport-specific efficiency, particularly during the season.
- Encourage players to become familiar with some of the theoretical aspects of training.
- The development of strength should start to reflect the specific needs of hockey. Place emphasis on exercising the muscles that are primarily used when performing technical skills (prime movers). Athletes who are weight training can start performing exercises that require fewer repetitions and a heavier weight. Maximum strength training, where fewer than four repetitions of an exercise are performed, should be avoided, particularly for athletes who are still growing.
- Make development of the aerobic capacity a high priority for all players.
- Progressively increase the volume and intensity of anaerobic training. Players are capable of coping with lactic acid accumulation.
- Improve and perfect the techniques of the sport. Select specific exercises that will ensure the skills are being performed with correct biomechanics and physiological efficiency. Difficult technical skills should be performed frequently during training sessions, incorporated into specific tactical drills, and applied in games.
- Improve individual and team tactics. Incorporate game-specific drills into tactical training sessions. Select drills that are interesting, challenging, and stimulating and require quick decisions, fast actions, prolonged concentration, and a high level of motivation from the players. They should demonstrate initiative, self-control, competitive vigor, and ethics and fair play in game situations.
- Increase the number of games progressively so that by the end of this stage the players are competing frequently (two games per week). It is also important to set objectives for games that focus on the development of specific skills, tactics, and physical abilities. Although winning becomes increasingly important, it should not be overemphasized.
- Athletes should practice mental training. Drills and exercises that develop concentration, attention control, positive thinking, self-regulation, visualization, and motivation should be structured to specifically enhance sport-specific performance.

- Towards the end of this stage of athletic development, the athletes should have no major technical problems, and the coach can move from a teaching to a coaching (training) role.

HIGH PERFORMANCE—19 YEARS AND OLDER

A well-designed training plan based on sound principles of long-term development will lead to high performance. Good results that were achieved during various stages of development will increase after hockey players have reached athletic maturation.

The primary objective during this stage of development is to achieve the highest possible performance. Winning is unquestionably the most important objective; however, it is extremely important to ensure that winning takes place within the rules and regulations of ice hockey. The values of ethics and fair play must be constantly reinforced. Athletes should be discouraged from taking illegal performance-enhancing drugs, such as steroids, to achieve international-caliber results. The following guidelines will help in designing a training program that will facilitate high-performance results.

GENERAL TRAINING GUIDELINES FOR HIGH PERFORMANCE

- Progressively increase the volume and intensity of training for the specific physical abilities and capacities, relative to the current physical and psychological state of individual athletes. Training should consist primarily of exercises that lead to adapting to the needs of hockey. Maintain multilateral development, especially during the pre-season.
- Specific exercises and drills in training sessions should simulate the rhythm and speed required in games.

- Specific technical skills and tactics should be perfected and mastered.
- Sport-specific mental training strategies should be perfected.
- Base training programs on sound scientific principles.

SPECIFIC TRAINING IMPLICATIONS

Anaerobic Alactic

The power of the alactic system is low before puberty in both boys and girls. The production of energy (ATP) is limited because of the smaller muscle mass in children, although adults and children possess approximately the same amount of ATP and CP in the resting muscle.

Anaerobic alactic system training can be performed at any age, provided the training loads are not excessive. This means that the total number of repetitions and sets must be lower than for more mature players, recovery time must be longer, and work times should not exceed eight to 10 seconds in duration.

Anaerobic Lactate

The production of energy from the lactic system is relatively low before puberty but increases appreciably during puberty. The activity of enzymes such as LDH (lactate dehydrogenase) and PFK (phosphofructokinase) is increased during this phase. Although the capacity of this system is improved during puberty, it is still well below adult levels. The development of the anaerobic system appears to be directly related to the increased production during puberty of testosterone levels in boys and estrogen levels in girls.

CHAPTER 13

The Training Program and Specific Exercises

The development of the physical abilities for ice hockey follows a specific plan or periodization. The proper sequence within the plan promotes the development of these abilities, such as strength, power, quickness, the development of the energy systems, etc.

In training the energy systems, the aerobic base is developed early in the program, and the anaerobic system training is introduced later. The strength program is periodized in such a way that the end result is the application of power to the movements in ice hockey. The strength programs begin with initial weeks of anatomical adaptation (AA), followed by the period of maximum strength development (MxS). The maximum strength period then leads to the development of power.

With such a foundation, plus the physiological benefits of maximum strength (MxS), skating for quickness is introduced and developed to the highest level possible. Skating for quickness should be seen as applying maximum power against the ice in order to generate the highest velocity in the shortest length of time. Often this is also called power skating. This type of maximum-velocity skating relies on the energy produced by the anaerobic alactic (ATP/CP) system.

Quickness and agility can begin to develop off-ice, and continue with specific on-ice, alactic drills.

STRUCTURE OF THE TRAINING PROGRAMS

The suggested programs are presented in the form of micro-cycles, or weeks of training. They are modeled according to the periodized plan laid out in Figure 13.1; therefore, the program progresses from phase to phase, culminating with the league games, without mentioning the actual phase. Each micro-cycle has a number, and at the same time refers to the month and the week of that month. To be consistent with the step-loading pattern explained in Chapter 1, you will notice that for each micro-cycle we specify the planned training demand, either low (L), medium (M), or high (H). In this way you can alternate training demands and have regeneration cycles, and as a result avoid continuous exhausting training, which may lead to over-reaching and even overtraining.

Please consider the suggested micro-cycles only as guidelines for training. Specific conditions may require slight changes to our suggested program. Understanding the

FIGURE 13.1: The Periodization of Training

LEGEND:

Ex = Exhibition games
Dev. = Develop
AA = Anatomical adaptation

MxS = Maximum strength
P = Power

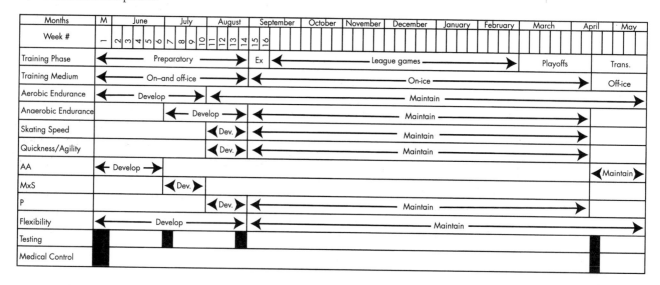

periodization of training for hockey, and the sequence of developing the dominant physical factors, will very quickly give you the knowledge to create individualized training plans. This will help you to create and apply your own program to your specific conditions.

Each micro-cycle is structured as follows:

- it states the training objectives of that week;
- it presents an outline of the program, in which we make specific training suggestions per day; and
- it offers a training program for all abilities to be trained in a given day.

The weekly structure of a given type of program follows a physiological rationale and the needs of alternating the energy systems explained earlier. Please also note that the micro-cycle is organized to allow morning and afternoon training sessions. When this is not specified, you may organize training as per your specific conditions, once a day only.

Structure of a Training Session

To increase effectiveness, a training session has to be very well organized. We suggest the following structure for doing this.

Part 1: *The warm-up* has the main scope of preparing the players physically and mentally for training. After gathering the team together, the coach/instructor has to tell the players the objectives of the day, and the means to be used to achieve those objectives. The actual warm-up follows, consisting of:
  – 10 minutes of jogging/skating/cycling, etc.
  – five minutes of calisthenics
  – five minutes of overall specific joint flexibility
  By the time the warm-up is over, some players may be sweating.

Part 2: *Perform the training session's objectives.* For increasing the efficiency of skill acquisition, speed and power elements have to be planned for in the early part of the session, when the nervous system is not fatigued. Anaerobic or aerobic drills/activities are planned at the end of Part 2 so that fatigue, the normal outcome of such training, does not impair learning or speed power development. Following speed power–maximum strength exercises/drills, players should perform a few stretching exercises to prevent muscle tightness, or even muscle pull.

Part 3: *Conclusion.* At this time the coach gives feedback to the players about whether and, if so, how the training objectives were achieved. Positive criticism is often necessary, especially during the preparatory phase, but the coach should always end his or her remarks on a positive note. Players should end the session with another five minutes of stretching and five to 10 minutes of light aerobic activity to flush lactic acid out of the system.

Monitoring a Training Program (Testing)

We strongly advise that testing, especially with professional, university, and junior teams, be regarded as a very useful means of monitoring players' improvement throughout the preparatory phase, and at the end of league games and playoffs. Testing is not, as is often the case, a once-a-year gimmick. A once-a-year test at the beginning of the training camp cannot have any impact on the overall fitness assessment of a team. It is also too late to be of use in improving any of the weaknesses detected during the testing. Further, to compare players' fitness levels with those of the previous year is also an exercise in futility. The time between these testing dates—one year—is too great to influence players to be motivated to make significant changes in their training. Testing for the midget, bantam, and pee wee may be done on a more limited basis, perhaps twice a year.

For testing to have an impact on fitness evaluation and monitoring of elite and junior teams, it has to be done at the following times:

- At the beginning of the program. These initial test results are compared with those of the tests done in the fourth week of June, the first week of August, and at the beginning of the training camp. The June test is very comprehensive and has the scope of testing all the hockey-specific physical abilities.
- The second test, in the fourth week of June, is used to calculate the load for the MxS phase.
- The third testing date, the first week in August, is also a MxS and P test.
- The test planned during the training camp is another comprehensive test, and can be used as both a monitoring device and a motivating technique. The improvements in all the fitness components should be positively reflected in the players' performance during a game and in their general effectiveness, and used by the coach to demonstrate to his players that they will have a very successful year at the elite level.

- Finally, the last test, at the end of the season, is also a comprehensive test. It should be used as a monitoring device to see how players fare at the end of the season, and whether the gains during the preparatory phase have been maintained throughout the season. Similarly, this data will also be used to compare the scores collected during the four tests of the next year's preparatory phase.
- A medical examination regarding the health status of each player is suggested for the beginning of the preparatory phase and at the end of the league/playoffs phase.

CORE EXERCISES FOR STRENGTH AND POWER FOR HOCKEY

From the multitude of exercises available for strength and power training for hockey, we have chosen those designed especially for the elite and junior teams (Figures 13.2 to 13.42). You will notice that for younger players we suggest more simple exercises (Figures 13.43 to 13.67). The core exercises suggested in our program (Figures 13.2 to 13.15) do not necessarily exclude others. They do, however, have to be used with care, always observing a careful progression, especially for younger players.

As you examine our suggested exercises for strength and power training, you will notice that exercises are selected to match the muscle groups used in hockey. Obviously, you can replace some exercises with others of your choice as long as they are for the muscle groups used in hockey.

Please do not lessen the importance of exercises for the back muscles, lower back and spine (erector spinae). These muscles are extremely important to maintain the trunk at a low level during fast, explosive forward skating. The closer the trunk is to horizontal, the easier it is for the player to apply leg force against the ice, and as a result be able to generate a high skating velocity. Mechanically this position is very advantageous, since the resultant force is as close as realistically possible to horizontal, and as such maximizes players' leg power. This is possible because the application of force against the ice is also very close to horizontal. The fastest hockey players do keep a low trunk position; however, to keep this position, a player needs strong back muscles.

CORE EXERCISES FOR STRENGTH DEVELOPMENT

FIGURE 13.2: Neck Flexion/Extension
Region: Neck
Primary muscles: Prevertebral muscles, sternocleidomastoids, deep posterior muscles, cervical region, trapezius

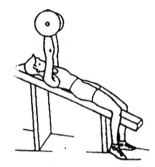

FIGURE 13.3: Incline/Flat Bench Press
Region: Chest; upper arms
Primary muscles: Pectoralis major, anterior deltoids, triceps

FIGURE 13.4: Shoulder Shrugs
Region: Shoulders
Primary muscles: Trapezius

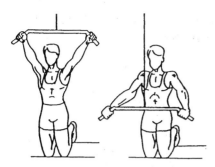

FIGURE 13.5: Front Lat Pull-downs
Region: Shoulder girdle
Primary muscles: Latissimus dorsi, upper pectoralis major, trapezius

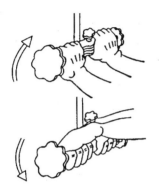

FIGURE 13.6: Wrist Flexion/Extension
Region: Wrist
Primary muscles: Flexor carpi radials, flexor carpi ulnaris, extensor carpi ulnaris

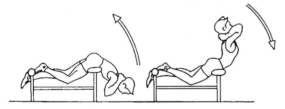

FIGURE 13.7: Back Extension/Hyperextension
Region: Lower back
Primary muscles: Erector spinae, gluteus maximus

FIGURE 13.8: Power Cleans to Chest Level
Region: Trunk, lower back, shoulders
Primary muscles: Quadriceps, gluteus maximus, erector spinae, hamstrings, trapezius, deltoids

FIGURE 13.9: Abdominal Curls; V sits, or Weighted Situps
Region: Trunk
Primary muscles: Rectus abdominis, obliques—externus/internus abdominis

FIGURE 13.10: Knee Lifts (resistance is provided by a rubber cord/towel hooked around the ankle and held at both ends by another player)
Region: Hips
Primary muscles: Iliopsoas

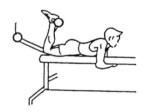

FIGURE 13.11: Leg Curls
Region: Upper legs, hips
Primary muscles: Hamstrings, gluteus maximus

FIGURE 13.12: Half Squats
Region: Upper body and lower legs
Primary muscles: Gluteus maximus, quadriceps, erector spinae, abdominals

FIGURE 13.13: Jump Half Squats

Region: Upper body and lower legs

Primary muscles: Gluteus maximus, quadriceps, erector spinae, abdominals, soleus, gastrocnemius, vasti lateralis and medialis

FIGURE 13.14: Reverse Leg Presses

Region: Upper legs, hips

Primary muscles: Quadriceps, gastrocnemius

FIGURE 13.15: Heel Raises

Region: Lower legs

Primary muscles: Gastrocnemius, soleus

EXERCISES FOR POWER DEVELOPMENT —COMBINED EXERCISES

During the last phase of the MxS (maximum strength) training, specific exercises for the enhancement of MxS and power have to be introduced. By including these exercises, gains in MxS will be progressively transformed into hockey-specific power (Figures 13.16 to 13.21).

As the start of regular league play fast approaches, power training becomes one of the most important training objectives. To maximize the level of power the players need, we suggest the use of many types of power and plyometric exercises (Figures 13.30 to 13.42).

FIGURE 13.16: Half squat, slow eccentric (lower the barbell) followed by a low jump half squat

FIGURE 13.17: One-leg incline press followed by two-leg jumps over low hurdles/cones (alternate leg presses)

FIGURE 13.18: Bench press, stressing a fast press followed by a drop pushup and culminating with side medicine ball (MB) throws toward a partner (alternate sides)

FIGURE 13.19: Reverse leg press followed by a quick sprint of 20 y/m (alternate legs continuously)

FIGURE 13.20: One-leg incline press followed by five to 10 bounding exercises (triple jump-like jumps from one leg to the other)

FIGURE 13.21: Slow eccentric (lower the barbell into a half squat) followed by fast concentric (the press phase). Two spotters should take the barbell off shoulders. Follow with 5 to 10 bounding exercises.

FIGURE 13.22: A series of 10 to 15 MB throws with partner: forward, overhead backward, and sideways. Emphasize the side throws, a movement which is very specific to hockey.

FIGURE 13.23: Drop pushups followed by a 20-y/m sprint

FIGURE 13.24: MB side or front throw followed by a 20-y/m sprint

FIGURE 13.25: Drop jump followed by a series of 5 to 8 (at most 10) high hops

FIGURE 13.26: Drop jump, immediately followed by a jump onto a box or bench

FIGURE 13.27: A series of jumps over 3 to 5 low boxes/benches followed by 5 to 8 bounding exercises

FIGURE 13.28: A series of jumps over 5 to 8 boxes, 2 feet (60 cm) high

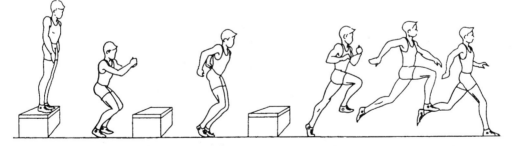

FIGURE 13.29: A series of direct jumps over 3 to 5 boxes (2 feet/60 cm high) followed by a 20-y/m sprint of maximum velocity

EXERCISES FOR POWER DEVELOPMENT —PLYOMETRICS

Power training and quickness, including quick footwork, is developed mostly through plyometric exercises. Of the many exercises available in this area, we suggest only a reduced number. For further information on this subject you may refer to *Power Training for Sports: Plyometrics for Maximum Power Development* by Tudor Bompa, second edition, published by the Coaching Association of Canada, 1996. In it, you will find 207 exercises for power training/plyometrics.

The ability of a player to skate with maximum speed comes from the force applied against the ice by knee and ankle extensors, which is why we emphasize hip, knee, and ankle force.

There are several misconceptions about specific power training for ice hockey; one is regarding the slide board. As you can see from this book, we do not suggest using a slide board for training elite hockey players simply because the action is too slow, especially the application of force at the end of the board. Just because the slide board imitates the skating action is not an acceptable argument. (We do, however, suggest it for younger players.) Instead, we suggest exercises for power development that include both exercises with weights and plyometrics. These exercises develop power, since the force application against the ground is fast and the leg muscles contract quickly and powerfully.

The exercises suggested below specify first the starting position (SP), followed by the description of the movement (M).

FIGURE 13.30: Two-Feet Slalom Jumps
(SP): Standing.
(M): Using both feet, take continuous diagonal jumps, progressing forward in slalom fashion.

FIGURE 13.31: Side Scissors
(SP): Standing.
(M): Jump vertically, switching legs in midair and landing on the outside leg.

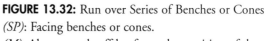

FIGURE 13.32: Run over Series of Benches or Cones
(SP): Facing benches or cones.
(M): Alternate takeoff leg for each repetition of the course.

FIGURE 13.33: Jump over the Bench
(SP): Facing the bench.
(M): Jump over the bench, turn around, and immediately jump over again.

FIGURE 13.34: Side Jumps over the Bench
(SP): Standing at the end of a bench (or a series of benches end to end), one side facing the bench.
(M): Swing arms and jump over the bench, land, prepare to jump on the spot, and jump over again. Advanced players should jump over continuously without preparing for another jump.

FIGURE 13.35: Front Scissors Splits
(SP): Standing, one leg forward and the other behind.
(M): Drive back leg forward into a jump. When legs are switched quickly in midair, land into a lunge and rebound immediately into another scissors split jump. Achieve maximal vertical height and an active takeoff. Although the exercise is performed on the spot, the player should also try to go forward.

FIGURE 13.36: Knee-tuck Jumps
(SP): Standing.
(M): Swing arms upward and actively press the feet against the ground for a vertical tuck jump. Land with flexed knees to absorb shock.

FIGURE 13.37: Reactive Box Jumps
(SP): Standing on box, facing the row of boxes
(M): Land on the ground, then take off explosively to jump to next box, using an active arm swing. Prepare for the next jump for one to two seconds and continue activity over all the boxes.

FIGURE 13.38: Drop. Pushup on a Gym Box
(SP): Palms supporting the body on a gym box (or low table or chair).
(M): Push upward explosively, and return to SP.

FIGURE 13.39: MB Scoop Throws
(SP): A half-squat position, feet apart, arms extended down between legs, holding the ball.
(M): Extend legs in an active takeoff while the arms swing upward, releasing the ball vertically upwards. After landing, catch the ball with both palms, return to a half-squat position, then repeat.

FIGURE 13.40: Two-Hand MB Side Throw or
(M): Alternate sides.

FIGURE 13.41: Abs Rainbows

(SP): Lying down, head near the lowest rung of a stall bar, hands gripping it.

(M): Lift legs and lower on both sides.

Variation: A "shock" reaction is achieved if the lift of the legs is opposed by a partner.

FIGURE 13.42: Abs Arches

(SP): Seated, back against the stall bars, arms above head, gripping the nearest rung.

(M): Press hips actively upward, arching the body (feet are on the ground, hands firmly gripping the rung). Lower the hips to the SP and continue the movement.

EXERSIZES FOR THE YOUNGER PLAYER

FIGURE 13.43: Running Up Two Stairs

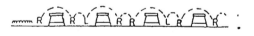

FIGURE 13.44: Running and Jumping over Low Gym Boxes (L = left leg; R = right leg)

FIGURE 13.45: Standing Jump

(SP): Standing.

(M): Jump vertically. While in midair, bring one leg forward, the other backward, in a scissors-like movement. Repeat, alternating legs.

FIGURE 13.46: Vertical Hops

(SP): Standing.

(M): Swing the arms upward and press actively against the ground for a vertical spring. Land, absorbing the shock, lowering the arms at hip level.

FIGURE 13.47: Wheelbarrow

Whereas this exercise is normally "walking" on the hands for the purpose of power training, the wheelbarrow is performed in small forward hops.

FIGURE 13.48: Plyometric Pushups (or Clap Pushups)

FIGURE 13.49: Twisted Abs (Trunk Twists)

FIGURE 13.53: MB Standing Chest Throw

FIGURE 13.50: MB Situp Throw
(SP): One partner standing, feet apart, holding the ball. The other seated, feet apart, knees slightly flexed.
(M): The ball is carefully tossed toward the chest of the seated partner. As it is caught, the partner rocks toward the floor and, using the momentum of an upper-body upward thrust, throws the ball back to the other partner.

FIGURE 13.54: MB Back Throw

FIGURE 13.55: MB Situp Throws
(SP): Partners sitting on the floor facing each other, with feet interlocked to secure good balance and support for the actions. One partner holds the ball above the head.
(M): The ball is thrown toward the partner, who catches it, rocks backward, and immediately changes the direction forward, releasing the ball toward his partner, for a maximal involvement of abdominal muscles.

FIGURE 13.51: Leg Thrusts (Burpees)
(Variation): Do the same on the floor.

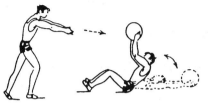

FIGURE 13.52: V Sits

FIGURE 13.56: Rope Skipping
Using single, alternate, or double leg action, where the emphasis is on continuous rebounding off the ground, rope skipping is one of the most commonly used plyometric exercises. Variations include circling, underneath, forward, backward, and sideways.

FIGURE 13.57: Sideways Skips

FIGURE 13.58: Stairs Crossover Run

FIGURE 13.59: Double-leg Jumps over Two Stairs

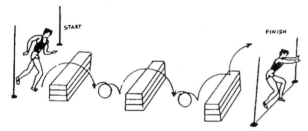

FIGURE 13.60: Obstacle Run

FIGURE 13.61: MB Abs Rolls

(SP): Lying on the back, arms overhead holding a medicine ball.
(M): With hips slightly flexed the performer then rolls over onto the stomach, arching the back, then keeps rolling over hips to complete the rotation.

Note: Throughout these continuous rotations in both directions, avoid touching the floor with the legs, upper body, and arms, in order to better involve the back and abdominal muscles.

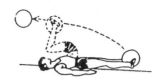

FIGURE 13.62: MB Back Roll and Throw

FIGURE 13.63: Leg and Trunk Extensions

FIGURE 13.64: Trunk Extensions

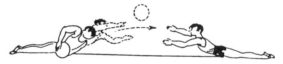

FIGURE 13.65: MB Side Throws

FIGURE 13.66: Situps

FIGURE 13.67: Squat Jumps

(SP): Standing, feet apart, hands behind the head.
(M): Move actively upward and forward. Land on toes, lower heels, and slightly bend your knees to absorb the shock, and repeat the sequence.

CHAPTER 14

Year-Round Fitness Programs for Elite Professional, National, and University Teams

INTRODUCTION

A year-round training program for an elite-level team has to consider the specific abilities to be trained for hockey players, as well as the sequence in which they have to be planned.

Figure 14.1 illustrates a periodized plan for such a team. This plan, which is an overall outline, considers a team that can start its training program in early June. The preparatory phase is only three months long, followed by a short training camp, exhibition games, and culminating with league games.

The plan outlined in this chapter considers a hypothetical team that does not play beyond April. The month of May is, then, a transition phase, where some basic, informal training is maintained, as suggested at the end of the chapter.

The proposed training is performed both on- and off-ice, as specifically outlined in each micro-cycle presented.

The sequence of developing the physical abilities in hockey follows the periodization of strength power, energy systems, and quickness. After developing the aerobic base, from early June on, it has to be maintained throughout the exhibition and league games. Following the first six weeks of

aerobic endurance, the anaerobic lactic, which is more specific for hockey, is introduced and developed throughout the last three weeks of July and the month of August. During this time, the coach should attempt to maximize the aerobic endurance.

TRAINING PROGRAM

The strength training program is periodized in such a way that the end product should be power and power-endurance. As such, after three weeks of anatomical adaptation (AA), maximum strength (MxS) is developed to the highest levels realistically possible. To lessen the high levels of stress typical for MxS, the development of this important strength component for hockey is achieved through two phases, one six weeks in duration and the other three weeks. Power (P) training starts after the first six weeks of MxS. The first phase of power training is three weeks long, and the second is four weeks. The second MxS period is planned in between. The reason for this alternation of MxS with P is that the players will reach higher levels of power than by using any other methods.

FIGURE 14.1: The Periodization of Training for an Elite Hockey Team

LEGEND:
C = Training camp
Pre-C = Pre-competitive/exhibition games
AA = Anatomical adaptation

MxS = Maximum strength
P = Power
P-E = Power-endurance

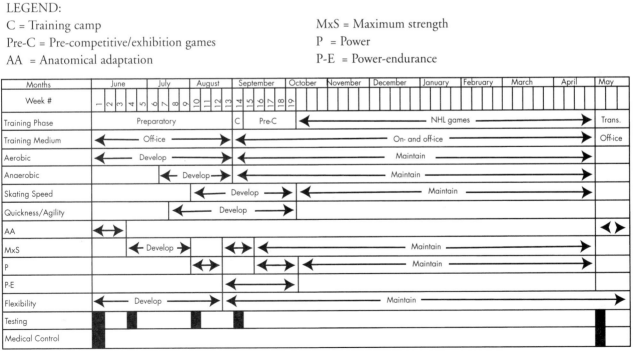

Power-endurance (P-E) is developed at the same time, with the second phase of MxS and following the first phase of P development.

All the above abilities have to be maintained through-out the league and playoff games. This is true for flexibility as well, the only specification here being that the maintenance of flexibility throughout the league games should also be used as a regeneration and stretch therapy method.

(Note: For conversion chart, see page 199.)

Micro-cycle No. 1

- June: Week 1
- Training demand: L

Training objectives:
- Introduce aerobic training – continuous, steady-state activity
- Start the AA program – 40% of 1RM
- Begin overall flexibility program
- First testing date at the end of the week

Outline of the program:

Days	Mon.	Tues.	Wed.	Thurs.	Fri.	Sat.	Sun.
AM						O_2	
PM	O_2	AA	O_2	AA			

Training program:
- Training the energy systems:
  - Aerobic training (O_2) = 1 x 30 minutes
    - Means of training – do one of the following:
      - cycling;
      - running, roller blading, cycling; or stationary bike – tension (T) 2.5; rotations per minute (rpm) = 80
    - Target heart rate (HR) – 160 to 166 beats/minute (b/m)

Note: Unless otherwise specified, the same type of work will be performed on each day planned for a given micro-cycle.

Anatomical Adaptation (AA) Training:

No.	Exercise	Load	# Reps.	# Sets	RI/sec.
1	Diagonal lunges (Chap. 5, #19)	30 kg	12 each leg	2	60
2	Incline bench press (Figure 13.3)	50%	15	3	60
3	Twisted abs (Figure 13.49)	—	12	2	30
4	Shoulder shrugs (Figure 13.4)	20 kg	10	2	30
5	Leg curls (Figure 13.11)	40 kg	6	2	60
6	Front lat pulldowns (Figure 13.5)	40 kg	10	2	60
7	Neck flexion/extension (Figure 13.2)	—	12	2	30
8	Back extension (Figure 13.7)	—	8	2	60
9	Wrist flexion/extension (Figure 13.6)	—	12	3	30
10	Heel raises (Figure 13.15)	60%	15	3	30
11	Biceps curls	50%	10	2	60
12	Half squats (Figure 13.12)	60%	10–12	3	60

Notes: For the exercises where the load is expressed in percentage, a test for 1RM is necessary to calculate the load.
- For exercises 7 and 9, take a resistance that allows the players to perform the indicated number of repetitions.
- Exercises may be changed/added/excluded.
- To calculate the load in pounds, multiply the load by 2.2.
- Testing: Comprehensive testing as per the protocol (see Chapter 9).
- — signifies using own body weight.

Micro-cycle No. 2

- June: Week 2
- Training demand: M

Training objectives:
- Develop aerobic endurance – continuous, steady state
- Develop AA – 50% of 1RM
- Develop overall flexibility

Outline of the program:

Days	Mon.	Tues.	Wed.	Thurs.	Fri.	Sat.	Sun.
AM						O_2	
PM	O_2	AA		O_2	AA		

Training program:
- Training the energy systems:
- O_2 = 1 x 45 minutes
  - Means of training:
    - cycling
    - running or rollerblading; or
    - stationary bike – T2.5; rpm = 80
  - Target HR—160 to 166 b/m

AA Training:

No.	Exercise	Load	# Reps.	# Sets	RI/sec.
1	Diagonal lunges	30 kg	12 each leg	3	60
2	Incline bench press	60%	12	3	60
3	Twisted abs	—	15	2	30
4	Shoulder shrugs	40 kg	8–10	2	30
5	Leg curls	40 kg	6–8	2	60
6	Front lat pulldowns	40 kg	10–12	1	60
7	Neck flexion/extension	—	12–15	2	30
8	Back extension	—	12–15	2	60
9	Wrist flexion/extension	—	10–12	3	30
10	Heel raises	60%	15	3	30
11	Biceps curls	60%	8–10	2	60
12	Half squats	60%	12–15	3	60

Micro-cycle No. 3

- June: Week 3
- Training demand: H

Training objectives:

- Develop aerobic endurance – long repetitions
- Develop AA – 60% of 1RM
- Develop overall flexibility

Outline of the program:

Days	Mon.	Tues.	Wed.	Thurs.	Fri.	Sat.	Sun.
AM						AA	
PM	O_2	AA	O_2	AA	O_2		

Training program:

- Training the energy systems:
  - O_2 = 2 x 25 minutes
    - Rest interval (RI) = 5 minutes
    - Means of training:
      - cycling
      - running, rollerblading, cycling or stationary bike – T 2.5; rpm = 80
    - Target HR – 160 to 166 b/m

AA Training:

No.	Exercise	Load	# Reps	#Sets	RI/sec
1	Diagonal lunges	30 kg	15 each leg	3	60
2	Incline bench press	70%	8	3	90
3	Twisted abs	—	18	3	60
4	Upright rowing with shoulder shrugs	40 kg	15	2	60
5	Leg curls	40 kg	8	2	60
6	Front lat pulldowns	40 kg	12–15	1	60
7	Neck flexion/extension	—	15	1	30
8	Back extension	—	10–12	3	60
9	Wrist flexion/extension	—	12–15	2	30
10	Heel raises	70%	12	3	60
11	Half squats	70%	10	3	60

MICRO-CYCLE NO. 4

- June: Week 4
- Training demand: L

Training objectives:
- Develop aerobic endurance – long repetitions
- Start the MxS program – 70% of 1RM
- Develop overall flexibility

Outline of the program:

Days	Mon.	Tues.	Wed.	Thurs.	Fri.	Sat.	Sun.
AM						MxS	
PM	O_2	MxS	O_2	MxS	AA	O_2	

Training program:
- Training the energy systems:
  - O_2 = 1 x 45 minutes + 1 x 20 minutes
    - RI = 5 minutes
    - Means of training:
      - cycling or rollerblading or running; or stationary bike – T 2.5; rpm = 80
    - Target HR – 164 b/m

Maximum Strength (MxS) Training:

No.	Exercise	Load	# Reps.	# Sets	RI/min.
1	Half squats	70%	12	3	2
2	Triceps extension	70%	8–10	2	2
3	Twisted abs	—	8–10	2	1
4	Reverse leg press (Figure 13.14)	70%	12	3	2
5	Shoulder shrugs	40 kg	10	2	1
6	Heel raises	70%	12	3	1
7	Incline bench press	70%	10	2	2
8	Power cleans to chest (Figure 13.8)	20 kg	12	2	2
9	Leg curls	40 kg	6–8	2	2

Notes: The load is expressed in percentage of 1RM (i.e., 70%).
- For twisted abs—hold a 11-pound (5-kg) weight or plate on the chest while performing the action (# reps. = for each side).
- Reverse leg press—perform same work for each leg separately.
- Calculate the load as close as possible to the indicated percentage.
- Test: for 1RM for each exercise where the load is expressed in percentage.

Micro-cycle No. 5

- June: Week 5
- Training demand: M

Training objectives:

- Improve aerobic endurance – long repetitions
- MxS – 80% of 1RM
- Develop overall flexibility

Outline of the program:

Days	Mon.	Tues.	Wed.	Thurs.	Fri.	Sat.	Sun.
AM						MxS	
PM	O_2	MxS	O_2	MxS	AA	O_2	

Training program:

- Training the energy systems:
  - O_2 = 3 x 30 minutes
    - RI = 5 minutes
    - Means of training:
    - cycling, rollerblading, running, or stationary bike – T 2.5; rpm = 80
    - Target HR – 164 to 168 b/m

MxS Training:

No.	Exercise	Load	# Reps.	# Sets	RI/min.
1	Half squats	85%	6	4	4
2	Cable elbow extension	85%	6	4	3
3	Twisted abs	—	12	2	3
4	Reverse leg press	85%	10	4	4
5	Shoulder shrugs	40 kg	12	2	3
6	Heel raises	85%	10	3	2
7	Incline bench press	85%	8	3	4
8	Power cleans to chest	30 kg	8	2	3
9	Leg curls	40 kg	8	1	2

Micro-cycle No. 6

- July: Week 1
- Training demand: H

Training objectives:

- Improve aerobic endurance – long repetitions
- MxS – 85% of 1RM
- Flexibility training – stress hips, groin, trunk rotation, and shoulders

Outline of the program:

Days	Mon.	Tues.	Wed.	Thurs.	Fri.	Sat.	Sun.
AM	O_2	O_2				O_2	
PM	MxS		MxS	O_2	MxS		

Training program:
- Training the energy systems:
  - O_2 = 1 x 20 minutes + 2 x 30 minutes + 1 x 10 minutes
    - RI = 5 minutes
    - Means of training:
      - cycling, rollerblading, running, or stationary bike – T 2.0; rpm = 80
    - Target HR – 164 to 168 b/m

Note: From this week on, aerobic (O_2) training could be performed earlier in the day to free the player for other activities.

MxS Training:

No.	Exercise	Load	# Reps.	# Sets	RI/min.
1	Half squats	85%	6	4	4
2	Cable elbow extension	85%	6	4	3
3	Twisted abs	—	12	2	3
4	Reverse leg press	85%	10	4	4
5	Shoulder shrugs	40 kg	12	2	3
6	Heel raises	85%	10	3	2
7	Incline bench press	85%	8	3	4
8	Power cleans to chest	30 kg	8	2	3
9	Leg curls	40 kg	8	1	2

Micro-cycle No. 7

- July: Week 2
- Training demand: M

Training objectives:
- Maximize aerobic endurance – steady state
- Introduce anaerobic, lactic acid (LA) system
- MxS – 80% of 1RM
- Flexibility training – stress hips, groin, trunk rotation, and shoulders
- Test for 1RM

Outline of the program:

Days	Mon.	Tues.	Wed.	Thurs.	Fri.	Sat.	Sun.
AM	O_2	LA	O_2	LA	O_2	LA	
PM	MxS		MxS		MxS		

Note: From this week on, the structure of a micro-cycle becomes more complex, at times with two training sessions per day. Those players who follow our program will see the difference between past and present programs. These players will notice a great improvement in their physical potential, which will drastically improve their game. A training session, such as LA training, could be performed either in the morning or in the afternoon.

Training program:
- Training the energy systems:
  - O_2 = 1 x 45 minutes
    - Means of training:
      - cycling, rollerblading, running, or stationary bike – T 2.5; rpm = 80
    - Target HR – 164 b/m
  - LA + O_2 = 6 to 8 x 3 minutes
    - stationary bike – T = 1.5 to 2; rpm = 80
    - RI = 2 to 3 minutes easy ride for compensation (recovery)
    - Target HR – 170 to 176 b/m

MxS Training:

No.	Exercise	Load	# Reps.	# Sets	RI/min.
1	Half squats	90%	5	4	4
2	Incline bench press	90%	5	3	4
3	Twisted abs	—	12	3	3
4	Reverse leg press	90%	5	4	3
5	Shoulder shrugs	40 kg	12	2	2
6	Heel raises	90%	5	3	2
7	Leg curls	40 kg	8	1	3
8	Power cleans to chest	40 kg	6	2	3

Note: Test for 1RM for exercises expressed in percentage

Micro-cycle No. 8

- July: Week 3
- Training demand: H

Training objectives:
- Maximize aerobic endurance
- Develop LA system
- MxS – 90% of 1RM
- Introduce drills for quickness and agility
- Flexibility training stressing hips and groin

Outline of the program:

Days	Mon.	Tues.	Wed.	Thurs.	Fri.	Sat.	Sun.
AM	O_2	Quickness and agility + LA	O_2	LA + quickness and agility			
PM	MxS		MxS	O_2	MxS		

Training program:

- Training the energy systems:
  - O_2 = 3 x 30 minutes
    - RI = 4 minutes
    - Means of training:
      - cycling, rollerblading, running, or stationary bike – T 2.5; rpm = 80
    - Target HR – 164 to 168 b/m
  - LA + O_2 = 8 x 3 minutes
    - stationary bike – T 3.0; rpm = 60 to 70
    - RI = 3 minutes easy ride for compensation (recovery)
    - Target HR – 174 to 178 b/m

MxS Training:

No.	Exercise	Load	# Reps.	# Sets	RI/min.
1	Half squats	95%	5	4	4
2	Incline bench press	95%	5	3	4
3	Twisted abs	—	12	3	3
4	Reverse leg press	95%	5	4	3
5	Shoulder shrugs	40 kg	12	2	2
6	Heel raises	95%	5	3	2
7	Leg curls	40 kg	8	1	3
8	Power cleans to chest	40 kg	6	2	3

Note: On Thursday, we suggest the LA training be done first, followed immediately by quickness and agility drills. The main reason for this is that the players have to perform quickness and agility drills under the fatiguing conditions of LA build-up.

Micro-cycle No. 9

- July: Week 4
- Training demand: H

Training objectives:

- Maximize aerobic endurance
- Develop LA system
- MxS – 95% of 1RM
- Develop quickness and agility
- Maximize the flexibility of hips and groin. Maintain overall flexibility.

Outline of the program:

Days	Mon.	Tues.	Wed.	Thurs.	Fri.	Sat.	Sun.
AM	O_2	Quickness and agility + LA	O_2	LA + quickness and agility			
PM	MxS		MxS	O_2	MxS		

Training program:
- Training the energy systems:
  - O_2 = 2 x 30 minutes + 2 x 10 minutes
    - RI = 5 minutes
      - Means of training:
        - cycling, rollerblading, or running, or stationary bike – T 2.5; rpm = 80
      - Target HR – 164 to 168 b/m
  - LA + O_2 = 6 x 2 minutes
    - stationary bike – 4.0 to 4.5; rpm = 80 to 90
    - RI = 3 to 4 minutes easy ride for compensation + 6 x 30 seconds
    - stationary bike – T 4.0; rpm = 140
    - RI = 2 minutes
  - Target HR – 174 to 180 b/m

MxS Training:

No.	Exercise	Load	# Reps.	# Sets	RI/min.
1	Half squats	95%	5	4	4
2	Incline bench press	95%	5	3	4
3	Twisted abs	—	12	3	3
4	Reverse leg press	95%	5	4	3
5	Shoulder shrugs	40 kg	12	2	2
6	Heel raises	95%	5	3	2
7	Leg curls	40 kg	8	1	3
8	Power cleans to chest	40 kg	6	2	3

Micro-cycle No. 10

- August: Week 1
- Training demand: L

Training objectives:
- Maximize aerobic endurance
- Improve LA system (preferably on-ice)
- Introduce skating for maximum speed
- Improve quickness and agility
- Develop power

Outline of the program:

Days	Mon.	Tues.	Wed.	Thurs.	Fri.	Sat.	Sun.
AM	O_2	Skating for speed + LA		O_2	Skating for speed + LA		
PM	P		P		P		

Note: From this micro-cycle on, drills for quickness and agility will be performed together with skating for speed.

Training program:
- Training the energy systems:
  - O_2 = 1 x 45 minutes
    - Means of training:
      - cycling, rollerblading running, or stationary bike – T 2.0; rpm = 80
    - Target HR – 164 b/m
  - $LA + O_2$ = 6 x 2 minutes
    - stationary bike – T 4.0; rpm = 80 to 90
    - RI = 3 to 4 minutes easy ride for compensation 6 x 1 minute
  - stationary bike – Tension 4.0; rpm = 80 to 90
    - RI = 4 minutes easy ride for compensation
  - Target HR – 176 to 182 b/m
  - Alactic (maximum skating speed) = 12 x 30 meters
    - RI = 2 to 3 minutes

Power Training:

No.	Exercise	Load	# Reps.	# Sets	RI/min.
1	Jump half squat (Figure 13.13)	30%	6	2	2
2	Knee lifts (Figure 13.10)	—	12–15 each leg	2	2
3	Bench press, drop pushup, and side MB throws (Figure 13.18)	40%	8	2	2
4	Scoop MB throws (Figure 13.39)	4-kg MB	8	2	2
5	Side scissors jumps (Figure 13.31)	—	12	2	1
6	Half squat, slow eccentric, and low jump half squat (Figure 13.16)	40%	6	2	3
7	Abs rainbows (Figure 13.41)	—	10	2	1

Note: Test MxS for 1RM to compare the results with the test organized in the first week of the MxS phase. Compare the scores to assess individual improvements.

Micro-cycle No. 11

- August: Week 2
- Training demand: H

Training objectives:
- Maximize aerobic endurance
- Maximize LA system (preferably on-ice)
- Develop skating for maximum speed
- Maximize quickness and agility
- Develop power

Outline of the program:

Days	Mon.	Tues.	Wed.	Thurs.	Fri.	Sat.	Sun.
AM	O_2	Speed + LA	O_2	Skating for speed + LA	O_2	Skating for speed + LA	
PM	P		P		P		

Training program:
- Training the energy systems:
  - O_2 = 3 x 20 minutes
    - RI = 4 minutes
    - Means of training:
      - cycling, rollerblading, running, or stationary bike – T 2.5; rpm = 80 to 90
    - Target HR – 164 to 168 b/m
  - LA = 12 x 1 minute
    - stationary bike – T 4.0; rpm = 80
    - RI = 4 minutes easy ride for compensation
  - Target HR – 176 to 182 b/m
  - Alactic (maximum skating speed) = 15 x 30 meters
    - RI = 3 minutes

Power Training:

No.	Exercise	Load	# Reps.	# Sets	RI/min.
1	Jump half squat	40%	6	3	3
2	Knee-tuck jumps (Figure 13.36)	—	12–15	2	1
3	Bench press, drop pushup, and side MB throws	40%	8	3	3
4	Abs rainbows (Figure 13.41)	—	10	2	1
5	Side jumps over bench (Figure 13.34)	—	3	2	2
6	Half squat, slow eccentric, and low jump half squat (Figure 13.16)	40%	3	3	3

Micro-cycle No. 12

- August: Week 3
- Training demand: H

Training objectives:
- Maximize aerobic endurance
- Maximize LA system (preferably on-ice)
- Improve skating for maximum speed
- Maximize quickness and agility
- Improve power

Outline of the program:

Days	Mon.	Tues.	Wed.	Thurs.	Fri.	Sat.	Sun.
AM	O_2	Skating for speed + LA		O_2	Skating for speed LA +		
PM	P		P		P		

Training program:
- Training the energy systems:
  - O_2 = 3 x 20 minutes + 3 x 5 minutes
    - RI = 4 minutes
    - Means of training:
      - cycling, rollerblading, running, or
        stationary bike – 20 minutes; T 2.5; rpm = 80
        –5 minutes; T 2.0; rpm = 90
  - Target HR – 164 to 170 b/m
  - $LA + O_2$ = 6 x 2 minutes
    - stationary bike – T 3.0; rpm = 80
    - RI = 3 to 4 minutes easy ride for compensation 6 x 30 seconds
      - stationary bike – T 4.5; rpm = 140
  - Target HR – 176 to 182 b/m
  - Alactic (skating speed) = 15 x 40 meters
  - RI = 3 to 4 minutes

Power Training:

No.	Exercise	Load	# Reps.	# Sets	RI/min.
1	Jump half squats	40%	6	3	3
2	Knee-tuck jumps	—	12–15	2	1
3	Bench press, drop push up, and side MB throws	40%	8	3	3
4	Abs rainbows	—	10	2	1
5	Side jumps over bench	—	3	2	2
6	Half squat, slow eccentric, and low jump half squat	40%	3	3	3

Micro-cycle No. 13

- August: Week 4
- Training demand: L (to regenerate prior to the start of training camp and the scheduled testing session)

Training objectives:
- Maintain aerobic endurance
- Maintain LA system (preferably on-ice)
- Improve skating for maximum speed
- Maintain quickness and agility
- Maintain MxS
- Introduce power-endurance training

Outline of the program:

Days	Mon.	Tues.	Wed.	Thurs.	Fri.	Sat.	Sun.
AM	O_2	Skating for speed + LA	O_2	Skating for speed + LA	O_2		
PM	MxS		P-E		MxS		

Training program:
- Training the energy systems:
  - O_2 = 1 x 30 minutes
    - Means of training:
      - cycling, rollerblading, running, or stationary bike – T 2.0; rpm = 80
    - Target HR – 160 to 164 b/m
  - LA = 6 x 30 seconds
    - stationary bike – T 2.0; rpm = 140
    - RI = 3 minutes easy ride for compensation
  - Target HR – 174 to 180 b/m
  - Alactic (skating speed) = 12 x 40 meters
  - RI = 4 minutes

MxS Training:

No.	Exercise	Load	# Reps.	# Sets	RI/min.
1	Half squats	70%	8–10	2	3
2	Incline bench press	70%	10	2	3
3	Twisted abs	—	12	2	2
4	Reverse leg press	70%	10	2	2
5	Heel raises	70%	12	2	2
6	Power cleans to chest	40 kg	8	1	2

Note: Perform each P-E exercise for the duration in minutes indicated above. Take a steady rhythm of execution to complete the set. From this micro-cycle on, flexibility has to be maintained throughout the league games, especially groin flexibility. Perform flexibility exercises during the warm-up, between strength exercises, and at the end of a training session.

Micro-cycle No. 14

- September: Week 1 of training camp
- Training demand: M

Training objectives:
- Organize and select the players for your team
- Maintain the training program for O_2 via long-duration drills
- Maintain LA and skating speed through specific drills
- Maintain MxS and P-E
- Testing: Comprehensive testing as per evaluation of fitness protocol in Chapter 11

Outline of the program:

Days	Mon.	Tues.	Wed.	Thurs.	Fri.	Sat.	Sun.
AM	Drills for alactic + LA	Drills for O_2	Drills for alactic + LA	Drills for O_2	Drills for alactic + LA	O_2 LA intensity (off-ice)	
PM	MxS		P-E		MxS		

Training program:
- Training the energy systems – organize drills for:
  - O_2 = 90-second to 5-minute specific drills
    - RI = 90 seconds for long drills to 2 minutes for shorter drills
    - Target HR – 168 to 176 b/m
  - LA = 20 to 90-second specific drills
    - RI = 1 to 3 minutes
    - Target HR – 176 to 188 b/m
  - Alactic = 5- to 10-second specific drills/skating for speed
    - RI = 1 to 2 minutes
  - Target HR – 164 to 184 b/m

Note: Alternate energy systems: alactic and lactic in the same day, alternated with O_2 drills. The coach should determine the number of drills for each energy system according to players' potential and the time spent on selecting the players for the team.

MxS Training:

No.	Exercise	Load	# Reps.	# Sets	RI/min.
1	Half squats	80%	6–8	3	3
2	Incline bench press	80%	6–8	2	2
3	Twisted abs	—	10	2	2
4	Reverse leg press	80%	8	2	2
5	Heel raises	80%	8–10	2	2

P-E Training:

No.	Exercise	Load	# Reps.	# Sets	RI/min.
1	Front scissors splits (Figure 13.35)	—	20 sec.	2	2
2	Side MB throws (Figure 13.40)	5–6 kg	30 sec.	3	2
3	Side jumps over benches	—	30 sec.	3	3
4	Abs rainbows	—	30 sec.	2	2

Note: MxS and P-E training should be planned three times a week. Training days could be different from those suggested above, but as much as possible one day apart. Considering that MxS could detrain in a few weeks, it is imperative that this type of strength be maintained throughout training camp and exhibition games.

Micro-cycle No. 15

- September: Week 2
- Training demand: M

Training objectives:
- Test the players in exhibition games
- Maintain energy systems' training
- Maintain MxS and P-E

Outline of the program:

Days	Mon.	Tues.	Wed.	Thurs.	Fri.	Sat.	Sun.
AM							
PM	MxS		P-E		MxS		

Training program:

- Training the energy systems: This depends on the schedule of exhibition game. As much as possible, train each of the three energy systems at least once a week. Any additional training session(s) should be dedicated to drills for the O_2 system. It is still too early in the season to eliminate O_2 training. Benefits from a solid aerobic base will be visible in the latter part of the league games and playoffs. Therefore, find more time for O_2 system training!
- MxS and P-E training: Plan these between days of games, especially when the team does not travel. If the team is away for several days, MxS can still be performed between days of exhibition games. The suggested exercises are very simple and therefore can be performed even in the fitness room of a hotel.

MxS Training:

No.	Exercise	Load	# Reps.	# Sets	RI/min.
1	Half squats	80%	6–8	3	3
2	Incline bench press	80%	6–8	2	2
3	Twisted abs	—	8–10	2	2
4	Half squat, slow eccentric, and low jump half squat	40%	6–8	2	3

P-E Training:

No.	Exercise	Load	# Reps.	# Sets	RI/min.
1	Front scissors splits (Figure 13.35)	20 sec.	2	2	
2	Side MB throws	4–6 kg	30 sec.	2	2
3	Side jumps over cones	20 sec.	2	3	
4	Twisted abs	—	12	2	2

Micro-cycles No. 16 to 19

- September: Week 3 – October: Week 1
- Training demand: M

Training objectives:

- Test the players in exhibition games
- Select players and form lines for the league games
- Maintain energy system training through specific drills
- Maintain MxS, P, and P-E

Outline of the program:

Days	Mon.	Tues.	Wed.	Thurs.	Fri.	Sat.	Sun.
AM							
PM	MxS		P-E		MxS		

Training program:

- Training the energy systems: Organize the training schedule and type of energy system to be trained according to the schedule of exhibition games. Be sure to maintain at least one, and if possible two, O_2 training(s).
- MxS, P, and P-E training: Plan each of these strength components once a week, as per your game schedule.

FITNESS TRAINING PROGRAM FOR LEAGUE GAMES

Training demand: M-L depending on games' schedule

Training objectives:

- Maintain training for the energy systems, especially alactic (for maximum speed and quickness) and O_2, at least from October through early March. The intensity of games and duration of shifts will maintain the LA system at an adequate level
- Maintain MxS and P

Training program:

MxS Training:

No.	Exercise	Load	# Reps.	# Sets	RI/min.
1	Jump half squats	60%	6–8	3	3
2	One-leg incline press and two-leg jump over hurdles (Figure 13.17)	60%	6+ 6–8 jumps	2	2
3	Bench press, drop pushups, and MB side throws	60%	6 + 12	2	2

P-E Training:

No.	Exercise	Load	# Reps.	# Sets	RI/min.
1	Half squats	80–90%	6–10	2	3
2	Bench press, and MB side throws	80–90%	6–10	2	2
3	Twisted abs	—	10	1	2
4	Half squat, slow eccentric, and low jump half squat	50%	6	3	3

FITNESS TRAINING PROGRAM FOR THE TRANSITION PHASE

Training demand: Low and informal

Training objectives:

- Relax mentally and physically
- Remove the fatigue acquired during the long league games and playoffs
- Maintain a basic fitness through fun, games, and other fitness activities chosen by the players
- Perform a basic, informal, low-intensity strength training, mostly for the muscles not used in hockey (upper body, knee flexors)

Number of training sessions per week: 2 to 3

Basic strength training: 1 to 2

Fun and games: 1 to 2

CHAPTER 15

Year-Round Fitness Programs for Junior Players (17 to 20 Years of Age)

INTRODUCTION

As junior hockey players are one step away from becoming elite (professional, university, or national) players, their fitness program should share several similarities with that of an elite player's, such as the structure of a micro-cycle (week), exercises, and most elements of periodization of training.

Our suggested fitness program (Figure 15.1) considers a team that starts the preparatory phase at the end of May, and the program itself has a duration of 14 weeks (end of August). Exhibition games are planned for the first two weeks in September (micro-cycles 15 and 16). There are, therefore, 16 micro-cycles (weeks) from the beginning of the program to the time of starting the league games. Playoffs are slated from early March to mid-April, followed by a transition of five weeks—mid-April to the third week of May.

Development of the physical abilities needed for hockey starts with 10 weeks of aerobic (O_2) endurance. The more hockey-specific anaerobic endurance (lactic acid tolerance) training is eight weeks long, followed by skating speed, for maximum skating velocity, and quickness and agility (four weeks long).

Although anaerobic alactic, lactic, and endurance training can start on- or off-ice, we strongly suggest that from early August on, everything be done on-ice for a better and more specific adaptation. The same is true for aerobic, skating speed, and quickness and agility drills; however, these can be started much earlier than early August, especially if on-ice training is possible. For specific on-ice drills, please refer to Chapter 5.

Strength training—anatomical adaptation (AA)—is planned from the first week of training, and lasts for six weeks. This basic strength training, aimed at developing the foundation for other elements of strength, is followed by maximum strength (MxS) and power (P) training, each of which has a duration of four weeks. As shown in Figure 14.1, flexibility training is planned for the entire duration of the training plan.

FIGURE 15.1: The Periodization of Training for a Junior Team

LEGEND:

Ex = Exhibition Games

Dev. = Develop

AA = Anatomical adaptation

MxS = Maximum strength

P = Power

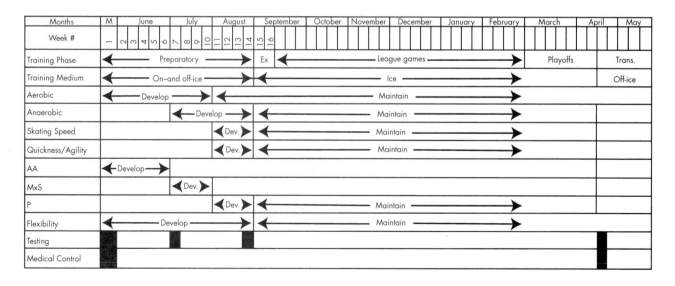

To avoid any detraining of the basic fitness components for hockey, they have to be maintained throughout the league games.

Testing to monitor fitness improvement is planned for the following times:

- First week of training (end of May)—a comprehensive testing (please refer to our suggested testing protocol, Chapter 9).
- First week of July—a test for one repetition maximum (1RM) in order to recalculate the percentage for strength training.
- Last week of August, before the start of exhibition games—a comprehensive testing session.
- Comprehensive testing is to be done at the end of the playoffs. This last test should be used to compare the scores achieved during the preparatory phase with those collected at the end of the playoffs. This comparison will allow the coach to comprehend a player's physiological behavior during the hockey season.

Finally, we strongly suggest that each player have a medical examination at the beginning of the program and at the end of the playoffs. Any eventual medical problems, especially cardiovascular and body alignment as detected by the physician, must be addressed as early in the program as possible.

TRAINING PROGRAM

Although we are very specific in our week-by-week training program, we expect you to apply it with common-sense flexibility, and adjust it according to your specific conditions and your players' potential.

For better adaptation, we suggest that training for a given fitness component be repeated for the entire week. For instance, if we propose aerobic (O_2) training for 40 minutes, apply the same duration to the other sessions planned in that week. The same is true for the other fitness components.

You will also notice that we are very specific regarding the exercises to perform for strength training. Although you may change some exercises to match your specific conditions, please make sure that the new exercises address the same muscle groups as those specified. Most of the exercises were either suggested in Chapter 13, or will be known to you or your strength and conditioning coach.

(Note: For conversion chart, see page 199.)

Micro-cycle No. 1

- May: Week 4
- Training demand: L

Training objectives:

- Begin overall flexibility program
- Begin aerobic training (O_2) – continuous, steady-state activity
- Start the AA program – 50% of 1RM
- First testing date at the end of the week

Outline of the program:

Days	Mon.	Tues.	Wed.	Thurs.	Fri.	Sat.	Sun.
AM						O_2	
PM	O_2	AA	O_2	AA			

Training program:
- Training the energy systems:
  - Aerobic training (O_2): 1 x 20 minutes continuous
  Means of training:
    - cycling
    - running or rollerblading; or
    - stationary bike – tension (T) 2.5; rotations per minutes (rpm) = 80
  - Target heart rate (HR) – 160 to 166 beats/minute (b/m)
- Flexibility training – please select your flexibility exercises from Chapter 6

Anatomical Adaptation (AA) Training:

No.	Exercise	Load	# Reps.	# Sets	RI/min.
1	Biceps curls	50%	10	2	1
2	Leg curls (Figure 13.11)	40%	6–8	2	1
3	Triceps extension	50%	6	2	1
4	Situps (Figure 13.66)	—	12	2	1
5	Incline bench press (Figure 13.3)	50%	10	2	1
6	Back extension (Figure 13.7)	—	10	2	1
7	Shoulder shrugs (Figure 13.4)	50%	10	2	1
8	Wrist flexion/extension (Figure 13.6)	50%	10	2	1
9	Neck flexion/extension (Figure 13.2)	—	10	2	1
10	Half squats (Figure 13.12)	50%	10	2	1
11	Heel raises (Figure 13.15)	50%	10	2	1
12	Diagonal lunges (Chapter 5 #19)	30 kg	10 each leg	2	1

Notes: For the neck flexion/extension exercise, choose a resistance that allows the player to perform the prescribed number of repetitions.
— signifies using own body weight.

Micro-cycle No. 2

- June: Week 1
- Training demand: M

Training objectives:
- Develop aerobic endurance – continuous steady state
- Develop AA program – 60% of 1RM
- Develop flexibility program

Outline of the program:

Days	Mon.	Tues.	Wed.	Thurs.	Fri.	Sat.	Sun.
AM						O_2	
PM	O_2	AA		O_2	AA		

Training program:

- Training the energy systems:
  - O_2 = 1 x 35 minutes continuous
    - Means of training: as in micro-cycle 1

Note: For the stationary bike program, please follow the suggested program for elite (pro) players.

- Target HR – 160 to 166 b/m

AA Training:

No.	Exercise	Load	# Reps.	# Sets	RI/min.
1	Biceps curls	60%	10	2	1
2	Leg curls	50%	6	2	1
3	Triceps extension	60%	10	2	1
4	Situps	—	12	3	1
5	Bench press	60%	10	2	1
6	Back extension	—	12	3	1
7	Shoulder shrugs	60%	10	2	1
8	Wrist flexion/extension	60%	10	2	1
9	Neck flexion/extension	—	10	2	1
10	Half squats	60%	10	2	1
11	Heel raises	60%	10	2	1
12	Diagonal lunges	30 kg	10 each leg	2	1

Micro-cycle No. 3

- June: Week 2
- Training demand: H

Training objectives:

- Develop aerobic endurance – continuous steady state
- Develop AA program – 70% of 1RM
- Develop flexibility

Outline of the program:

Days	Mon.	Tues.	Wed.	Thurs.	Fri.	Sat.	Sun.
AM						AA	
PM	O_2	AA	O_2	AA	O_2		

Training program:
- Training the energy systems:
  - O_2 = 1 x 40 minutes continuous
    - Means of training: as in micro-cycle 1
  - Target HR – 160 to 166 b/m

AA Training:

No.	Exercise	Load	# Reps.	# Sets	RI/min.
1	Biceps curls	70%	10	2	1
2	Leg curls	50%	6–8	2	2
3	Triceps extension	70%	10	2	1
4	Twisted abs, (Figure 13.49)	—	15	3	2
5	Bench press	70%	10	2	2
6	Back extension	—	12	3	2
7	Shoulder shrugs	70%	10	2	1
8	Wrist flexion/extension	70%	10	2	1
9	Neck flexion/extension	—	10	2	1
10	Half squats	70%	10	2	2
11	Heel raises	70%	10	2	1
12	Diagonal lunges	30 kg	10	2	2

Micro-cycle No. 4

- June: Week 3
- Training demand: L

Training objectives:
- Develop aerobic endurance
- Develop AA program – 60% of 1RM
- Develop flexibility
- Lighter load than micro-cycle 3

Outline of the program:

Days	Mon.	Tues.	Wed.	Thurs.	Fri.	Sat.	Sun.
AM						AA	
PM	O_2	AA	O_2	AA	O_2		

Training program:
- Training the energy systems:
  - O_2 = 1 x 40 minutes continuous
  - Means of training: as in micro-cycle 1
    - Target HR – 160 to 166 b/m
- AA training at 60% 1RM

AA Training:

No.	Exercise	Load	# Reps.	# Sets	RI min.
1	Biceps curls	60%	10	2	1
2	Leg curls	60%	8	2	2
3	Triceps extension	60%	10	2	1
4	Twisted abs	—	15	3	2
5	Bench press	60%	10	2	2
6	Back extension	—	12	3	2
7	Wrist flexion/extension	—	10	2	1
8	Shoulder shrugs	60%	10	2	1
9	Half squats	60%	10	2	2
10	Heel raises	60%	10	2	1

Micro-cycle No. 5

- June: Week 4
- Training demand: M

Training objectives:
- Develop aerobic endurance
- Develop AA program – 65% of 1RM

Outline of the program:

Days	Mon.	Tues.	Wed.	Thurs.	Fri.	Sat.	Sun.
AM						AA	
PM	O_2	AA	O_2	AA	O_2		

Training program:
- Training the energy systems:
  - O_2 = 1 x 45 minutes
  - Means of training: as in micro-cycle 1
    - Target HR – 164 to 168 b/m

AA Training:

No.	Exercise	Load	# Reps.	# Sets	RI/min.
1	Biceps curls	65%	10	2	1
2	Leg curls	60%	8	2	2
3	Triceps extension	65%	10	2	1
4	Twisted abs	—	18	3	2
5	Bench press	65%	10	2	2
6	Back extension	—	15	3	2
7	Wrist flexion/extension	—	10	2	1
8	Shoulder shrugs	65%	10	2	1
9	Half squats	65%	10	2	2
10	Heel raises	65%	10	2	1

Micro-cycle No. 6

- June: Week 5
- Training demand: M

Training objectives:

- Develop aerobic endurance – long repetitions
- Develop AA
- Develop flexibility

Outline of the program:

Days	Mon.	Tues.	Wed.	Thurs.	Fri.	Sat.	Sun.
AM						O_2	
PM	O_2	AA	O_2	AA			

Training program:

- Training the energy systems:
  - O_2 = 2 x 25 minutes
  - Means of training: as in micro-cycle 1
    - Rest interval (RI) = 5 minutes
    - Target HR – 164 to 166 b/m

AA Training:

No.	Exercise	Load	# Reps.	# Sets	RI/min.
1	Biceps curls	65%	10	2	2
2	Leg curls	60%	8	2	2
3	Triceps extension	65%	10	2	2
4	Twisted abs	—	18	3	2
5	Bench press	65%	10	2	2
6	Back extension	—	15	3	2
7	Wrist flexion/extension	—	10	2	1
8	Shoulder shrugs	65%	10	2	2
9	Half squats	65%	10	2	2
10	Heel raises	70%	10	2	2

Micro-cycle No. 7

- July: Week 1
- Training demand: H

Training objectives:

- Develop aerobic system
- Develop lactic acid (LA) system
- Develop MxS
- Develop flexibility

Outline of the program:

Days	Mon.	Tues.	Wed.	Thurs.	Fri.	Sat.	Sun.
AM	O_2		O_2			O_2	
PM	MxS	LA	MxS	LA	MXS		

Training program:

- Training the energy systems:
  - O_2, Wednesday = 1 x 40 minutes
  - Means of training: as in micro-cycle 1
    - Target HR – 160 to 166 b/m
  - O_2, Monday and Saturday = long intervals – 3 x 10 minutes
    RI = 5 minutes
  - Means of training: as in micro-cycle 1
    - Target HR – 168 to 172 b/m
  - LA + O_2 = 6 x 2 minutes
    - RI = 3 minutes
    - Target HR – 172 to 176 b/m

Maximum Strength (MxS) Training:

No.	Exercise	Load	Reps.	Sets	RI/min.
I	Half squats	70%	10	3	3
2	Triceps extension	70%	10	2	2
3	Twisted abs	—	15	2	2
4	Reverse leg press (Figure 13.14)	70%	10	2	2
5	Shoulder shrugs	70%	10	2	2
6	Heel raises	70%	12	3	2
7	Bench press	70%	10	2	2
8	Power cleans to chest (Figure 13.8)	20 kg	10	2	3
9	Leg curls	60%	8	2	3

Note: For twisted abs, hold a weight of 5 kg against the chest (i.e., a disc).

Micro-cycle No. 8

- July: Week 2
- Training demand: L

Training objectives:

- Develop aerobic system
- Develop LA system
- Develop MxS
- Develop flexibility

Outline of the program:

Days	Mon.	Tues.	Wed.	Thurs.	Fri.	Sat.	Sun.
AM						O_2	
PM	O_2	AA	O_2	AA			

Training program:

- Training the energy systems:
  - O_2, Wednesday = 1 x 30 minutes
  - Means of training: as in micro-cycle 1
    - Target HR – 160 to 166 b/m
  - O_2, Monday and Saturday = 1 x 5 minutes + 2 x 10 minutes + 2 x 5 minutes
  - Means of training: as in micro-cycle 1
    - RI = 5 minutes
    - Target HR – 168 to 174 b/m
  - LA = 6 x 90 seconds
    - RI = 4 minutes
    - Target HR – 174 to 176 b/m

AA Training:

No.	Exercise	Load	# Reps.	# Sets	RI/min.
I	Half squats	80%	8	3	3–4
2	Triceps extension	80%	8	2	2–3
3	Twisted abs	—	10	2	2
4	Reverse leg press	80%	8	2	2
5	Shoulder shrugs	75%	8–10	2	2
6	Heel raises	80%	10–12	2	2
7	Bench press	80%	8	2	3
8	Power cleans to chest	20 kg	10	2	3
9	Leg curls	60%	8	2	2

Micro-cycle No. 9

- July: Week 3
- Training demand: M

Training objectives:

- Develop aerobic system
- Develop LA system
- Develop MxS
- Develop flexibility

Outline of the program:

Days	Mon.	Tues.	Wed.	Thurs.	Fri.	Sat.	Sun.
AM	O_2	O_2				O_2	
PM	MxS	LA	MxS	LA	MxS		

Training program:

- Training the energy systems
  - O_2, Wednesday = 1 x 40 minutes
  - Means of training: as in micro-cycle 1
    - Target HR – 162 to 168 b/m
  - O_2, Monday and Saturday = 8 x 3 minutes
  - Means of training: as in micro-cycle 1
    - RI = 5 minutes
    - Target HR – 174 to 178 b/m
  - LA = 6 to 8 x 60 seconds
    - RI = 3 to 4 minutes
    - Target HR – 176 to 182 b/m

MxS Training:

No.	Exercise	Load	# Reps.	# Sets	RI/min.
1	Half squats	85%	5–6	3	4
2	Triceps extension	85%	6	2	3
3	Twisted abs	—	20	2	2
4	Reverse leg press	85%	5–6	2	3
5	Shoulder shrugs	80%	8	2	3
6	Heel raises	85%	8–10	2	3
7	Bench press	85%	6	2	3–4
8	Power cleans to chest	20 kg	10	2	3
9	Leg curls	70%	6	2	2

Micro-cycle No. 10

- July: Week 4
- Training demand: H

Training objectives:

- Develop aerobic system
- Develop LA system
- Develop MxS
- Develop flexibility

Outline of the program:

Days	Mon.	Tues.	Wed.	Thurs.	Fri.	Sat.	Sun.
AM	O_2		O_2			O_2	
PM	MxS	LA	MxS	LA	MxS		

Training program:

- Training the energy systems:
  - O_2, Wednesday = 1 x 45 minutes
  - Means of training: as in micro-cycle 1
    - Target HR – 162 to 168 b/m
  - O_2, Monday and Saturday = 8 x 3 minutes
  - Means of training: as in micro-cycle 1
    - RI = 4 minutes
    - Target HR – 174 to 178 b/m
  - LA = 8 x 60 seconds
    - RI = 3 minutes
    - Target HR – 176 to 182 b/m

AA Training:

No.	Exercise	Load	# Reps.	# Sets	RI/min.
I	Half squats	90%	3–4	3	4
2	Triceps extension	90%	4	2	4
3	Twisted abs	—	20	2	3
4	Reverse leg press	90%	3–4	2	4
5	Shoulder shrugs	85%	4–5	2	3
6	Heel raises	90%	6–8	2	3
7	Bench press	90%	3–4	2	3-4
8	Power cleans to chest	20 kg	10	2	3
9	Leg curls	70%	8	2	2

MICRO-CYCLE NO. 11

- August: Week 1
- Training demand: L

Training objectives:

- Maintain aerobic system
- Develop LA system
- Start power training program
- Develop quickness and agility
- Develop skating speed

Outline of the program:

Days	Mon.	Tues.	Wed.	Thurs.	Fri.	Sat.	Sun.
AM		Quickness and agility + LA		LA + quickness and agility		Skating speed + O_2	
PM	P		Skating speed + P		P		

Note: Please observe that on Thursday, LA training is planned to be performed prior to the quickness and agility drills. Under these conditions, the players are trained to perform quick and agile drills while under the fatiguing conditions of LA training.

Training program:

- Training the energy systems:
  - O_2 = 1 x 45 minutes
  - Means of training: as in micro-cycle 1
    - Target HR – 162 to 168 b/m
  - LA = 6 x 90 seconds
    - RI = 4 minutes
    - Target HR – 176 to 182 b/m
  - Alactic (maximum skating speed) = 8 x 33 yards (30 m)
    - RI = 2 minutes
- Quickness and agility drills: please refer to Chapter 5

Power (P) Training:

Note: Perform each exercise as dynamically as possible.

No.	Exercise	Load	# Reps.	# Sets	RI/min.
1	Scoop MB throws (Figure 13.39)	4–kg MB	15	2	2
2	Twisted abs	—	15	2	1
3	Bench press	50%	10	3	2
4	Side jumps over bench (Figure 13.34)	—	20 sec.	2	2
5	Reverse leg press	50%	8–10	2	3
6	MB side throw and 20-m sprint (Figure 13.24)	4-kg MB	6	3	3
7	Half jump, slow eccentric, and a low jump half squat (Figure 13.16)	40%	6	2	3

Note: MB = medicine ball.

Micro-cycle No. 12

- August: Week 2
- Training demand: M

Training objectives:

- Maintain aerobic system
- Develop alactic and LA systems (preferably on-ice)
- Develop power
- Develop skating speed
- Develop quickness and agility

Outline of the program:

Days	Mon.	Tues.	Wed.	Thurs.	Fri.	Sat.	Sun.
AM	Quickness and agility drills	Skating speed + LA		Skating speed + LA	Quickness and agility drills	Skating speed + O$_2$	
PM	P		P		P		

Training program:

- Training the energy systems:
  - O$_2$ = 2 x 5 minutes + 2 x 10 minutes + 1 x 5 minutes
  - Means of training: as in micro-cycle 1
  - RI = 5 minutes
    - Target HR – 168 to 174 b/m
  - LA = 4 x 2 minutes + 4 x 45 seconds
  - RI = 4 minutes
  - Target HR – 174 to 182 b/m
  - Alactic (maximum skating speed) = 8 x 44 yards (40 m)
  - RI = 2 minutes

P Training:

No.	Exercise	Load	# Reps.	# Sets	RI/min.
1	Scoop MB throws	4-kg MB	15	2	2
2	Twisted abs	—	18	2	1
3	Bench press	60%	18–12	3	2
4	Side jumps over bench	—	30 sec.	3	3
5	Reverse leg press	50%	12	2	2
6	MB side throw and 20-m sprint	4-kg MB	8	3	3
7	Jump squats (Figure 13.13)	40%	8	2	2
8	Back extension	—	12	2	2

Note: The take-off for jump half squats is low (8 inches/20 cm), but the push against the ground is dynamic.

Micro-cycle No. 13

- August: Week 3
- Training demand: H

Training objectives:

- Maintain aerobic system
- Develop alactic and LA systems (preferably on-ice)
- Develop power
- Develop quickness and agility
- Develop skating speed

Outline of the program:

Days	Mon.	Tues.	Wed.	Thurs.	Fri.	Sat.	Sun.
AM	Quickness and agility drills	Skating speed + LA		Skating speed + LA	Quickness and agility drills	Skating speed + O$_2$	
PM	P		P		P		

Training program:

- Training the energy systems:
  - O$_2$ = 2 x 20 minutes + 2 x 5 minutes
  - Means of training: as in micro-cycle 1
    - RI = 3 minutes
    - Target HR – 168 to 174 b/m
  - LA = 8 x 45 seconds (preferably on-ice)
    - RI = 3 minutes
    - Target HR – 176 to 182 b/m
  - Alactic = 12 x 33 yards (30 m)
    - RI = 3 minutes

P Training:

No.	Exercise	Load	# Reps.	# Sets	RI/min.
1	Side jumps over bench	—	15	2	2
2	Reverse leg press	50%	18	2	1
3	Twisted abs	—	18–12	3	2
4	Jump squats	50%	30 sec.	3	3
5	Bench press	60%	12	2	2
6	Jump over boxes (Figure 13.29)	box height 30–40 cm	8	2	3
7	Back extension		15	2	2

Micro-cycle No. 14

- August: Week 4
- Training demand: L to peak for exhibition and league games

Training objectives:

- Maintain aerobic system
- Develop alactic and LA systems (preferably on-ice)
- Develop power
- Develop quickness and agility
- Develop skating speed

Outline of the program:

Days	Mon.	Tues.	Wed.	Thurs.	Fri.	Sat.	Sun.
AM	Quickness + agility drills	LA		LA	Quickness + agility drills	O$_2$	
PM	P		P		P		

Training program:

- Training the energy systems:
  - O$_2$ = 2 x 20 minutes (low intensity)
  - Means of training: as in micro-cycle 1
    - RI = 5 minutes
    - Target HR – 162 to 166 b/m
  - LA = 6 x 30 seconds
    - RI = 3 minutes
  - Alactic = 8 x 44 yards (40 m)
    - RI = 3 minutes

P Training:

No.	Exercise	Load	# Reps.	# Sets	RI/min.
1	Jump over boxes	30–40 cm	8	2	2
2	Twisted abs	—	20	3	2
3	Jump squats	60%	8–10	3	3–4
4	Bench press	60%	12	2	2
5	Back extension	—	15	2	2

Micro-cycles No. 15 and 16

- September: Weeks 1 and 2
- Training demand: M

Training objectives:

- Test players in exhibition games
- Select lines and validate them in exhibition games
- Maintain energy systems' training
- Maintain power training

Outline of the program:

Days	Mon.	Tues.	Wed.	Thurs.	Fri.	Sat.	Sun.
AM							
PM	P		P		P		

Training program:

- Training the energy systems – organize specific drills for:
  - O_2 = 1 to 3 minutes
  - Means of training: as in micro-cycle 1
    - RI = 2 to 3 minutes
      - Target HR – 170 to 178 b/m
  - LA = 30 to 60 seconds
    - RI = 3 minutes
      - Target HR – 176 to 182 b/m
  - Alactic = 5- to 15-second specific drills and skating speed
    - RI = 2 minutes
      - Target HR – 164 to 174 b/m

P Training:

Plan three power training sessions per week, as per the plan below.

FITNESS TRAINING PROGRAM FOR LEAGUE GAMES

No.	Exercise	Load	# Reps.	# Sets	RI/min.
1	Half squats	—	50%	8	2
2	Side MB throws (Figure 13.40)	4-kg MB	30 sec.	2	2
3	Twisted abs	—	15	2	2
4	Reverse leg press	60%	8	2	2

Training demand: M-L as per games' schedule and players' level of fatigue

Training objectives:

- Maintain training the energy systems through specific drill suggested above (micro-cycles 15 and 16)
- Maintain strength training with loads specific for MxS and P

Training program:

No.	Exercise	Load	# Reps.	# Sets	RI/min.
1	Half squats	—	50%	8	2
2	Side MB throws	4-kg MB	30 sec.	2	2
3	Twisted abs	—	15	2	2
4	Reverse leg press	60%	8	2	2

FITNESS TRAINING PROGRAM FOR THE TRANSITION PHASE

Training Demand: L and informal

Training objectives:

- Relax mentally and physically
- Remove the fatigue acquired during league games and playoffs
- Maintain a decent fitness level through fun, and games, all of them outdoors
- Informal O_2 basic strength and flexibility training

Number of training sessions per week: 1 to 3

Basic strength and stretching: 1

Fun and games: 1 to 2

CHAPTER 16

Year-Round Fitness Programs for Midget Players (16 to 17 Years of Age)

INTRODUCTION

The periodization model for midget players, Figure 16.1, lays down the overall program for all of the abilities needed for this age group, as well as the breakdown of the yearly plan into various phases.

The preparatory phase runs from early June to the end of August. The main objective of this phase is to create a stress-free environment in which coaches will have the time, without the pressure of games, to work on technical and physical fundamentals. Although this program refers to16- and 17-year-old players, they still have room for learning— to refine technique and lay down the physical foundation

for league games (mid-September to February) and playoffs (March and part of April).

Players who follow the program will have a much better chance of making an elite (junior, university, or professional) team, since their technical and tactical skills, as well as physical potential, will be superior.

A well-planned preparatory phase will allow the athlete to work on the aerobic base for more than three months. It will also permit six weeks of anaerobic training and eight weeks to work on quickness and agility (on- and off-ice). After nine weeks of strength training work, based on strength via anatomical adaptation (AA), the program leads

FIGURE 16.1: The Periodization of Training for Midget Players
LEGEND: Ex = Exhibition Games
           Dev = Develop
           AA = Anatomical Adaptation
           P = Power

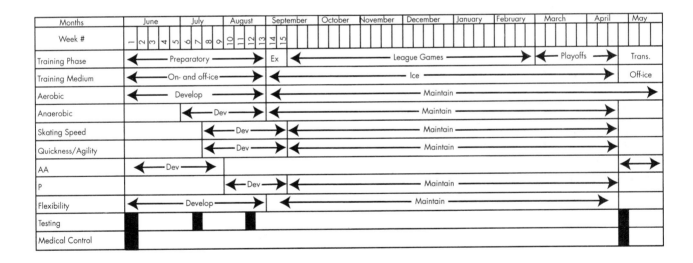

to hockey-specific strength. Six weeks are allocated to power training, and, finally, flexibility is developed throughout the preparatory phase and maintained during league games.

The main benefits of this program, with an obvious progression, are a faster and stronger endurance base, as well as increased the probability of injury-free players. If you follow the suggested program, these things will clearly be an advantage of your players.

The program also incorporates dates for fitness evaluation:

- First week in June—comprehensive testing. Use this data in the future to monitor the players' progress (see our testing protocol in Chapter 9).
- Second week in July—testing one repetition maximum (1RM). This is to calculate the percentage for strength training.
- Third week in August—comprehensive testing as per our testing protocol.
- At the end of the league games, for those players who did not make the playoffs, or at the end of the playoffs for those who did—comprehensive testing.

Finally, we strongly suggest to every coach and parent that each player have two medical assessments every year,

one at the beginning of the program and another at the end of the program (first week of the transition phase). The scope of these medical assessments is to ensure that players are healthy and that any medical problems, especially those related to the cardiovascular system and body alignment, are detected early in the player's hockey career. These tests will ensure the prevention of some medical problems and permit sufficient time to work on correcting others.

TRAINING PROGRAM

The suggested program represents a progression from the first day of training in early June to the exhibition games in early September, and league games from mid-September through the playoffs.

You can follow the suggested program as is or make a few changes according to your own particular conditions. Similarly, you can alter the suggested amount of work for the same reasons. It is, however, very important to follow the intent of the program, and not necessarily every single detail of it. The same is true for the exercises suggested below—you can change an exercise as long as its replacement addresses the same muscle group.

(Note: For conversion chart, see page 199.)

Micro-cycle No. 1

- June: Week 1
- Training demand: L

Training objectives:

- Develop O_2 endurance at lower intensity
- AA training – 40% of 1RM
- Overall flexibility
- First comprehensive testing and medical assessment

Outline of the program:

Mon.	Tues.	Wed.	Thurs.	Fri.	Sat.	Sun.
O_2	AA			O_2	AA	

Training program:
- Training the energy systems:
  - O_2 training = 1 x 30 minutes
    - Means of training:
      - cycling, running, rollerblading, slide board or
        stationary bike – tension (T) 2.0; rotations per minute (rpm) = 70
  - Target heart rate (HR) – 154 to 164 beats per minute (b/m)

Note: Unless otherwise specified, do the same type of training for each activity in each day of the micro-cycle. The main benefit will be a better adaptation to that type of activity.

Anatomical Adaptation (AA) Training:

No.	Exercise	Load	# Reps.	# Sets	RI/min.
1	Pushups	10	2	2	
2	Neck flexion/extension (Figure 13.2)	—	10	1	1
3	Situps (Figure 13.66)	—	12–15	2	2
4	Forward lunges (Chapter 5 #19)	—	12 each leg	2	2
5	Wrist flexion/extension (Figure 13.6)	—	15	2	2
6	Knee lifts (Figure 13.10)	—	10	1	1
7	Back extension (Figure 13.7)	—	12	1	2
8	Reverse leg press (Figure 13.14)	40%	12	2	2
9	Biceps curls	40%	12	1	2
10	Lateral step-ups	—	10 each leg	1	2
11	Shoulder shrugs (Figure 13.4)	40%	12	2	2
12	Burpees (Figure 13.51)	—	10	2	2
13	Lateral raise	5 kg	8	1	1

Note: For neck flexion/extension and wrist flexion/extension exercises, select the resistance that allows the players to perform the suggested number of repetitions. A lateral raise is performed with a dumbbell held in each hand; raise arms laterally to strengthen the deltoid muscles.
— signifies using own body weight.

Micro-cycle No. 2

- June: Week 2
- Training demand: M

Training objectives:
- Develop O_2 endurance – long repetitions (reps)
- AA training – 50% of 1RM
- Overall flexibility, but start by stressing ankles, knees, hips, and shoulders
- Test for 1RM for bench press, half squats, and upright rowing

Outline of the program:

Mon.	Tues.	Wed.	Thurs.	Fri.	Sat.	Sun.
O_2	AA			O_2	AA	O_2

Training program:
- Training the energy systems:
  - O_2 = 2 x 20 minutes
    RI = 5 minutes
    - Means of training: as in micro-cycle 1
      - stationary bike – T 2.0; rpm = 80
    - Target HR – 160 to 168 b/m

AA Training:

No.	Exercise	Load	# Reps.	# Sets	RI/min.
1	Incline bench press (Figure 13.3)	50%	8–10	2	2
2	Neck flexion/extension	—	12	1	1
3	V sits (Figure 13.52)	—	8–10	2	2
4	Lateral lunges	10 kg	12 each leg	2	2
5	Wrist flexion/extension (Figure 13.7)	—	15	1	1
6	Knee lifts	—	15	1	1
7	Back extension	—	15	1	2
8	Half squats (Figure 13.12)	50%	8–10	2	2
9	Upright rowing	50%	8	1	2
10	Heel raises (Figure 13.15)	50%	12	1	2
11	Shoulder shrugs (Figure 13.14)	40%	12–15	2	2
12	Burpees	—	12	2	2
13	Lateral raise	5 kg	10	1	1

Note: For lateral lunges, hold an 11-pound (5-kg) dumbbell in each hand.

Micro-cycle No. 3

- June: Week 3
- Training demand: H

Training objectives:
- Improve O_2 endurance – long reps
- Improve AA training – 50% of 1RM
- Stress specific flexibility training

Outline of the program:

Mon.	Tues.	Wed.	Thurs.	Fri.	Sat.	Sun.
O_2	AA			O_2	AA	O_2

Training program:
- Training the energy systems:
  - O_2 = 3 x 15 minutes
    RI = 6 minutes
    - Means of training: as in micro-cycle 1
      - stationary bike – T 2.0; rpm = 80
    - Target HR – 160 to 168 b/m

AA Training:

No.	Exercise	Load	# Reps.	# Sets	RI min.
1	Bench press	50%	12	2	2
2	Neck flexion/extension	—	15	1	1
3	V sits	—	12	2	1
4	Lateral lunges	10 kg	15 each leg	2	2
5	Wrist flexion/extension	—	15	1	1
6	Knee lifts	—	17	1	1
7	Back extension	—	15	1	2
8	Half squats	50%	10–12	2	2
9	Upright rowing	50%	10	1	1
10	Heel raises	50%	15–20	1	1
11	Shoulder shrugs	50%	12	2	2
12	Burpees	—	12	2	2
13	Lateral raise	5 kg	12	1	1

Micro-cycle No. 4

- June: Week 4
- Training demand: L

Training objectives:

- Improve O_2 endurance
- Improve AA training – 50% of 1RM
- Specific flexibility training

Outline of the program:

Mon.	Tues.	Wed.	Thurs.	Fri.	Sat.	Sun.
O_2	AA			O_2	AA	O_2

Training program:

- Training the energy systems:
  - O_2 = 2 x 20 minutes
    - RI = 5 minutes
    - Means of training: as in micro-cycle 1
      - stationary bike – T 2.0; rpm = 80
  - Target HR – 160 to 166 b/m

AA Training:

No.	Exercise	Load	# Reps.	# Sets	RI/min.
1	Bench press	50%	10	2	2
2	Neck flexion/extension	—	12	1	1
3	V sits	—	10	2	2
4	Lateral lunges	10 kg	15 each leg	1	2
5	Wrist flexion/extension	—	15	1	1
6	Knee lifts	—	15	1	1
7	Back extension	—	15	1	2
8	Half squats	50%	10	2	2
9	Upright rowing	50%	10	1	1
10	Heel raises	50%	15	1	2
11	Shoulder shrugs	50%	10	2	2
12	Burpees	—	10–12	1	2
13	Lateral raise	5 kg	10	1	1

Micro-cycle No. 5

- June: Week 5
- Training demand: M

Training objectives:

- Improve O_2 endurance
- AA training – 60% of 1RM
- Specific flexibility training
- Test for 1RM and 40 laps specific O_2 endurance: O_2 testing on Monday and 1RM on Tuesday

Outline of the program:

Mon.	Tues.	Wed.	Thurs.	Fri.	Sat.	Sun.
O_2	AA	O_2	AA	O_2	AA	

Training program:

- Training the energy systems:
  - O_2 = 3 x 15 minutes
    - RI = 5 minutes
    - Means of training: cycling, rollerblading, running, or stationary bike – T 2.5; rpm = 70
    - Target HR – 164 to168 b/m

AA Training:

No.	Exercise	Load	# Reps.	# Sets	RI/min.
1	Bench press	60%	8	2	2
2	Neck flexion/extension	—	15	1	1
3	V sits		12	2	2
4	Lateral lunges	20 kg	10 each leg	2	2
5	Wrist flexion/extension		15	1	1
6	Knee lifts	—	15	1	1
7	Back extension	—	15	1	2
8	Half squats	60%	8	2	2
9	Upright rowing	60%	8	2	2
10	Heel raises	60%	15	2	1
11	Shoulder shrugs	60%	10	2	2
12	Burpees	—	12	2	2
13	Lateral raise	5 kg	12	1	1

Micro-cycle No. 6

- July: Week 1
- Training demand: H

Training objectives:

- Improve O_2 endurance
- Introduce anaerobic lactic acid (LA) system training
- AA training – 60% of 1RM
- Specific flexibility training

Outline of the program:

Mon.	Tues.	Wed.	Thurs.	Fri.	Sat.	Sun.
AA	O_2	AA	LA	AA		

Training program:

- Training the energy systems:
  - O_2 = 1 x 10 minutes + 1 x 20 minutes + 1 x 10 minutes + 1 x 5 minutes
    - RI = 4 minutes
    - Means of training: cycling, rollerblading, running, or stationary bike – T 2.5; rpm = 70
    - Target HR – 164 to 168 b/m
    - Lactic acid (LA) + O_2 = 4 x 2 minutes
    - RI = 3 minutes
      - stationary bike – T 2.0; rpm = 80
    - Target HR – 174 to 178 b/m

AA Training:

No.	Exercise	Load	# Reps.	# Sets	RI/min.
1	Bench press	60%	8	3	2
2	Twisted abs (Figure 13.49)	—	15	3	2
3	Diagonal lunges	20 kg	12 each leg	2	2
4	Wrist flexion/extension	—	17	1	1
5	Knee lifts	—	19	1	1
6	Back extension	—	15	1	2
7	Upright rowing	60%	10	3	2
8	Half squats	60%	8	3	2
9	Heel raises	60%	12	2	1
10	Leg curls (Figure 13.11)	30%	8	1	1
11	Jump over bench (Figure 13.33)	—	12	2	2
12	Lateral raise	5 kg	15	1	1

Micro-cycle No. 7

- July: Week 2
- Training demand: L

Training objectives:

- Improve O_2 endurance
- Develop LA system
- AA training – 60% of 1RM
- Specific flexibility training
- Test 1RM to recalculate percentage for AA training

Outline of the program:

Mon.	Tues.	Wed.	Thurs.	Fri.	Sat.	Sun.
AA	O_2	AA	LA	O_2	AA	

Training program:

- Training the energy systems:
  - O_2 = 2 x 20 minutes
    - RI = 5 minutes
    - Means of training: cycling, rollerblading, running or stationary bike – T 2.0; rpm = 70
    - Target HR – 164 to 168 b/m
  - LA + O_2 = 4 x 2 minutes
  - RI = 3 minutes
    - stationary bike – T 2.0; rpm = 80
  - Target HR – 174 to 178 b/m

AA Training:

No.	Exercise	Load	# Reps.	# Sets	RI/min.
1	Bench press	60%	8	2	2
2	Twisted abs	—	12	2	2
3	Diagonal lunges	20 kg	10 each leg	2	2
4	Wrist flexion/extension	—	15	15	1
5	Knee lifts	—	15	1	1
6	Back extension	—	15	1	2
7	Upright rowing	60%	10	2	2
8	Half squats	60%	8	2	2
9	Heel raises	60%	10	2	1
10	Leg curls	40%	8	1	1
11	Jump over bench	—	12	2	2

Micro-cycle No. 8

- July: Week 3
- Training demand: M

Training objectives:

- Improve O_2 endurance
- Develop LA system
- Introduce drills for quickness and agility (see Chapter 5)
- Introduce drills for skating speed (alactic training)
- AA training – 70% of 1RM
- Specific flexibility training

Outline of the program:

Days	Mon.	Tues.	Wed.	Thurs.	Fri.	Sat.	Sun.
AM	AA	Q_2	AA		O_2	Skating speed + quickness and agility	
PM	LA		Skating speed + quickness and agility	LA	AA		

Note: Starting with this cycle, we strongly advise you to organize two training sessions for the next six weeks. Please organize your players' program and type of training as suggested above. It is equally important that, except for strength training, all other types of training be performed on-ice.

- Training the energy systems:
  - O_2 = 4 x 10 minutes
    - RI = 4 minutes
    - Means of training: cycling, rollerblading, running or stationary bike – T 2.5; rpm = 70–80
    - Target HR – 164 to 168 b/m
  - LA = 8 x 1 minute
    - RI = 3 minutes
    - Target HR – 174 to 180
  - Alactic training (skating speed) = 8 x 33 yards (30 m)
    - RI = 2 to 3 minutes
- Quickness and agility training: Please perform all drills as suggested in Chapter 5, on- and off-ice.

AA Training:

No.	Exercise	Load	# Reps.	# Sets	RI/min.
1	Bench press	70%	7–8	3	2
2	Twisted abs	—	8	2	1
3	Diagonal lunges	20 kg	12 each leg	2	2
4	Wrist flexion/extension	—	15	2	1
5	Knee lifts	—	15	1	1
6	Back extension	—	15	2	2
7	Upright rowing	70%	8	2	2
8	Half squats	70%	6	2	3
9	Heel raises	70%	10–12	2	1
10	Leg curls	40%	8	1	2
11	Jump over bench	—	12	2	2

Note: For twisted abs, hold a weight of 5 kg at chest level.

Micro-cycle No. 9

- July: Week 4
- Training demand: H

Training objectives:

- Improve O_2 endurance
- Develop LA system
- Develop quickness and agility
- Develop the alactic system (skating speed)
- AA training – 70% of 1RM
- Specific flexibility

Outline of the program:

Days	Mon.	Tues.	Wed.	Thurs.	Fri.	Sat.	Sun.
AM	AA	Q_2	AA		O_2	Skating speed + quickness and agility	
PM	LA		Skating speed + quickness and agility	LA	AA		

Training program:
- Training the energy systems:
  - $O_2 =$ 2 x 10 minutes + 1 x 15 minutes + 2 x 5 minutes
    - RI = 4 minutes
    - Means of training: cycling, rollerblading, running or stationary bike – T 2.5; rpm = 80
      - Target HR – 168 to 170 b/m
  - LA = 8 x 1 minute
  - RI = 3 minutes
    - Target HR – 174 to 180 b/m
  - Alactic (skating speed) = 10 x 30 to 44 yards (40 m)
    - RI = 3 minutes

AA Training:

No.	Exercise	Load	# Reps.	# Sets	RI/min.
1	Incline bench press	70%	8	3	2
2	Twisted abs	—	10	3	2
3	Diagonal lunges	20 kg	12 each leg	3	2
4	Wrist flexion/extension	—	15	1	1
5	Knee lifts	—	15	1	1
6	Back extension	—	15	2	2
7	Upright rowing	70%	8	2	2
8	Half squats	70%	6	3	3
9	Heel raises	70%	12	3	1
10	Leg curls	40%	8	1	2
11	Jump over bench	—	15	3	2

Micro-cycle No. 10

- August: Week 1
- Training demand: L

Training objectives:
- Improve O_2 endurance
- Develop LA system
- Develop quickness and agility through specific drills (Chapter 5)
- Develop skating speed (alactic training)
- Introduce power (P) training
- Specific flexibility

Outline of the program:

Days	Mon.	Tues.	Wed.	Thurs.	Fri.	Sat.	Sun.
AM	P	O_2	P		O_2	Quickness + agility	
PM	Skating speed + LA		Quickness + agility	P			

Note: For many midget teams, the month of August represents the start of on-ice training. As such, our suggested program is made for on-ice as well as off-ice training (for the teams who might not have access to ice training).

Training program:
- Training the energy systems:
  - O_2 = 90 seconds to 3 minutes, most/all on-ice specific drills
    - RI = 1 to 2 minutes
    - Target HR – 168 to 176 b/m
  - LA = 20- to 60-second specific drills
    - RI = 2 to 3 minutes
    - Target HR – 176 to 186 b/m
  - Alactic = 5- to 10-second specific drill/skating for speed
    - RI = 2 to 3 minutes
    - Target HR – 164 to 180 b/m

Note: All energy systems' training should preferably be on-ice. The number of repetitions for on-ice drills for energy systems' training has to be decided by the coach, according to the specific conditions.

Training program:
- Training the energy systems:
  - O_2 = 4 x 10 minutes
  - RI = 4 minutes
    - Means of training: cycling, rollerblading, running or stationary bike – T 2.5; rpm = 70 – 80
    - Target HR – 168 to 170 b/m
  - LA + O_2 = 6 x 2 minutes
  - RI = 3 to 4 minutes
    - Target HR – 174 to 180 b/m
  - Alactic = 8 x 33 yards (30 m)
  - RI = 3 minutes

Power (P) Training:

No.	Exercise	Load	# Reps.	# Sets	RI/min.
1	Half squats	60%	6	2	2
2	Incline bench press	60%	8	1	1
3	MB situp throw (Figure 13.50)	4-kg MB	10	2	2
4	Squat jumps (Figure 13.67)	40%	8	1	3
5	MB back throws (Figure 13.54)	4-kg MB	10	2	1
6	Jump over bench	—	8–10	1	2
7	Two-hand MB side throws Figure 13.40	4-kg MB	12	2	2

Note: MB = medicine ball

Micro-cycle No. 11

- August: Week 2
- Training demand: M

Training objectives:

- Improve O_2 endurance
- Develop LA system
- Develop skating speed
- Develop P
- Develop quickness and agility
- Specific flexibility

Outline of the program:

Days	Mon.	Tues.	Wed.	Thurs.	Fri.	Sat.	Sun.
AM	P	O_2	P		O_2	Quickness + agility	
PM	Skating speed + LA		Quickness + agility	Skating speed + LA	P		

Training program:

Note: On-ice training as per micro-cycle 10

- Training the energy systems:
  - O_2 = 3 x 5 minutes + 1 x 10 minutes + 1 x 5 minutes
  - RI = 1 to 2 minutes
  - LA = 8 x 30 seconds
    - RI = 4 minutes
  - Target HR – 174 to 182 b/m
  - Alactic = 10 x 33 yards (30 m)
  - RI = 3 minutes

P Training:

No.	Exercise	Load	# Reps.	# Sets	RI/min.
1	Half squats	70%	6	2	2
2	Incline bench press	70%	8	1	1
3	MB situp throw	4-kg MB	12	2	1
4	Squat jumps	40%	8	1	2
5	MB back throws (Figure 13.54)	3-kg MB	10	2	1
6	Side jumps over bench (Figure 13.34)	—	10	1	2
7	MB side throws (Figure 13.65)	4-kg MB	12	2	1

Micro-cycle No. 12

- August: Week 3
- Training demand: H

Training objectives:

- Maintain O_2 endurance
- Improve LA system
- Develop skating speed
- Improve P
- Improve quickness and agility
- Comprehensive testing

Outline of the program:

Days	Mon.	Tues.	Wed.	Thurs.	Fri.	Sat.	Sun.
AM	P	O_2	P		O_2	Quickness + agility	
PM	Skating speed + LA		Quickness + agility	Skating speed + LA	P		

Training program:

Note: On-ice training as per micro-cycle 10. If on-ice training is not possible, consider the following off-ice program:

- Training the energy systems:
  - O_2 = 6 x 5 minutes
    - Means of training: as per micro-cycle 10
      - stationary bike – T 2.0; rpm = 80
  - LA = 8 x 30 seconds
    - RI = 4 minutes
      - stationary bike – T 2.5; rpm = 80
    - Target HR – 176 to 184 b/m
  - Alactic = 12 x 33 yards (30 m)
    - RI = 3 minutes

P Training:

No.	Exercise	Load	# Reps.	# Sets	RI/min.
1	Half squats	70%	6	3	2
2	Incline bench press	70%	8	1	1
3	MB situp throw	4-kg MB	15	2	1
4	Squat jumps	40%	6	2	2
5	MB back throws	4-kg MB	12	2	1
6	Side jumps over bench	—	2	2	2
7	MB side throws	4-kg MB	15	2	2

Micro-cycle No. 13

- August: Week 4
- Training demand: L in order to peak for the upcoming exhibition games

Training objectives:

- Continue to improve LA system while O_2 training is maintained
- Improve skating speed
- Improve P
- Improve quickness and agility

Outline of the program:

Days	Mon.	Tues.	Wed.	Thurs.	Fri.	Sat.	Sun.
AM	P	O_2	P				
PM	Skating speed + LA		Quickness + agility	LA	O_2 easy		

Training program:

Note: On-ice training as per micro-cycle 10.

- Training the energy systems:
  - O_2 = 2 x 20 minutes
    - RI = 4 minutes
    - Means of training as per micro-cycle 10
      - stationary bike – T 2.0; rpm = 70
    - Target HR – 160 to 168 b/m
  - LA = 8 x 30 seconds
    - RI = 4 minutes
      - stationary bike – T 2.5; rpm = 90 to 100
    - Target HR – 174 to 180 b/m
  - Alactic = 8 x 33 yards (30 m)
    - RI = 3 minutes

P Training

No.	Exercise	Load	# Reps.	# Sets	RI/min.
1	Half squats	60%	6	2	2
2	Drop pushups (Figure 13.38)	—	6	2	2
3	MB situp throws (Figure 13.50)	4-kg MB	6	1	2
4	Two-hand MB side throws	4-kg MB	12	2	2

Micro-cycle No. 14 and No. 15

- September: Weeks 1 and 2
- Training demand: M-L

Training objectives:

- Test your players in the exhibition games
- Organize/select players
- Maintain energy systems training through specific drills
- Maintain strength, power, and flexibility training

Training program:

- Training the energy systems: Organize the on- and off-ice training according to the schedule of exhibition games.
- O_2 = specific 90-second to 3-minute drills
    - RI = 1 to 2 minutes
    - Target HR – 160 to 168 b/m
- LA = 20- to 60-second specific, non-stop, high-intensity drills
    - RI = 2 to 3 minutes
    - Target HR – 176 to 186 b/m
- Alactic = 5- to 15-second specific drills/skating for speed
    - RI = 2 minutes
    - Target HR – 164 to 180 b/m

Note: The coach should determine the number of training days and the number of drills per training session as per the game schedule, players' fatigue and training potential. Alternate alactic and lactic energy systems on the same day, and O_2 on the other days.

P Training:

No.	Exercise	Load	# Reps.	# Sets	RI/min.
1	Half squats	70%	6	2	3
2	Incline bench press	70%	6	2	2
3	Twisted abs	—	12	2	
4	Two-hand MB side throws	4-kg MB	12	1	2

Note: Strength and power training should be maintained by planning two, maximum three, short training sessions per week, following on-ice sessions.

FITNESS TRAINING PROGRAM FOR LEAGUE GAMES

- Training demand: M-L depending on game schedule

Training objectives:

- Maintain training for energy systems, especially the O_2 training and alactic for maximum speed, and quickness and agility.
- Maintain P training.
- Maintain flexibility: between drills/exercises, and at the end of the training session/games. Stress groin flexibility.
- Training the energy systems: as per micro-cycle 10.

Training program for strength and P:

No.	Exercise	Load	# Reps.	# Sets	RI/min.
1	Half squats	70%	6–8	2	3
2	Incline bench press	70%	6–8	2	3
3	Twisted abs	—	8–12	1–2	2
4	Two-hand MB side throws	4-kg MB	10–12	1–2	2

Year-Round Fitness Programs for Pee Wee (12 to 13 Years of Age) and Bantam (14 to 15 Years of Age) Players

INTRODUCTION

In the long-term approach to training hockey players, the training for pee wee and bantam players has a crucial role; these are the first groups for which we propose formal training. The reason for combining the training programs for both categories of players is that from the viewpoint of growth and development they have many similarities. Between the ages of 12 and 15, which comprises both categories, these players are either experiencing or just ending puberty; therefore, from the training perspective we treat them together and suggest the same training program.

Our proposed training program for pee wee and bantam players should be viewed as the foundation of overall physical development for the years to come, progressively leading to the levels required by professional teams.

Figure 17.1 represents the periodization of training for these players. Please observe that:

- The preparatory phase is very short—13 weeks (June to the end of August). Under the present game-oriented system of training, with eight months of playing time, there is not enough time to work on the foundation of fitness, and technical and tactical skills.
- The aerobic foundation is planned to be built over 13 weeks, and maintained thereafter.
- The anaerobic endurance cannot be planned for longer than six weeks because of the lack of time and the need to build an aerobic endurance first.
- Unless some players can train on-ice earlier than the month of August, there are only four weeks before the start of exhibition and league games for the development of skating speed. Obviously, this activity has to be performed on-ice. If ice is unavailable, you can do sprinting, such as in track and field, for a distance of 22 yards to 44 yards (20 m to 40 m).
- The quickness and agility phase is six weeks long, which preferably has to be trained on-ice, or you can follow the types of exercises we suggest in Chapter 5.
- Strength training has only two components—anatomical adaptation (AA) for nine weeks and power (P) for only four weeks. This is explained by the fact that it is more important to train the foundation of strength training (AA) than power for this age group.

- As in the previous programs, flexibility is a year-round concern for both injury prevention and faster recovery. The developmental phase is 13 weeks long, from which point on it has to be maintained throughout the league schedule.
- We propose three testing sessions for the purpose of monitoring players' improvement:
  – First week in June, a comprehensive testing as per our testing protocol (please see Chapter 9).
  – First week in August, also a comprehensive testing. This date coincides with the end of the AA phase and the beginning of the P phase. Since this date is just three weeks from the beginning of exhibition and league games, test results could effectively be used by the coach to asses his or her players' physical potential.
  – The final testing session is planned for the end of the playoffs, which is also the beginning of the transition phase. Use the information from this comprehensive testing session to make comparisons between the players' first tests and the last one.
- An important component in our overall planning is the suggested medical assessment, which has to be done at the beginning of the training program and at the end of the playoffs. The scope of the medical is to assess players' health, and to detect any potential medical problems, especially those related to the cardiovascular system and body alignment. The detection of any such medical problems in the early years of a player's hockey career is an advantage, since certain problems could be addressed and hopefully corrected.

TRAINING PROGRAM

It is important to mention that you should view the suggested program only as a guideline, adapting it to your specific conditions and basing it on your players' background. This program may be adequate for some players and too difficult for others; therefore, use your expertise to adjust it to individual needs. Similarly, based on your specific conditions, you may have to change some exercises. The new exercises you incorporate into training must, however, focus on the same muscle groups as our suggested exercises, since we selected them to be as specific to hockey as possible.

(Note: For conversion chart, see page 199.)

FIGURE 17.1: The Periodization of Training for Pee Wee and Bantam Players

LEGEND:

Ex	= Exhibition Games
Dev	= Develop
AA	= Anatomical Adaptation
P	= Power

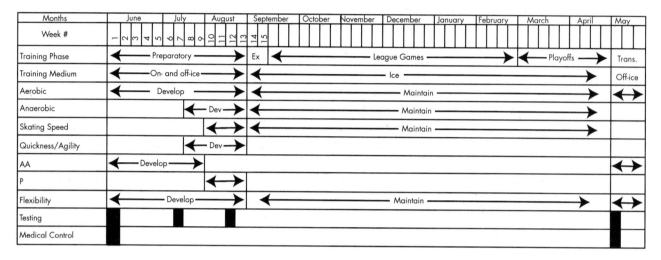

Please also observe that in the early phase of strength train-ing—the AA phase—the number of exercises is high. This number declines as regular season games approach, and the focus becomes hockey-specific exercises only. Finally, please observe that some exercises suggested in this program were also used in the programs of other age groups, and some are introduced specifically for this age group.

Micro-cycle No. 1

- June: Week 1
- Training demand: L

Training objectives:

- Introduce aerobic (O_2) endurance
- Begin strength training—anatomical adaptation (AA)
- First comprehensive testing (as per our testing protocol)
- Pass medical

Outline of the program:

Mon.	Tues.	Wed.	Thurs.	Fri.	Sat.	Sun.
O_2	AA		O_2		AA	

Training program:
- Training the energy systems:
  - O_2 training = 2 x 15 minutes
  - Rest interval (RI) = 5 minutes
  - Means of training: either one of
    - cycling, running, rollerblading, slide board
  - Target heart rate (HR) – 150 to 162 beats per minute (b/m)

Flexibility training to be performed throughout the program:
- At the end of the warm-up
- During the rest interval between sets in any forms of strength training
- At the end of strength training sessions

Anatomical Adaptation (AA) Training:

No.	Exercise	Load	# Reps.	# Sets	RI/min.
1	Step-ups (on bench)	5 kg each hand	15	2	2
2	Lateral raise	2.5 kg each hand	8	1	1
3	Wrist flexion/extension (Figure 13.6)	—	12	2	1
4	Forward lunges (Chapter 5 #19)	5 kg	10 each leg	2	2
5	Chin-ups (Chapter 9)	—	Maximum	1	2
6	Trunk extensions (Figure 13.64)	—	8	2	1
7	Pushups	—	10–15	2	2
8	Situps (Figure 13.66)	—	10–12	2	1
9	Shoulder shrugs (Figure 13.4)	10 kg	12–15	2	1
10	Leg and trunk extensions (Figure 13.63)	—	8–10	1	1
11	Half squats (Figure 13.12)	10 kg each hand	12	2	2
12	Burpees (Figure 13.51)	—	8	1	1
13	Neck flexion/extension (Figure 13.2)	—	8–10	1	1

Note: Lateral raise: standing, a 5.5-pound (2.5-kg) dumbbell in each hand. Raise arms laterally to horizontal and return.
- For wrist flexion/extension and neck flexion/extension, use a resistance that allows the player to perform the number of repetitions suggested in the program.
- For all types of lunges, hold a dumbbell in each hand as per load suggestion.
- For half squats, hold an 11-pound (5-kg) dumbbell in each hand, on the side of the body.
- — signifies that no load, but rather own body weight is used for that exercise(s).
- To convert kg into lbs, multiply the figure by 2.2 (i.e., 10 kg = 22.2 lbs.)

Micro-cycle No. 2

- June: Week 2
- Training demand: M

Training objectives:
- Develop O_2 endurance
- AA strength training
- Develop overall flexibility

Outline of the program:

Mon.	Tues.	Wed.	Thurs.	Fri.	Sat.	Sun.
O_2	AA		O_2		AA	

Training program:
- Training the energy systems:
  - O_2 = 2 x 15 minutes
    - RI = 5 minutes
  - Means of training: as in micro-cycle 1
    - Target HR – 150 to 162 b/m

AA Training:

No.	Exercise	Load	# Reps.	# Sets	RI/min.
1	Step-ups	5 kg	18	2	2
2	Lateral raise	2.5 kg	10	1	1
3	Wrist flexion/extension	—	12	1	1
4	Forward lunges	5 kg	12 each leg	2	1
5	Chin-ups	—	Maximum	1	2
6	Trunk extensions	—	10	2	1
7	Pushups	—	15	2	2
8	Situps	—	15	1	2
9	Shoulder shrugs	10 kg	15	2	1
10	Leg and trunk extensions		10	1	1
11	Half squats	10 kg	12	2	2
12	Burpees	10	1	1	1

Micro-cycle No. 3

- June: Week 3
- Training demand: H

Training objectives:
- Develop O_2 endurance
- Develop AA strength
- Develop overall flexibility

Mon.	Tues.	Wed.	Thurs.	Fri.	Sat.	Sun.
O_2	AA		O_2		AA	

Outline of the program:

Training program:
- Training the energy systems:
  - O_2 = 1 x 30 minutes
  - Means of training: as in micro-cycle 1
    - Target HR – 160 to 164 b/m

AA Training:

No.	Exercise	Load	# Reps.	# Sets	RI/min.
1	Step-ups	5 kg	20	2	2
2	Lateral raise	2.5 kg	12	1	1
3	Wrist flexion/extension	—	8	2	1
4	Forward lunges	—	15 per leg	2	1
5	Chin-ups	—	Maximum	1	2
6	Trunk extensions	—	10	2	1
7	Pushups	—	18	2	2
8	Situps	—	15	2	2
9	Shoulder shrugs	10 kg	15	2	1
10	Leg and trunk extensions		12	1	1
11	Half squats	10 kg	15	2	2
12	Burpees	7	2	1	1

Micro-cycle No. 4

- June: Week 4
- Training demand: L

Training objectives:

- Develop O_2 endurance
- AA strength
- Develop overall flexibility

Outline of the program:

Mon.	Tues.	Wed.	Thurs.	Fri.	Sat.	Sun.
O_2	AA		O_2		AA	

Training program:

- Training the energy systems:
  - O_2 = 1 x 30 minutes
  - Means of training: as in micro-cycle 1
  - Target HR – 160 to 164 b/m

AA Training:

No.	Exercise	Load	# Reps.	# Sets	RI/min.
1	Lateral step-ups	5 kg	15	2	2
2	Lateral raise	5 kg	10	1	1
3	Wrist flexion/extension	—	10	2	1
4	Diagonal lunges	5 kg	10 each leg	2	2
5	Trunk extensions	—	8	2	1
6	Pushups	—	12	2	1
7	Abs arches (Figure 13.42)	—	10	1	1
8	Rope climbs/hand and hold	—	2/15 sec.	2	2
9	Shoulder shrugs	20 kg	12	1	2
10	Half squats	10 kg	15	2	2
11	Burpees	—	10	2	2
12	Running up two stairs (Figure 13.43)	—	2 min.	2	2
13	Heel raises	10 kg	15	1	1

Note: For rope climbs the number of repetitions refers to number of climbs (i.e., 2), whereas for hang and hold it is in seconds (i.e., 15 seconds).

Micro-cycle No. 5

- June: Week 5
- Training demand: M

Training objectives:

- Develop O_2 endurance
- AA strength
- Develop overall flexibility

Outline of the program:

Mon.	Tues.	Wed.	Thurs.	Fri.	Sat.	Sun.
O_2	AA		O_2		AA	

Training program:

- Training the energy systems:
  - O_2 = 1 x 10 minutes + 2 x 20 minutes
  - RI = 5 minutes
  - Means of training: as in micro-cycle 1
  - Target HR – 164 to 168 b/m

AA Training:

No.	Exercise	Load	# Reps.	# Sets	RI/min.
1	Lateral step-ups	5 kg	18	2	2
2	Lateral raise	5 kg	8	2	1
3	Wrist flexion/extension	—	12	2	1
4	Diagonal lunges	5 kg	10 each leg	2	2
5	Trunk extensions	10	2	1	
6	Incline press (Figure 13.3)	20 kg	15	2	1
7	Abs rainbows (Figure 13.41)	—	8 each side	1	1
8	Biceps curls	10 kg	12	2	1
9	Shoulder shrugs	20 kg	15	1	1
10	Half squats	10 kg	8	2	2
11	Burpees	—	10	2	2
12	Running up two stairs	—	2 min.	2	2
13	Heel raises	10 kg	12	1	1

Micro-cycle No. 6

- July: Week 1
- Training demand: H

Training objectives:

- Improve O_2 endurance
- Improve adaptation to AA strength
- Improve overall flexibility

Outline of the program:

Mon.	Tues.	Wed.	Thurs.	Fri.	Sat.	Sun.
O_2	AA		O_2		AA	

Training program:

- Training the energy systems:
  - O_2 = 1 x 5 minutes + 2 x 20 minutes + 2 x 5 minutes
  - RI = 5 to 6 minutes
  - Means of training: as in micro-cycle 1
  - Target HR – 164 to 170 b/m
- Flexibility training is to be performed throughout the program.

AA Training:

No.	Exercise	Load	# Reps.	# Sets	RI/mins.
1	Reverse leg press (Figure 13.14)	40%	10 each leg	2	2
2	Wrist flexion/extension	—	12	1	1
3	Back extension (Figure 13.7)	—	8	1	1
4	Trunk twists (Figure 13.49)	—	8–10	2	1
5	Incline bench press	20 kg	12	2	2
6	Biceps curls	20 kg	12	1	2
7	Diagonal lunges	10 kg each hand	8 each leg	2	2
8	Half squats	10 kg	15	2	2
9	Running up two stairs	—	2 min.	2	2
10	Shoulder shrugs	20 kg	12	1	1
11	MB back roll and throws (Figure 13.62)	4-kg MB	8	1	1

Notes: Running up two stairs is to be timed in minutes.
- MB = medicine ball

Micro-cycle No. 7

- July: Week 2
- Training demand: L

Training objectives:

- Improve O_2 endurance
- Improve adaptation to AA strength
- Improve overall flexibility

Outline of the program:

Mon.	Tues.	Wed.	Thurs.	Fri.	Sat.	Sun.
O_2	AA		O_2		AA	

Training program:
- Training the energy systems:
  - O_2 = 3 x 15 minutes
  - RI = 5 to 6 minutes
  - Means of training: as in micro-cycle 1
  - Target HR – 162 to 168 b/m

Micro-cycle No. 8

- July: Week 3
- Training demand: M

Training objectives:

- Improve O_2 endurance
- Improve AA strength
- Introduce anaerobic lactic acid (LA) system training
- Introduce quickness and agility drills (on-ice if possible)
- Improve overall flexibility

Outline of the program:

Mon.	Tues.	Wed.	Thurs.	Fri.	Sat.	Sun.
Quickness and agility + AA	LA + O_2	AA		Quickness and agility + AA	LA + O_2	

Note: Training for Quickness and Agility can be performed before AA, or separately, one in training in the morning and the other in the afternoon.

Training program:

- Training the energy systems:
  - O_2 = 1 x 15 minutes + 1 x 10 minutes + 2 x 15 minutes + 2 x 5 minutes
    - RI = 4 to 5 minutes
    - Target HR – 164 to 172 b/m
  - Lactic acid (LA) training = 5 x 1 minutes
    - RI = 3 minutes
    - Means of training:
      - on-ice drills, rollerblading, or slide board
    - Target HR – 174 to 178 b/m
  - Alactic training = Drills of 5 to 15 seconds for quickness and agility as per Chapter 5

AA Training:

No.	Exercise	Load	# Reps.	# Sets	RI/min.
1	Reverse leg press	40%	12	2	2
2	Wrist flexion/extension	—	12	1	1
3	Back extension	—	10	1	1
4	Trunk twists	—	10–12	2	1
5	Incline bench press	40%	10	2	2
6	Biceps curls	20 kg	12	1	1
7	Diagonal lunges	10 kg each hand	10 each leg	2	2
8	Half squats	20 kg	12	2	2
9	Shoulder shrugs	20 kg	15	1	1
10	Running up two stairs	—	2.5	2	3
11	MB back roll and throws	4-kg MB	10	1	1

Micro-cycle No. 9

- July: Week 4
- Training demand: H

Training objectives:

- Improve O_2 endurance
- Improve AA strength
- Develop LA system
- Develop quickness and agility
- Improve specific flexibility

Outline of the program:

Mon.	Tues.	Wed.	Thurs.	Fri.	Sat.	Sun.
Quickness and agility + AA	LA + O_2	AA		Quickness and agility + AA	LA + O_2	

Training program:

- Training the energy systems:
  - O_2 = 1 x 15 minutes + 3 x 10 minutes + 2 x 5 minutes
    - RI = 5 minutes
    - Target HR – 166 to 172 b/m
  - LA = 2 x 1 minute + 2 x 2 minutes + 2 x 30 seconds
    - RI = 3 minutes
    - Target HR – 174 to 180 b/m
  - Alactic = Specific drills of 5 to 15 seconds

AA Training:

No.	Exercise	Load	# Reps.	# Sets	RI/min.
1	Reverse leg press	50%	12	2	2
2	Wrist flexion/extension	—	15	1	1
3	Back extension	—	12	2	2
4	Trunk twists	—	12	2	1
5	Incline bench press	50%	10–12	2	2
6	Biceps curls	20 kg	15	1	1
7	Diagonal lunges	10 kg each hand	15 each leg	2	2
8	Half squats	20 kg	15	2	2
9	Shoulder shrugs	20 kg	15	1	1
10	Running up two stairs	—	3	1	3
11	MB back roll and throws	4-kg MB	12	1	1

Micro-cycle No. 10

- August: Week 1
- Training demand: L

Training objectives:

- Improve O_2 endurance
- Introduce power (P) training
- Develop LA system
- Develop quickness and agility
- Introduce skating speed (for maximum skating velocity)
- Improve specific flexibility
- Second comprehensive testing as per our testing protocol

Outline of the program:

Mon.	Tues.	Wed.	Thurs.	Fri.	Sat.	Sun.
Quickness and agility + P	LA + O_2	Skating speed + P	LA + O_2	Quickness and agility + P	Skating speed + O_2	

Note: Since in each day there are two qualities to train, they can be performed one after the other, or separately in the morning and afternoon.

- All energy systems' training should, preferably on on-ice.
- For alactic training, specific drills, please consider the suggestions made in Chapter 5.

Training program:

- Training the energy systems:
  - O_2 = 2 x 20 minutes
    - RI = 4 minutes
    - Target HR – 162 to 168 b/m
  - LA = 6 x 30 seconds
    - RI = 2 minutes
    - Target HR – 176 to 182 b/m
  - Alactic = specific drills of 5 to 15 seconds
  - Skating speed = 8 x 33 yards (30 m)
    - RI = 3 minutes

P Training:

No.	Exercise	Load	# Reps.	# Sets	RI min.
1	Side jumps over bench (Figure 13.34)	—	15 sec.	2	3
2	V sits (Figure 13.52)	—	8	2	2
3	MB scoop throws (Figure 13.39)	4-kg MB	10	1	3
4	Trunk extensions	—	8	2	2
5	Run over benches (Figure 13.32)	—	15 sec.	2	2
6	Abs rainbows (Figure 13.41)	—	8 per side	1	2
7	MB side throws (Figure 13.65)	4-kg MB	6	2	3
8	Sideways skips (Figure 16.57)	—	8 each leg	2	3
9	Half squats	40%	10	2	2

Note: Side jump over bench and run over bench is to be timed in seconds.

MICRO-CYCLE NO. 11

- August: Week 2
- Training demand: M

Training objectives:

- Improve O_2 endurance
- Develop P
- Develop LA system
- Improve quickness and agility
- Improve skating speed
- Improve specific flexibility

Outline of the program:

Mon.	Tues.	Wed.	Thurs.	Fri.	Sat.	Sun.
Quickness and agility + P	LA + O_2	Skating speed + P	LA + O_2	Quickness and agility + P	Skating speed + O_2	

Training program:

- Training the energy systems:
  - O_2 = 6 x 5 minutes (specific drills)
    - RI = 2 minutes
    - Target HR – 170 to 174 b/m
  - LA = 2 x 30 seconds + 4 x 1 minute + 2 x 30 seconds
    - RI = 3 minutes
    - Target HR – 176 to 182 b/m
  - Skating speed = 8 x 44 yards (40 m)
    - RI = 3 minutes

P Training:

No.	Exercise	Load	# Reps.	# Sets	RI/min.
1	Side jumps over bench	—	25 sec.	2	3
2	V sits	—	8	2	2
3	MB back throws (Figure 13.54)	4-kg MB	12	1	2
4	MB scoop throws	4-kg MB	10	2	3
5	Trunk extension	—	10	2	2
6	Run over benches	—	15	2	3
7	Abs rainbows	—	10 per side	2	2
8	MB side throws	4-kg MB	8	2	2
9	Half squats	50%	10	2	2

Micro-cycle No. 12

- August: Week 3
- Training demand: H

Training objectives:

- Improve O_2 endurance
- Develop P
- Develop LA system
- Improve skating speed
- Improve quickness and agility
- Improve specific flexibility

Outline of the program:

Mon.	Tues.	Wed.	Thurs.	Fri.	Sat.	Sun.
Quickness and agility + P	LA + O_2	Skating speed + P	LA + O_2	Quickness and agility + P	Skating speed + O_2	

Training program:

- Training the energy systems:
  - O_2 training = 6 x 5 minutes (specific drills)
  - RI = 2 minutes
    - Target HR – 170 to 174 b/m
  - LA = 2 x 30 seconds + 4 x 1 minute + 2 x 30 seconds
    - RI = 3 minutes
    - Target HR – 176 to 182 b/m
  - Skating speed = 8 x 44 yards (40 m)
    - RI = 3 minutes

P Training:

No.	Exercise	Load	# Reps.	# Sets	RI min.
1	Side jumps over bench	—	30 sec.	2	3
2	Abs arches (Figure 13.41)	—	10	2	2
3	MB back throws	4-kg MB	12	2	3
4	MB scoop throws	4-kg MB	15	2	3
5	Trunk extensions	—	8	2	2
6	Abs rainbows	—	12 per side	2	2
7	MB side throws	4-kg MB	12	3	2
8	Half squats	50%	12	2	2

Micro-cycle No. 13

- August: Week 4
- Training demand: L to facilitate peaking for the exhibition and league games

Training objectives:

- Maintain O_2 endurance
- Improve P
- Maintain LA
- Improve skating speed
- Improve quickness and agility
- Improve specific flexibility

Outline of the program:

Mon.	Tues.	Wed.	Thurs.	Fri.	Sat.	Sun.
Quickness and agility + P	Skating speed	O_2	Quickness and agility + P (low reps)	Skating speed + LA (low reps)	O_2 (easy)	

Training program:

- Training the energy systems:
  - O_2 training = 4 x 5 minutes (specific drills)
    - RI = 3 minutes
    - Target HR – 170 to 174 b/m
  - LA = 4 x 1 minute
    - RI = 3 minutes
    - Target HR – 176 to 180 b/m
  - Skating speed = 8 x 33 yards (30 m)
    - RI = 3 minutes

P Training:

No.	Exercise	Load	# Reps.	# Sets	RI/min.
1	Side jumps over bench	—	30 sec.	2	3
2	Abs arches	—	10	2	2
3	MB back throws	4-kg MB	12	2	3
4	MB scoop throws	4-kg MB	15	2	3
5	Trunk extensions	—	8	2	2
6	Abs rainbows	—	12 per side	2	2
7	MB side throws	4-kg MB	12	3	2
8	Half squats	50%	12	2	2

Micro-cycle No. 14 and No. 15

- September: Weeks 1 and 2
- Training demand: M-L

Training objectives:

- Test your players in exhibition games
- Organize/select players and form/test lines
- Maintain energy systems' training
- Improve P, quickness and agility, and speed skating
- Maintain specific flexibility

Training program:

- Training the energy systems: Organize your training program according to the schedule of exhibition games.
  - O_2 = 2- to 3-minute specific, non-stop, drills
    - RI = 2 minutes
    - Target HR – 166 to 172 b/m
  - LA = 20- to 60-second specific, non-stop, high-intensity drills
    - RI = 3 minutes
    - Target HR – 174 to 178 b/m
  - Alactic = 5- to 15-second specific drills/skating for speed
    - RI = 2 minutes
    - Target HR – 166 to 176 b/m
- P Training = Maintain at least two sessions for P training

Note: Determine the number of training days, the number of specific drills, and repetitions, according to the schedule of games and the fatigue level of your players.

- Constantly alternate energy systems' training: a day of O_2 training with one when LA and alactic are training together (alactic first, followed by LA).

FITNESS TRAINING PROGRAM FOR LEAGUE GAMES

- Training demand: M-L depending on schedule of games

Training objectives:

- Maintain training for energy systems as per drills suggested in micro-cycles 14 and 15.
- Maintain P training.
- Maintain flexibility: end of each warm-up, between drills and power exercises, and at the end of each training session.

Training Program:

P Training:

No.	Exercise	Load	# Reps.	# Sets	RI min.
1	Half squats	60%	8	2	3
2	Trunk extension	—	8	2	2
3	Twisted abs	—	8	2	2
4	MB side throws	4-kg MB	8–10	2	3

CHAPTER 18

Conditioning Program for Under Age 12 (Pre-pubescent)

In the pre-puberty years, we believe that formal conditioning of children should be limited, and the emphasis should be on skill development, enjoyment of games, and development of confidence, with a smaller emphasis on competitive games. We suggest a ratio of 3:1 or 4:1 of practices to games, with games at the lower ages of 6 to 8 being two or three cross-ice games with the objective of maximum participation.

We also suggest that the children experience and participate in a number of different sports throughout the year, with the commitment to hockey being six to seven months only. Other sports such as soccer, basketball, baseball, gymnastics, and track and field, tend to develop the general motor skills and fitness. In addition, the children are not over-exposed to a sport that they may tire of if the total time commitment and intensity become overwhelming. The objective of a child's involvement in hockey should be to develop the basic skills of skating, stick handling, and passing, with an emphasis on shooting when more strength is developed. A lighter or smaller puck would be an advantage, at least up to age 10.

We suggest that league games for 8 years and over be only once per week, and that they not begin until the middle of October after four to six weeks of skill training has taken place. Informal scrimmage games can substitute for formal games until mid-October. Exhibition games can be started in the last two weeks of October, with league competition commencing in early November and continuing until the end of February. Playoffs would be completed by the end of March.

As has been mentioned, the primary focus of the hockey training of children up to and including age 11 should be on the acquisition of skills. Formal off-ice training is not necessary, as fitness can generally be related to play in all types of different sports.

Some considerations related to training of the following factors for children under 12 years:

ALACTIC SYSTEM

All-out repetitions of three to 10 seconds produce little or no accumulation of lactic acid. As children have less muscle mass than an adult, the reserves of ATP and CP are not as large and therefore the alactic capacity is limited. The total number of repetitions and sets must be lower, and this should be taken into consideration when designing on-ice training sessions. Development of the alactic system through training is limited in this age group.

LACTATE SYSTEM

Before puberty, children can make very little progress in the development of this system. They also have difficulty recovering from effort that leads to large amounts of lactic acid accumulation. Children can usually tolerate work intensities of 20 seconds, but longer work intensities up to 50–60 seconds should be avoided in training sessions. The development of this system is also limited in pre-pubescent children.

AEROBIC SYSTEM

The one aspect of energy system training that can be improved upon up to puberty is the aerobic system. Studies have shown up to a 55% improvement in VO_2 max of trained children aged 6 to 11 years, compared to children of the same age who did not perform the endurance program (Ekblum, 1968). Training methods should emphasize medium to long duration efforts at a constant speed below the anaerobic threshold. Team sports such as hockey, soccer, and basketball are excellent informal methods of training the aerobic system, as well as many play games such as tag, British bulldog, etc.

Generally, children develop the energy systems through informal games and skill training sessions. Formal training of the anaerobic energy systems, supervised by an adult, may tend to put undue stress on children, especially involving the lactate system. Children who take part in spontaneous games tend to stop when they are fatigued, and therefore, do not endanger themselves. The anaerobic systems cannot be developed fully at this age, and only aerobic training can be highly productive.

STRENGTH DEVELOPMENT

Before the age of 10 to 11, strength development is similar in both boys and girls. Formal strength training during this pre-pubertal period is not recommended, as the testosterone levels are not sufficient to produce noticeable strength gains. This does not preclude, however, activities that do not overload the muscles to any great extent. Some examples of exercises that promote muscle development are pushups, chins, situps, trunk extensions, use of light medicine balls, and low hopping and bounding. At approximately age 11 or 12, as children near puberty, lightweight exercises to develop form and technique can be introduced, as well as some forms of circuit training with light or without weights. Overhead lifts should be avoided.

Studies regarding the effects of strength training in the pre-pubertal period are contradictory, and this type of training should not be emphasized with this age group.

SPEED DEVELOPMENT

Between the ages of 7 and 10 years, there can be a significant increase in the speed of movement. This increase seems to plateau around age 10 and does not improve significantly again until puberty, when the efficiency of the central nervous system and reaction time develop further. It is not recommended, however, to emphasize speed training in children, but rather develop speed through improvements in technique. Speed can be improved at this age through play with relay races, games requiring reactions and quick starts, hopping, skipping, and short sprints.

In summary, we recommend the following:

1. No competitive regularly scheduled games until age 9.
2. A practice to game ratio of 3:1 (one practice could be off-ice).
3. Six weeks of skill acquisition and training sessions starting the first week of September.
4. Exhibition games starting in mid-October.
5. A four-month competitive season lasting until the end of February, with no more than one or two games a week.
6. No formal systemized on- and off-ice training of anaerobic alactic and lactate systems. On-ice drills involving these systems should be modified with shorter work and longer rest periods.
7. On- and off-ice aerobic training with games and/or low intensity endurance training can be instituted.
8. Modified strength work using body exercises such as pushups, situps, chins, etc., can be introduced at ages 10 and 11, as well as modified circuit training.
9. An overall emphasis on skill development in the training sessions. Emphasis should be on the skills of skating, passing, and stick handling. Smaller nets and lighter or smaller pucks are recommended up to age 8, or even 10.
10. The objectives of fun, success, and developing confidence, and a de-emphasis on stressful competition and winning. We recommend resource books such as *Fun and Games* (CHA, 1995) be used by coaches to help reach these objectives.
11. Children should be involved in many sports in different seasons, and hockey should not become a year round activity with this age group.

Appendix

MAXIMUM WEIGHT CHART

If for any reason, (i.e., equipment) an athlete cannot lift the load necessary to calculate 1RM, but only 3, 4, or 5RM, etc., one can still figure out his or her 1RM by using the chart below. In order to calculate 1RM, perform the maximum number of repetitions with the load available (say 4 repetitions with 250 lbs.), and then:

1. Choose from the top of the chart the column headed "4" — the number of repetitions you did.
2. Find the row with "250 lbs."—the maximum load you had available.
3. Find the number where column (4) and row "250" meet.
4. This number is your 1RM at that given time.

(Note: For conversion chart, see page 199.)

Pounds	10	9	8	7	6	5	4	3	2
5	7	6	6	6	6	6	6	5	5
10	13	13	13	12	12	11	11	11	11
15	20	19	19	18	18	17	17	16	16
20	27	26	25	24	24	23	22	22	21
25	33	32	31	30	29	29	28	27	26
30	40	39	38	36	35	34	33	32	32
35	47	45	44	42	41	40	39	38	37
40	53	52	50	48	47	46	44	43	42
45	60	58	56	55	53	51	50	49	47
50	67	65	63	61	59	57	56	54	53
55	73	71	69	67	65	63	61	59	58
60	80	77	75	73	71	69	67	65	63
65	87	84	81	79	76	74	72	70	68
70	93	90	88	85	82	80	78	76	74
75	100	97	94	91	88	86	83	81	79
80	107	103	100	97	94	91	89	86	84
85	113	110	106	103	100	97	94	92	89
90	120	116	113	109	106	103	100	97	95
95	127	123	119	115	112	109	106	103	100
100	133	129	125	121	118	114	111	108	105
105	140	135	131	127	124	120	117	114	111
110	147	142	138	133	129	126	122	119	116
115	153	148	144	139	135	131	128	124	121
120	160	155	150	145	141	137	133	130	126
125	167	161	156	152	147	143	139	135	132
130	173	168	163	158	153	149	144	141	137
135	180	174	169	164	159	154	150	146	142
140	187	181	175	170	165	160	156	151	147
145	193	187	181	176	171	166	161	157	153
150	200	194	188	182	176	171	167	162	158
155	207	200	194	188	182	177	172	168	163
160	213	206	200	194	188	183	178	173	168
165	220	213	206	200	194	189	183	178	174
170	227	219	213	206	200	194	189	184	179

Pounds	10	9	8	7	6	5	4	3	2
175	233	226	219	212	206	200	194	189	184
180	240	232	225	218	212	206	200	195	189
185	247	239	231	224	218	211	206	200	195
190	253	245	238	230	224	217	211	205	200
195	260	252	244	236	229	223	217	211	205
200	267	258	250	242	235	229	222	216	211
205	273	265	256	248	241	234	228	222	216
210	280	271	263	255	247	240	233	227	221
215	287	277	269	261	253	246	239	232	226
220	293	284	275	267	259	251	244	238	232
225	300	290	281	273	265	257	250	243	237
230	307	297	288	279	271	263	256	249	242
235	313	303	294	285	276	269	261	254	247
240	320	310	300	291	282	274	267	259	253
245	327	316	306	297	288	280	272	265	258
250	333	323	313	303	294	286	278	270	263
255	340	329	319	309	300	291	283	276	268
260	347	335	325	315	306	297	289	281	274
265	353	342	331	321	312	303	294	286	279
270	360	348	338	327	318	309	300	292	284
275	367	355	344	333	324	314	306	297	289
280	373	361	350	339	329	320	311	303	295
285	380	368	356	345	335	326	317	308	300
290	387	374	363	352	341	331	322	314	305
295	393	381	369	358	347	337	328	319	311
300	400	387	375	364	353	343	333	324	316
305	407	394	381	370	359	349	339	330	321
310	413	400	388	376	365	354	344	335	326
315	420	406	394	382	371	360	350	341	332
320	427	413	400	388	376	366	356	346	337
325	433	419	406	394	382	371	361	351	342
330	440	426	413	400	388	377	367	357	347
335	447	432	419	406	394	383	372	362	353
340	453	439	425	412	400	389	378	368	358
345	460	445	431	418	406	394	383	373	363
350	467	452	438	424	412	400	389	378	368
355	473	458	444	430	418	406	394	384	374
360	480	465	450	436	424	411	400	389	379
365	487	471	456	442	429	417	406	395	384
370	493	477	463	448	435	423	411	400	389
375	500	484	469	455	441	429	417	405	395
380	507	490	475	461	447	434	422	411	400
385	513	497	481	467	453	440	428	416	405
390	520	503	488	473	459	446	433	422	411
395	527	510	494	479	465	451	439	427	416
400	533	516	500	485	471	457	444	432	421
405	540	523	506	491	476	463	450	438	426
410	547	529	513	497	482	469	456	443	432
415	553	535	519	503	488	474	461	449	437
420		542	525	509	494	480	467	454	442
425		548	531	515	500	486	472	459	447
430		555	538	521	506	491	478	465	453
435		561	544	527	512	497	483	470	458

Pounds	10	9	8	7	6	5	4	3	2
440		568	550	533	518	503	489	476	463
445		574	556	539	524	509	494	481	468
450		581	563	545	529	514	500	486	474
455		587	569	552	535	520	506	492	479
460		594	575	558	541	526	511	497	484
465		600	581	564	547	531	517	503	489
470		606	588	570	553	537	522	508	495
475		613	594	576	559	543	528	514	500
480		619	600	582	565	549	532	519	505
485		626	606	588	571	554	539	524	511
490		632	613	594	576	560	544	530	516
495		639	619	600	582	566	550	535	521
500		645	625	606	588	571	556	541	526
505		652	631	612	594	577	561	546	532
510		658	638	618	600	583	567	551	537
515		665	644	624	606	589	572	557	542
520		671	650	630	612	594	578	562	547
525		677	656	636	618	600	583	569	553
530		684	663	642	624	606	589	573	558
535		690	669	648	629	611	594	578	563
540		697	675	655	635	617	600	584	568
545		703	681	661	641	623	606	589	574
550		710	688	667	647	629	611	595	579
555		716	694	673	653	634	617	600	584
560		723	700	679	659	640	622	605	589
565		729	706	685	665	646	628	611	595
570		735	713	691	671	651	633	616	600
575		742	719	697	676	657	639	622	605
580		748	725	703	682	663	644	627	611
585		755	731	709	688	669	650	632	616
590		761	738	715	694	674	656	638	621
595		768	744	721	700	680	661	643	626
600		774	750	727	706	686	667	649	632
605		781	756	733	712	691	672	654	637
610		787	763	739	718	697	678	659	642
615		794	769	745	724	703	683	665	647
620		800	775	752	729	709	689	670	653
625		806	781	758	735	714	694	676	658
630		813	788	764	741	720	700	681	663
635		819	794	770	747	726	706	686	668
640		826	800	776	753	731	711	692	674
645		832	806	782	759	737	717	697	679
650		839	813	788	765	743	722	703	684
655		845	819	794	771	749	728	708	689
660		852	825	800	776	754	733	714	695
665		858	831	806	782	760	739	719	700
670		865	838	812	788	766	644	724	705
675		871	844	818	794	771	750	730	711
680		877	850	824	800	777	756	735	716
685		884	856	830	806	783	761	741	721
690		890	863	836	812	789	767	746	726
695		897	869	842	818	794	772	751	732
700		903	875	848	824	800	778	757	737

Pounds	10	9	8	7	6	5	4	3	2
705		910	881	855	829	806	783	762	742
710		916	888	861	835	811	789	768	747
715		923	894	768	841	817	794	773	753
720		929	900	873	847	823	800	778	758
725		935	906	879	853	829	806	784	763
730		942	913	885	859	834	811	789	768
735		948	919	891	865	840	817	795	774
740		955	925	897	871	846	822	800	779
745		961	931	903	876	851	828	805	784
750		968	938	909	882	857	833	811	789
755		974	944	915	888	863	839	816	795
760		981	950	921	894	869	844	822	800
765		987	956	927	900	874	850	827	805
770		994	963	933	906	880	856	832	811
775		1,000	969	939	912	886	861	838	816
780		1,006	975	945	918	891	867	843	821
785		1,013	981	952	924	897	872	849	826
790		1,019	988	958	929	903	878	854	832
795		1,026	994	964	935	908	883	859	837
800		1,032	1,000	970	941	914	889	865	842
820		1,058	1,025	994	965	937	911	886	863
840		1,084	1,050	1,018	988	960	933	908	884
860		1,110	1,075	1,042	1,012	983	956	930	905
880		1,135	1,100	1,067	1,035	1,006	978	951	926
900		1,161	1,125	1,091	1,059	1,029	1,000	973	947
920		1,187	1,150	1,115	1,082	1,051	1,022	995	968

TABLE MADE BY STRENGTH TECH INC., BOX 1381, STILLWATER, OK 74076, U.S.A.

COPIED DIRECTLY FROM: *PERIODIZATION OF STRENGTH* (4TH EDITION),
PAGES 267, 268, 269, 270, 271
AUTHOR: TUDOR O. BOMPA   PUBLISHER: VERITAS PUBLISHING (1996)

Conversion Chart

To Convert	To	Multiply by	Divide by
pound	kilograms	0.4536	
kilograms	pounds	2.2046	
yards	meters	0.9144	
meters	yards		0.9144
inches	centimeters	2.54	
centimeters	inches		2.54

Bibliography

Almstead, J., ed. *On the Attack: A Drill Manual*. Ottawa, ON: Canadian Amateur Hockey Association, 1990.

Altar, M. *Sports Stretch*. Champaign, IL: Human Kinetics, 1990.

Arnheim, D.D. *Essentials of Athletic Training*, 3rd edition. St. Louis: Mosby Year Book, Inc., 1995.

Bacon, T. "The planning and integration of mental training programs" in *Scientific Periodical on Research and Technology in Sport*. Ottawa, ON: Coaching Association of Canada, 10, (1989): 1.

Baechle, T. *Essentials of Strength Training and Conditioning*. Champaign, IL; Human Kinetics, 1994.

Balch, F.; Balch A. *Prescription for Nutritional Healing*, 2nd edition. New York, NY: Avery Publishing, 1997.

Blimkie, C.J.R. "Age- and sex-associated variation in strength during childhood: Anthroprometric, morphologic, neurologic, biomechanical, endocrinologic, genetic and physical correlates," in C. Gisolfi and D. Lamb (eds.), *Youth Exercise and Sport*, vol. 2 (99–163) from *Perspectives in Exercise. Science and Sports Medicine*. Indianapolis, IN: Benchmark, 1989.

———. "Heat stress and athletic performance: Survival of the sweatiest," in *Scientific Periodical on Research and Technology in Sport*. Ottawa, ON: Coaching Association of Canada.

Bompa, T. *Some aspects of the athlete's psychological recovery following the strain of performance*. Conference on Research in Sports Psychology, Bucharest, 1969.

———. *Power Training for Sport: Plyometrics for Maximum Power Development*. Gloucester, ON: Coaching Association of Canada; and Oakville, New York, London: Mosaic Press, Oakville, ON, 1993.

———. *Theory and Methodology of Training*. Dubuque, IA: Kendall/Hunt, 1994.

———. *Periodization: Theory and Methodology of Training*. Champaign, IL: Human Kinetics, 1999.

———. *Total Training for Young Champions*. Champaign, IL: Human Kinetics, 1999.

———. *Periodization Training for Sports: Programs for Peak Strength for 35 Sports*. Champaign, IL: Human Kinetics, 1999.

Botterill, C., and Winston, G. "Psychological skill development," in *Scientific Periodical on Research and Technology in Sport*. Ottawa, ON: Coaching Association of Canada, 1984, August.

Botterill, C. "Energizing," in *Scientific Periodical on Research and Technology in Sport*. Ottawa, ON: Coaching Association of Canada, 1986, December.

Bowers, R., Foss, M., and Fox, E. *Physiological Basis of Physical Education and Athletics*. Dubuque, IA: Wm. C. Brown, 1986.

Bowers, R., and Fox, E. *Sports Physiology*. Dubuque, IA: Wm. C. Brown, 1992.

Boyle, M. "Elite Conditioning," in *Off-season Training for Ice Hockey*. Boston: Boston University Press, 1994.

Brook, G., and Fahey, T. *Fundamentals of Human Performance*. New York: Macmillan, 1987.

CHA. *Coach Level Manual*. Ottawa, ON: Canadian Hockey Association, 1989.

———. *Intermediate Level Manual*. Ottawa: Canadian Hockey Association, 1989.

———. *Fun and Games*. Ottawa, ON: Canadian Hockey Association, 1995.

———. *The Incredible Hockey Drill Book*. Toronto, ON: Key Porter Books, 1994.

———. *Complete Hockey Instruction*. Toronto, ON: Key Porter Books, 1995.

———. *Coaching: The Art and the Science*. Toronto, ON: Key Porter Books, 1997.

Chevalier, N. "Understanding the imagery and mental rehearsal processes in athletics," in *Scientific Periodical on Research and Technology in Sport*. Ottawa, ON: Coaching Association of Canada, 1983, October.

Clark, N. *Sports Nutrition Guidebook*. Champaign, IL: Leisure Press, 1990.

Coaching Association of Canada. *Coaching Theory Level 1*. National Coaching Certification Program. Ottawa, ON: Coaching Association of Canada, 1992(a).

———. *Coaching Theory Level 2*. National Coaching Certification Program. Ottawa, ON: Coaching Association of Canada, 1992(b).

———. *Coaching Theory Level 3*. National Coaching Certification Program. Ottawa, ON: Coaching Association of Canada, 1992(c).

———. *Coaching Assessment Workbook*, 1994.

Coyle, E.F., Martin, W.H., Sinacor, D.R., Joyner, M.J., Hagber, J.M., and Holloszy, J.O. "Time course of loss of adaptations after stopping prolonged intense endurance training" in *Journal of Applied Physiology*, 57, 1984: 1857–64.

Cox, R. *Sport Psychology: Concepts and Applications*. Dubuque, IA: Wm. C. Brown, 1994.

Csikszentmihalyi, M. "The flow experience," in D. Goleman and R. Davidson, eds., *Consciousness: Brain States of Awareness and Mysticism*. New York, NY: Harper & Row, 1979.

Davis, H., "Cognitive style and nonsport imagery in elite hockey performance" in *Perceptual and Motor Skills*, 71, 1990: 795–801, 1990.

Ellis, A., and Grieger, R. *Handbook of Rational-Emotive Therapy*. New York, NY: Springer Publishing, 1977.

Fleck, J., and Kraemer, W. *Designing Resistance Training Programs*. Champaign, IL: Human Kinetics, 1997.

Green, H. "Metabolic aspects of intermittent work with specific regard to ice hockey," in *Canadian Journal of Applied Sport Science*, 4 (4) (1989): 29–33.

Greenspan, M.J., and Feltz, D.L. "Psychological interventions with athletes in competitive situations: A review," in *The Sport Psychologist*, 3, (1989): 219–36.

Gwartney, D., and Stout, J. "Androstenedione: Physical and ethical considerations relative to its use as an ergogenic aid" in *Strength and Conditioning Journal*, 21 (1) (1999): 65–6.

Harre, D. "Principles of Sport Training" *Sportverlag*, Berlin, 1982.

Haslam, I. "A conceptual framework for planning imagery training," in *Scientific Periodical on Research and Technology in Sport*. Ottawa: Coaching Association of Canada, 1990.

Holt, L. *Scientific Stretching for Sport*. Ottawa, ON: Coaching Association of Canada, 1989.

Kolonay, B. "The effects of visual motor behavioral rehearsal on athletic performance," in R. Martens, *Coaches' Guide to Sport Psychology*. Champaign, IL: Human Kinetics, 1977.

Kostka, V. *Czechoslovakian Youth Ice Hockey Training System*. Ottawa, ON: Canadian Hockey Association, 1979.

Kurtz, T. *Science of Sports Training*. Island Pond, VT: Stadion, 1991.

Lane, J.F. "Improving athletic performance through visual-motor rehearsal," in R.M. Suinn, ed., *Psychology in Sports: Methods and Applications*. Minneapolis MN: Burgess, 1980: 316–20.

Larivière, G., Godbout, D., and Lamontague, M. *Physical Fitness and Technical Skill Appraisal of Ice Hockey Players*. Ottawa, ON: Canadian Hockey Association, 1997.

Liitsola, S., and Heikkila, L. *Finnish Dryland Training Manual*. Ottawa, ON: Canadian Hockey Association, 1997.

Loehr, J. "The Ideal Performance State," in *Scientific Periodical on Research and Technology in Sport*. Ottawa: ON: Coaching Association of Canada, 1983, January.

MacAdam, D., and Reynolds, G. *Hockey Fitness*. Champaign, IL: Leisure Press, 1988.

MacDougall, J., Wenger, H., and Green, H. *Physiological Testing of the High-Performance Athlete*. Champaign, IL: Human Kinetics, 1991.

Martens, R. Paper presented at the Medical and Scientific Aspects of Elitism in Sport Conference, Brisbane, Australia, in R. Martens, *Coaches' Guide to Sport Psychology*. Champaign, IL: Human Kinetics, 1982, September.

———. *Coaches' Guide to Sport Psychology*. Champaign, IL: Human Kinetics, 1987.

Maslow, A. "Humanistic science and transcendent experiences," in *Journal of Humanistic Psychology*, 5 (2) (1965): 219–26.

Matveyev, L. *Fundamentals of Sport Training*. Moscow: Progress, 1981.

Neilson, K.L. "Injuries in female distance runners," in B.L. Drinkwater (ed.), *Female Endurance Athletes*. Champaign, IL: Human Kinetics, 1986: 149–61.

Neilson, R., ed. *Roger Neilson's Hockey Clinic*. Peterborough, ON, 1990–98.

Nideffer, R. M. *The Inner Athlete*. New York, NY: Thomas Y. Cromwell, 1976.

———. *The Ethics and Practice of Applied Sports Psychology*. Ithaca, NY: Mouvement, 1981.

———. *Athletes' Guide to Mental Training*. Champaign, IL: Human Kinetics, 1985.

———. *Psyched to Win*. Champaign, IL: Leisure Press, 1992.

Noakes, Tim. *Lore of Running*. Champaign, Illinois: Leisure Press, 1991.

Nudel, D.B., ed. *Pediatric Sports Medicine*. New York: PMA Publishing Corp., 1989.

Onestak, D.M. "The effects of progressive relaxation, mental practice, and hypnosis on athletic performance: A review," in *Journal of Sport Behavior*, 14 (1991): 247–82.

Orlick, T. *Psyching for Sport: Coaches' Training Manual*, Champaign, IL: Leisure Press, 1986(b).

———. *Psyching for Sport: Mental Training for Athletes*. Champaign, IL: Leisure Press, 1986(a).

———. *In Pursuit of Excellence*. Champaign, IL: Human Kinetics, 1990.

Ozolin, N. *Athlete's Training System for Competition*. Moscow: Phyzkultura Sport, 1971.

Proceedings of NCCP Level V Seminar. Ottawa, ON: Canadian Amateur Hockey Association, 1973, 1975, 1977, 1978, 1979, 1981, 1983, 1985.

Pechtl, V. "The basis and methods of flexibility training," in Harre, D., ed. *Trainingslehre.* Berlin: Sportverlag, 1982.

Plisk, S., and Kreider, R. "Creatine controversy?" in *Strength and Conditioning Journal,* 21 (1) (1999): 14–21.

Poliquin, C. "Variety in strength training" in *Scientific Periodical on Research and Technology in Sport.* Ottawa, ON: Coaching Association of Canada, 1988, August.

Poliquin, C. "Training for improving relative strength in sports," in *Scientific Periodical on Research and Technology in Sport.* Ottawa, ON: Coaching Association of Canada, 1991.

Radcliffe, J., and Farentinos, R. *Plyometrics: Explosive Power Training.* Champaign, IL: Human Kinetics, 1988.

Ramsay, J.A., Blimkie, C.J.R., Smith, K., Gavner, S., MacDougall, J.D., and Sale D.G. "Strength training effects in prepubescent boys" in *Medicine and Science in Sports and Exercise,* 22 (1990): 605–14.

Ravizza, K. "Peak experience in sport," in *Journal of Humanistic Psychology,* 17 (1977): 35–41.

Rhodes, T., and Twist, P. *The Physiology of Ice Hockey. A Testing and Training Manual.* Vancouver, BC: University of British Columbia Press, 1990.

Rowland, T. "Developmental aspects of physiological function relating to aerobic exercise in children" in *Sports Medicine,* 10 (4) (1990): 253–66.

Rushall, B. "On-site psychological preparations for athletes," in *Scientific Periodical on Research and Technology in Sport.* Ottawa, ON: Coaching Association of Canada, 1981, December.

Rushall, B.S., Hall, M., and Rushall, A. "Effects of three types of thought content instructions on skiing performance" in *The Sport Psychologist,* 2 (1988): 283–97.

Sale, D. "Strength training in children," in C.V. Gisolfi and D.R. Lambs, eds. *Perspective in Exercise and Sport Science.* Carmel, IN: Benchmark, 1989: 165–216.

Seabourne, T., Weinberg, A., Jackson, A., and Suinn, R. "Effect of individualized, non–individualized, and package intervention strategies on karate performance," in *Journal of Sport Psychology,* 7 (1985): 40–50.

Sharkey, B. *Coaches' Guide to Sport Physiology.* Champaign, IL: Human Kinetics, 1993.

Sewall, L., and Micheli, L.J. "Strength training for children," in *Journal of Pediatric Orthopedics,* 6 (1986): 143–6.

Singer, R. *Handbook of Sport Psychology.* Champaign, IL: Human Kinetics Press, 1993.

Suedfeld, P., and Bruno, T. "Flotation and imagery in the improvement of athletic performance," in *Journal of Sport and Exercise Physiology,* 12 (1990): 308–10.

Suinn, R. *Seven Steps to Peak Performance.* Toronto, ON: Hans Huber, 1986.

Twist, P. *Complete Conditioning for Ice Hockey.* Champaign, IL: Human Kinetics, 1997.

Vander, J.A., Sherman, J.H., and Luano, D.S. *Human Physiology: The Mechanisms of Body Function.* New York: McGraw-Hill Publishing Company, 1990.

Vernacchia, R., McGuide, R., and Cook, D. *Coaching Mental Excellence.* Portola Valley, CA: Wade, 1996.

Vrijens, J. "Muscle strength development in the pre and post pubescent age," in *Medicine and Sport,* 11 (1978): 152–58.

Weinberg, R.S. (1990), "Anxiety and motor performance: Where to go from here?" in *Anxiety Research,* 2 (1990): 227–42.

Weltman, A., Janney, C., Rians, C.B., Strand, K., Berg, B., Tippett, S., Wise, J., Cahill, B.R., and Katch, F.I. "The effects of hydraulic-resistance strength training in prepubertal males," in *Medicine and Science in Sports and Exercise,* 18 (1986): 629–83.

Wenger, H. *Fitness: The Key to Success.* Vancouver, BC: British Columbia Amateur Hockey Association, 1992.

———. *Fitness for High Performance Hockey.* Victoria, BC: Tafford Publishing, 1997.

Williams, M.H. *Nutritional Aspects of Human Physical and Athletic Performance.* Springfield, IL: Charles C. Thomas, 1985.

Williams, J. "Integrating and implementing a psychological skills program," in *Applied Sports Psychology,* J. M. Williams (ed.). Palo Alto, Mayfield, 1986: 301–24.

Williams, J.D., Rippon, G., Stone, B.M., and Annett, J. "Psychophysiological correlates of dynamic imagery," in *British Journal of Psychology,* 86 (1995): 283–300.

Wilson, V., and Cummings, M. *Learned Self-Regulation.* Toronto, ON: WSAM, 1997.

Wise, G. *Off Season Training Program.* Toronto, ON: York University, 1998.

About the Authors

Tudor O. Bompa, Ph.D., revolutionized Western training methods when he introduced his groundbreaking theory of periodization in Romania in 1963. After adopting his training system, the Eastern Bloc countries dominated international sports through the 1970s and 1980s. Dr. Bompa has personally trained 11 Olympic Games medalists (including four gold medalists) and has served as a consultant to coaches and athletes worldwide. A professor at York University, Toronto, Canada, Tudor Bompa has authored several important books on the theory and methodology of training that are used worldwide. Dr. Bompa's work has been translated into nine languages, and he has made presentations on training theories in more than 30 countries.

Dave Chambers, Ph.D., is a professor emeritus in the coaching program in the Department of Kinesiology and Health Science at York University. Dave has coached for over 30 years at the amateur, high school, Junior A, university, professional, and international levels, and was recognized as a "Master Coach" by the Canadian Hockey Association. He coached in the National Hockey League for three years, has coached two national teams to gold medals in World Championships and university teams to a number of league championships and one national title, and has won five "Coach of the Year" awards. Dave has written a number of books and articles on coaching and ice hockey and has made numerous presentations worldwide.

Books

TUDOR BOMPA

Power Training for Sport: Plyometrics for Maximum Power Development. Gloucester, ON: Coaching Association of Canada; and Oakville, New York, London: Mosaic Press, 1993.

Periodization: Theory and Methodology of Training. Champaign, IL: Human Kinetics, 1999.

Total Training for Young Champions. Champaign, IL: Human Kinetics, 1999.

Periodization Training for Sports: Programs for Peak Strength for 35 Sports. Champaign, IL: Human Kinetics, 1999.

DAVE CHAMBERS

The Incredible Hockey Drill Book. Toronto, ON: Key Porter Books, 1994.

Coaching: The Art and the Science. Toronto, ON: Key Porter Books, 1997.

Complete Hockey Instruction (3rd edition). Toronto, ON: Key Porter Books, 1999.

TUDOR BOMPA TRAINING SYSTEM

Tudor Bompa has developed a certification program in training, planning and periodization. For more information, please call the Tudor Bompa Training System at 905-478-2666 or reggier@truestarhealth.com.